Cultural Contacts in the North Atlantic Region: The Evidence of Names

Cultural Contacts in the North Atlantic Region: The Evidence of Names

Edited by
Peder Gammeltoft
Carole Hough
Doreen Waugh

Published by
NORNA, Scottish Place-Name Society and
Society for Name Studies in Britain and Ireland
2005

ISBN 0-9551838-0-4

The printing of this book is made possible by a gift to the University of Cambridge in memory of Dorothea Coke, Skjaeret, 1951.

The publishers are also grateful for the Grant Aid received from the Shetland Amenity Trust to assist with the printing of the book.

Printed by
The Shetland Times Ltd.,
Gremista, Lerwick,
Shetland, ZE1 0PX

Table of contents

List of contributors and editors

Dr **Gunnstein Akselberg**. Professor at the Department of Scandinavian Languages and Literature, University of Bergen, Norway.

John R. Baldwin. Part-time Lecturer/Tutor at the Office of Lifelong Learning, University of Edinburgh, Scotland.

Eileen Brooke-Freeman. Place Names Project Officer, Shetland Amenity Trust, Lerwick, Shetland.

Dr **Katherine Campbell**. Lecturer at the Department of Celtic and Scottish Studies, University of Edinburgh, Scotland.

Richard Coates. Professor and Head of the Department of Linguistics and English Language, University of Sussex. Honorary Director of the Survey of English Place-Names, England.

Dr **Barbara E. Crawford**. Honorary Reader at the School of History, University of St. Andrews, Scotland.

Dr **Gillian Fellows-Jensen**. Former Reader at the Institute of Name Research, University of Copenhagen, Denmark.

Dr **Peder Gammeltoft**. Associate Professor at the Institute of Name Research, University of Copenhagen, Denmark.

Dr **Alison Grant**. Tutor in the Department of English Language, University of Glasgow, Scotland.

Dr **Carole Hough**. Reader at the Department of English Language, University of Glasgow, Scotland.

Arne Kruse. Senior Lecturer, Scandinavian Studies, Division of European Languages and Cultures, University of Edinburgh, Scotland.

Dr **Gunnel Melchers**. Professor Emeritus at the Department of English, University of Stockholm, Sweden.

W.F.H. Nicolaisen. Honorary Professor of English, School of Language and Literature, University of Aberdeen, Scotland.

Dr **Berit Sandnes**. Norwegian Lecturer at the Department of Nordic Studies and Linguistics at the University of Copenhagen, Denmark.

Dr **Tom Schmidt**. Professor at the Section for Name Research, Department of Scandinavian Studies and Comparative Literature, University of Oslo, Norway.

David Sellar. Honorary Fellow at the Faculty of Law, University of Edinburgh, Scotland.

Svavar Sigmundsson. Head of the Place Name Institute, National Museum of Iceland, Iceland.

Dr **Inge Særheim**. Professor at the Department of Cultural Studies and Languages, University of Stavanger, Norway.

Dr **Doreen Waugh**. Honorary Fellow at the Department of Celtic and Scottish Studies, University of Edinburgh and Honorary Research Fellow, Department of English Language, University of Glasgow, Scotland.

Diana Whaley. Professor of Early Medieval Studies, University of Newcastle upon Tyne, England.

Introduction

The essays in this volume echo in written form the oral presentations offered at a unique event which took place in Lerwick (Shetland), April 4-8, 2003: The first ever joint meeting of the Scottish Place-Name Society, the Society for Name Studies in Britain and Ireland, and NORNA, the Society for Name Studies in the Nordic Countries. Some of the participants belonged to all three organisations but, on the whole, the conference provided an opportunity for scholars with similar, even identical interests to meet for the first time, to listen to each other and to exchange views on topics of common interest. The judiciously chosen title of the conference – *Cultural Contacts in the North Atlantic Region* – reflected well the purpose of the gathering, organised by Dr Doreen Waugh, herself a Shetlander but over many years active in the field of name studies, nationally and internationally, with particular emphasis on its Northern, even Nordic, dimensions.

The focus on contact allowed, indeed encouraged, conference participants to concentrate on connections, similarities and mutual influences, rather than the somewhat more 'parochial' concerns of the three societies represented at the conference. For the members of NORNA which is dedicated to name research in the six Nordic countries (Norway, Sweden, Denmark, Iceland, the Faeroes, and Finland) this was not an innovative approach as the organisation's basic tenets stress co-operation and internationality, in its conferences as well as its publications, but the Northern Isles at least may well have become a little closer to, if not part of, NORNA territory as a result of the conference. The members of the Society for Name Studies in Britain and Ireland present were also accustomed to looking across the borders of their respective 'homelands' (England, Wales, Scotland and Ireland) but their northern horizons may well have been widened in Lerwick. Of the triad of organisations involved in the joint meeting, it was only the Scottish Place-Name Society which had a more limited range of concerns, both geographically and thematically, but since 1469 the relevant geography has included Orkney and Shetland, and the single-mindedness of their activities gave them a thematic advantage.

Against that background, the nature of the conference, however, provided room for personal interaction as well as for scholarly exchange, and in the end all participants could look upon themselves as both contributors and beneficiaries. The publication of this volume is intended to reinforce that basic outlook for those who were present in Lerwick in April 2003, and to draw attention to the spirit as well as the substance of the gathering, for those who missed the original oral presentations.

This collection of essays cannot, of course, replicate the special atmosphere of the conference itself and its climate of fruitful interchange but it nevertheless makes it possible, in a more permanent fashion, to gauge, and for some to relive, the sense of being part of a 'cultural region' which crosses current political boundaries, and of the very 'regionality' which has found an expression in its inventory and heritage of names. Bringing together views, ideas, analyses and interpretations from Iceland to the Isle of Man and from Unst to the Danelaw, these essays examine concerns which are of interest locally as well as in a wider setting, thus reshaping the map of a region often mistaken for being at the margin to one with a firmly centred world view, with the sea not as a hostile separator but as an opportune connector and the numerous coastscapes not as inhospitable defences but as inviting opportunities. There could have been no more appropriate location than Shetland, a kind of maritime crossroads, to host a conference devoted to such matters.

A brief foreword such as this, cannot, indeed must not, evaluate or analyse individual pieces in the cluster of essays it introduces in this volume. That is the task of their readers who will have to make up their own minds as to their quality and persuasiveness. It is, however, not out of place to point to the remarkable variety of responses which the over-arching theme, *Cultural Contacts in the North Atlantic Region*, has brought forth, and one can do so in the knowledge that there is a plethora of others out there which would have been equally suitable if somebody had made one of them his or her choice. It is only to be expected that the majority of the responses are concerned mainly with the Northern Isles, both Shetland and Orkney (Akselberg, Baldwin, Brooke-Freeman, Campbell, Crawford, Fellows-Jensen, Gammeltoft, Melchers, Sandnes, Sigmundsson, Særheim, Waugh) but that others would venture further afield: the west of Scotland (Kruse), the Isle of Man (Sellar), Norway (Schmidt), Ayrshire (Grant), England (Coates, Whaley). Especially attractive are papers which involve (potential) comparisons of more than one part of the region (Akselberg, Crawford, Schmidt, Sellar, Sigmundsson). In tune with much modern scholarship, many of these essays look for patterns or for names as parts of systems, although there are also investigations of individual name types and elements, sometimes in conjunction with a search for their spatial distribution.

As a result, this volume is more than a record of what went on at the conference: it is an independent collection of essays which gains cohesion from a central theme, as well as a sense of place and a view of the world. It is therefore a volume to be highly recommended to everybody interested in the North Atlantic Region, on the one hand, and to students of names, on the other.

W.F.H. Nicolaisen

Names Composed in -*staðir* in Shetland and Western Norway. Continuity or Discontinuity?

Gunnstein Akselberg

1. *Staðir* names – structure and interpretation of the specifier

Nordic scholars have been interested in *staðir* names as an onomastic farmstead name category for over a hundred years (cf. Akselberg 1984, 2000a, 2000b). They have been particularly interested in the last element, the generic *staðir*, and one of the main questions has been: 'What is the etymology of the *staðir* element?' Another main interest has been the first element, the specifier, and much discussed questions have been: 'What do the specifiers tell us?' and 'Are the specifiers common or proper nouns?'

In this paper I will focus on the interpretation of the first element, the specifier, and I will only incidentally discuss the interpretation of the last element *staðir*. My main purpose is to investigate if there is any continuity in the way the *staðir* names are composed and the way the specifiers are or can be interpreted in Shetland, compared with the *staðir* names in Norway, especially Western Norway.

2. Cultural contacts between the Northern Isles and Norway, and the distribution of *staðir* names

If we look at a map, we will notice that there is but a short distance from Bergen and Western Norway to Shetland – and to Orkney, the Faroe Islands, Caithness and Northern England. From Bergen to Lerwick it is 300 km (200 miles) (see Figure 1).

Every year there is a big ship race from Bergen to the Northern Isles, and the fastest modern sailing boats use 24-30 hours in good weather and good wind (cf. www.shetland-race.no). But even as early as in the Viking era a ship could sail within 24-48 hours to the Northern Isles. The physical contact represented by the ship routes across the North Sea was one important factor behind Norwegian cultural influence in the Northern Isles, Scotland and Britain – and vice versa – in the Middle Ages.

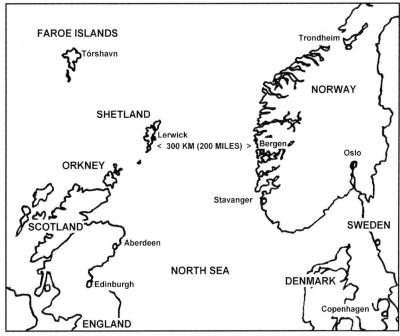

*Figure 1. The geographic situation of Shetland in relation
to Western Norway.*

In 1263 we know it was possible to sail from Western Norway to Shetland
with a big fleet in less than 48 hours (Helle 1982: 69, *Soga om Håkon
Håkonsson*: 344), and sometimes it would be possible to sail this distance in
24 hours (Gunnes 1976: 44). At the end of the 13th century we know it took
36-48 hours from Western Norway to Northern England and Scotland with
good sailing conditions (Helle 1982: 69). Normally, it would take 9-14 days
to England and Scotland from Bergen, while from Bergen to Trondheim and
from Bergen to Oslo would normally take 14 days (Helle 1982: 68). From
Western Norway to Iceland it normally took 4-7 days (Helle 1982: 69).

In the High Middle Ages there were regular trading routes from
Bergen to England, often with ships called *búza/bússa*,[1] 'big broad ships'.
One of these ships was Lysebussen, ON *Lysibúza* or *Lysibússa*, a boat which
belonged to the monastery of Lyse (Norw.: Lysekloster), 27 km south of
Bergen, which had regular routes to England with connections to Fountains
Abbey, Lyse's mother monastery.[2] Lyse was one of the pioneers in trading

with East England and frequently kept their own personnel and ship there from about 1200 till 1350 (Helle 1982: 368).[3]

Through the centuries even small rural areas in Western Norway have been in close contact with the North Atlantic Isles. There have for instance been close ties with my home town Voss, approximately 100 kilometers to the east of Bergen, and the *kongsbóndi* and his familly at Kirkjubœr, the old Faroese township in the vicinity of Tórshavn.[4]

One of the important Nordic influences has been the linguistic impact represented e.g. by pronouns like *they* (ON *þeir*), *them* (ON *þeim*) and *their* (ON *þeira*) on modern English, the Norn language of the Orkneys and thousands of place names scattered around in this vast north west Germanic/Nordic area.

Even the medieval architecture in the North Atlantic Isles is influenced by the architecture in Western Norway. The secular timber house of Finnesloftet in Voss, built about 1250, and Storastovo ('The big house') at Aga, Ullensvang i Hardanger, also from the 13th century, may have been the inspiration for the large timber hall at Kirkjubær, the old bishop's residence (op.cit.: 252-257).[5] In Norway it was customary in the Middle Ages to put up buildings on an assembly site, near the workshop, mark the logs, take them down, transport them to the final site and reconstruct the building there (cf. Berg 1995: 249): 'A bishop, a good customer from the Faroes, was certainly served in the same manner' (op.cit.: loc.cit.).

But even before the Viking period the cultural contact and impact was rather substantial, and we know today that Christianity was known very early in the western parts of Norway, amongst other things because of Christian influence from Ireland (Birkelid 1973; Krag 1995; Rindal 1996: 6; Bagge 2001: 57; Akselberg 2002). From long before the High Middle Ages there has been a continuity and regularity in the cultural contacts and impacts across the North Sea.

The sea and the fjords were the highways in those days, and it was far easier and more convenient to go to the North Atlantic Isles from Western Norway than to go to the eastern and northern parts of Norway. Until the 19th century it took a long time to go to Trondheim, and especially Oslo was far away. In the Middle Ages there was no alternative to crossing the mountains – which would take ages. Even in the beginning of the 20th century it took three nights to go by steamboat to the capital Oslo.[6] Due to rough sea, skerries, streams and wind, the modern ferry in regular service between Bergen and Denmark still stays overnight in Egersund or in Hanstholm (Denmark) on her way to Bergen in heavy weather.

7

3. *Staðir* names – an important Nordic farm name category

What impact these close connections had in the Middle Ages on the material, cultural and mental conditions in the Western Islands, Caithness and northern parts of England, has been an important subject to Norwegian scholars for over a hundred years. And this issue has been a prominent topic of dicussion among onomasticians.[7] In an onomastic context the study of *staðir* names has been important because this is one of the largest farm name categories in Norway, Sweden and Iceland, and because these names are said to be most productive in the Viking age – a period when emigrants from Norway settled in the North Atlantic Isles.[8]

The quantitative distribution of *staðir* names is interesting in this context, and the distribution is as shown in Figure 2, see next page (cf. Stemshaug 1985: 102).

In England there are possibly some *staðir* names in Cumberland and Westmoreland which was colonized by settlers from Norway. *Staðir* names are absent in Danelagen (cf. Sandred 1963).

Norway	ca.	2,500
Sweden	ca.	2,000
Iceland	ca.	1,160
Denmark	ca.	230
Shetland	ca.	35
Orkney		22
Man		12
Faroes		1
Caithness		1

Figure 2. The quantitative distribution of staðir *names.*

Norway has the greatest number of *staðir* names, and the distribution of *staðir* names in relation to other farm name groups in Norway is like this (a 'church farm' tells us about the farm's high social status) (cf. Stemshaug 1985: 97):

vin:	ca. 1,000 names, church farms:	67	(6,7 %)
heimr:	ca. 1,000 names, church farms:	39	(3,9 %)
staðir:	ca. 2,500 names, church farms:	63	(2,5 %)
land:	ca. 2,000 names, church farms:	35	(1,8 %)
setr:	ca. 900 names, church farms:	5	(0,6 %)
ruðr:	ca. 2,900 names, church farms:	0	(0 %)

Figure 3. The Norwegian distribution of staðir *names compared with other farm name groups.*

This distribution is one of the the main reasons why many Norwegian scholars have devoted their time to the *staðir* names. In most parts of Norway, most of the *staðir* names are clustered in the eastern part of the country and in Trøndelag, while Agder and the south-west of Norway have comparatively few. Compared with the distribution of farm names composed with the generics -*vin* and -*heimr*, *staðir* names have, generally speaking, a distribution complementary to *land* names in South West Norway and Agder. This may be the result of a competition between two groups of contemporarily productive names, according to Oluf Rygh (1898b: 63, 71f.).

The main reason for the high *staðir* concentration in Iceland is thought to be immigration from Western Norway in the viking period. There are many studies on the Icelandic *staðir* names (Vilmundarson 1971, 1980, 1982), as are the studies on *staðir* names in Denmark (cp. Sørensen 1958a), Sweden (cp. Linde 1946, 1951) and Norway (cp. Hovda 1971, Akselberg 1984), but so far only few scholars have addressed the *staðir* names of Shetland.

4. *Staðir* names in Shetland

4.1. Jakob Jakobsen's and John Stewart's staðir onomasticon

As yet there is no thorough study especially dedicated to the *staðir* names of Shetland. However, two persons have devoted much time to place names in Shetland generally: Jakob Jakobsen (1864-1918), especially in the book *The Place Names of Shetland* (1938), and John Stewart (1903-1977) in his *Shetland Place Names* (1987). In these books there is little about Shetland *staðir* names. Jakobsen has one and a half pages about these names, and Stewart has about five and a half pages. The result of their investigations is that there are about 35 *staðir* names in Shetland. Jakobsen is of the opinion that there are about 23-27 names, while by Stewart's estimate there are roughly 35.[9]

4.1.1. Jakobsen (1936) and Stewart's (1987) common staðir *onomasticon*

Jakobsen (1936) and Stewart (1987)[10] agree about 23 Shetland place names as *staðir* names, i.e. they interpret the generic in 23 names as a *staðir* element. In Shetland -*staðir* is represented as the modern generic forms -*sta* or -*ster*.

A. Modern generic -*sta* representing -*staðir*

Staðir is most frequently represented by the modern -*sta*, i.e. in 19 different place names:

Asta, Tingwall, Mainland.[11]
Ballista (Jakobsen)/Baliasta (Stewart), Unst.
Basta, Yell.
Bøsta (Jakobsen)/Busta (Stewart), Delting, Mainland.
Girlsta, Tingwall, Mainland.[12]
Grimista, Lerwick, Mainland.
Grista, Tingwall, Mainland.
Gunnista, Bressay.
Hagersta (Jakobsen)/ Haggersta (Stewart), Whiteness, Mainland.
Hoversta, Bressay.
Kalsta (Jakobsen)/Calsta (Stewart), Roe, Northmaven.
Klusta (Jakobsen)/Clousta (Stewart), Aithsting, Mainland.
Oddsta, Fetlar.
Ongersta (Jakobsen)/Ungirsta (Stewart), Haroldswick, Unst.
Ringasta, Dunrossness, Mainland.
Skatsta (Jakobsen)/Scatsta (Stewart), Delting, Mainland.
Tresta, Fetlar.
Tresta, Aithsting, Mainland.
Ulsta, Yell.

B. Modern generic -*ster* representing -*staðir*

In Shetland the -*ster* element in place names is most commonly an abbreviation of *seter* (O.N. *setr/sætr*), but it does represent a *staðir*-element in a few cases. Jakobsen and Stewart agree upon four such interpretations:

1. Elvister, Walls, Mainland.
2. Brinnister (Jakobsen)/Brindister (Stewart), Gulberwick, Mainland.
3. Flamister/Flamaster (Jakobsen)/Flamister (Stewart), Nesting, Mainland.
4. Skellister, Nesting, Mainland.

4.1.2. Jakobsen (1936) and Stewart's (1987) disagreement about the generic

In five instances, Jakobsen and Stewart disagree on the interpretation of the generic by Stewart recategorizing one of Jakobsen's *staðir* names as a *staðr* name, and two of Jakobsen's non-*staðir* names as *staðir* names:

1. Pundsta, Cunningsburgh, Mainland, is interpreted as a *staðir* name by Jacobsen (101) and as a *staðr* name by Stewart (257).
2. Benston, Nesting, Mainland, is interpreted by Jakobsen (149) as a *tún* name, while Stewart (254) claims it is a *staðir* name.
3. Lumbister, Yell, is according to Jakobsen a *bólstaðr* name (27), but to Stewart it is a *staðir* name (253).
4. Grista, *Grista* 1570-1799. *Griðstaðir*. 'from *grið*, m. sanctuary, refuge' (Stewart 255); 'prob. O.N. "griða-staðr", a sanctuary, refuge' (Jakobsen 100).

Sotersta, Sandsting, Mainland, and Kebister, Tingwall, Mainland, mentioned by Jakobsen in the overview (101), is interpreted as respectively a *staðr* name, '*sætr-staðr*' (95), and a *bólstaðr* name, 'a *Kirkebostad*'(27).

4.1.3. Additional staðir *names by Stewart (1987)*

In addition to the *staðir* onomasticon dealt with by Jakobsen, Stewart deals with nine additional *staðir* names. The main reason for this discrepancy is that Stewart had access to traditional written and oral forms not known to Jakobsen. These names are:

1. Ancesti, Bressay.
2. Bailister, Tingwall, Mainland.
3. Bardister, Walls, Mainland.
4. Grimista, Quarff.
5. Hoversta, Unst.
6. Oxensta, Dunrossness, Mainland.
7. Quendista, Dunrossness, Mainland.
8. Vollister, Yell.
9. Wethersta, Delting, Mainland.
10. Yugasta, Fetlar.

4.2. Jakobsen's and Stewart's interpretations of the specifier[13]

Jakobsen and Stewart agree on many interpretations of the specifier (4.2.1.),

11

but they also disagree in some cases (4.2.2.). Stewart is explicitly clear in all his interpretations, whereas Jakobsen is often vague (4.2.3.).

4.2.1. Common interpretation of specifiers (Jakobsen 1936 and Stewart 1987)

– Ballista/Baliasta, *Bollastöðum* 13th century.xiii *Bollastaðir.* 'the man's name Bolli' (Stewart 253); 'Bollastaðir' (Jakobsen 100), 'Bolli, m.' (Jakobsen 149).

– Basta, *Bosta* 1577-1623. *Bessastaðir/*Bassastaðir.* 'the name Bassi' (Stewart 253); '*Bessa-staðir; cf. "Bessigarth"' (Jakobsen 100). About *Bessigert* Jakobsen writes: '*Bessa-garðr (Bersi, Bessi, m.); to this possibly also *Basta* ...: *Bassa- or Bessa-staðir?' (Jakobsen 149).

– Bøsta/Busta, *Byrstad* 1498. *Bœjarstaðir/*Býjarstaðir.* 'from boer, býrr, m. farm' (Stewart 254); 'see bœr' (Jakobsen 100, cf. 27).

– Elvister, *Ilvista* 1624-96. *Ölvisstaðir, *Eilífsstaðir.* 'the man's name Ölvir' (Stewart 255); 'probably: *Eilífs or Ölvis' (Jakobsen 149).

– Girlsta, *Griddilstay* 1574-9. *Geirhildarstaðir.* 'the woman's name Geirhild' (Stewart 255); '*Geirhildar-staðir' (Jakobsen 150).

– Grimista (Lerwick), *Gremsta* 1507. *Grímsstaðir/*Grímustaðir.* 'the woman's name Gríma ... the man's name Grímr' (Stewart 256); '*Gríms-staðir' (Jakobsen 100), 'probably: *Gríms-staðir' (Jakobsen 150).

– Gunnista, *Gunnelista* 1507. *Gunhildarstaðir/*Gunnarsstaðir.* 'the woman's name Gunnhildr' (Stewart 256); '*Gunnars- or *Gunnhildar-staðir' (Jakobsen 100)

– Oddsta, *Odstay* 1558-1613. *Oddstaðir.* 'the name Oddr' (Stewart 253); '*Odds-staðir' (Jakobsen 100, 152).

– Ringasta, *Regusta* 1507. *Hringsstaðir.* 'the name Hringr, later Ringr' (Stewart 257); '*Hrings-staðir' (Jakobsen 101).

– Skellister, *Schellesta* 1507. *Skjaldarstaðir.* 'the man's name Skjöldr' (Stewart 254); 'probably: *á "Skjaldar-stöðum", containing the man's name "Skjöldr"' (Jakobsen 153).

– Ullsta, *Ulstadh* 1485. *Úlfsstaðir.* 'the name Úlfr' (Stewart 253); 'Úlfsstaðir?' (Jakobsen 101).

4.2.2. Different interpretation of specifiers (Jakobsen 1936 and Stewart 1987)

- *Hoversta* (Bressay), Hoverista 1507-1733. **Hafrstaðir/*Hávarðastaðir.* 'the man's name Hávarðr' (Stewart 256); 'prob. **Hafrs-staðir* ' (Jakobsen 100), 'must be derived from the man's name "Hafr"' (Jakobsen 151). See *Hoversta* (Unst) below (4.2.5).
- *Kalsta/Calsta*, Calstay 1507-1672. **Kaldstaðir/*Kalastaðir.* 'the man's name Kali' (Stewart 254); '**kald-staðir*' (Jakobsen 100).
- *Klusta/Clousta*, Cloustay 1507-1623. **Klóstaðir/*Klaufastaðir.* 'The name may be Klóstaðir, from kló, f., claw, used as a nickname. It is more probably Klaufastaðir, from the man's surname Klaufi' (Stewart 255); '**kló-staðir*? ... metaphorically also denoting headland or tongue of land' (Jakobsen 100).

4.2.3. Unclear interpretation of specifiers by Jakobsen 1936

- Asta, *Osta* 1568. **Ásustaðir.* 'from the very common woman's name Ása' (Stewart 255); 'Asta' Jakobsen (100).
- Brinnister/Brindister, *Brynista* 1507. **Brandsstaðir/*Branda-staðir.* 'from the man's name Brandr ... from the man's name Brandi' (Stewart 256); '"Brindista"' (Jakobsen 101).
- Flamister/Flamaster, *Flamesta* 1577-1656. **Flámstaðir.* 'No personal name or surname in Flam is known. Staðir does not combine with hill names, and the name is probably a setr one, a derivative of Norse flá, f., a level part on a hillside. This occurs elsewhere in Shetland: e.g. da Flaam aa Filla, on an islet near Skerries' (Stewart 254); '*Flamaster* or *Flamister*' (Jakobsen 101).
- Hagersta/Haggersta, *Hagrascath* 1524. **Hallgeirrstaðir/ *Hallgerðarstaðir.* 'The man's name Hallgeirr ... the woman's name Hallgerðr' (Stewart 256); 'cf. Hagrister (Nm.) under "setr"' (Jakobsen 100).
- Ongersta/Ungirsta, *Unustaðir* 13th century.xiv **Unnstaðir.* 'from the woman's name Una (Landnámabók), Unnr or Unna' (Stewart 252); 'Ongersta' (Jakobsen 100).
- Skatsta/Scatsta, *Skatsta* 1507. **Skatastaðir.* 'the name Skati' (Stewart 254); '"Scattersta"' (Jakobsen 101).
- Tresta (Aithsting, Mainland), *Traista* 1507-1628. **Tréstaðir.* 'see Tresta, Fetlar' (Stewart 255); 'Older form: "Trusta"' (Jakobsen 101). See *Tresta* below.

– Tresta (Fetlar), *Tresta* 1628. **Tréstaðir*. 'Thrasi's farm, is a possibility: the name is found in Landnámabók, and recorded in Troms in Norway and possibly the Western Isles of Scotland in placenames. However, the name occurs again in Shetland, and as both places are likely sites for that Shetland rarity a tree, the explanation may simply be tré-staðir, from tré, n., a tree' (Stewart 254); Jakobsen, see above.

4.2.4. Jakobsen's interpretation of specifiers in doubtful staðir names

– Pundsta (Cunningsburgh, Mainland) 'pund-staðir' (Jakobsen 101), 'pund' (203f.). Jakobsen suggests that the specifier *pund* may be a Celtic word. 'Gaelic *pund* denotes the same' as English pound 'fold, enclosure' (204).

4.2.5. Stewart's (1985) interpretation of specifiers in additional names

– Ancesti, *Ustensta* 1577. **Øysteinsstaðir*. 'The man's name Øy-steinn ... Eysteinn' (Stewart 256).
– *Bailister*, Balyesta 1577-1628. **Ballastaðir*. 'from the man's name Balli ... but cf. Baliasta, Unst' (Stewart 255), i.e. *Bollastaðir* and *Bolli* m.
– Bardister, *Bardesta* 1507-1716. **Barðastaðir*. 'from the man's name Barði ... or ... Barðr' (Stewart 255).
– Benston, *Bennasta* 1507. **Beinastaðir*. 'from the man's name Beini ... The late appearance of the 'ston' ending suggests that it is not the dative stöðum' (Stewart 254).
– Grimista (Quarff), *Gremesta* 1628. **Grímustaðir* 'See Grimista, supra' (Stewart 256), i.e. the woman's name *Gríma*.
– Hoversta (Unst), *Hoversta* 1558-1733. **Hafrstaðir*. 'the name Hafr' (Stewart 253).
– Lumbister, *Lumbista* 1517-1656. **Lambastaðir*. 'the name Lambi' (Stewart 253).
– Oxensta, *Oxnasta* 1507. **Oxnastaðir*. 'oxen farm' (Stewart 257).
– Quendista, *Cwindistay* 1506. **Kvarndalstaðir*. 'Quendale is not far away. The name Quendista is now unknown, though Broo still remains' (Stewart 257).
– Vollister, *Valista* 1576. **Valastaðir*. 'The name Vali' (Stewart 253)
– Wethersta, *Vedderista* 1507. **Viðarastaðir*. 'the name Viðarr' (Stewart 254).
– Yugasta, this name is preserved in oral memory. **Jóðgeirsstaðir*. 'the man's name Jóðgeirr or Jólgeirr' (Stewart 253).

4.3. Jakobsen's and Stewart's interpretation of the specifier – a conclusion

The analysis in 4.2. above tells us the following:

1.: Jakobsen and Stewart agree that there are 11 personal names as specifiers, and five names with a specifier that is not a personal name.

2.: In two cases Jakobsen prefers a non-personal specifier, while Stewart prefers a personal name interpretation in those instances.

3.: In eight cases Jakobsen is unclear in his interpretation of the specifier, while Stewart interprets six of these specifiers as personal names.

4.: In 10 out of 12 additional names Stewart interprets the specifier as a personal name.

5.: Stewart is nearly always categorical in his interpretations. In only two (three?) cases he provides a discussion of his interpretation of the specifier, and only once for the generic.

6.: Jakobsen, on the other hand, is more frequently qualifiying his interpretation, i.e. eight cases for the specifier.

7.: In 29 of 35 cases Stewart interprets the specifier as a personal name, i.e. 83 %. Jakobsen interprets explicitly the specifier as a personal name in 11 out of 24 cases, i.e. 45 %.

4.4. A discussion of Jakobsen's and Stewart's interpretations of specifiers[16]

4.4.1. Appellatives which may denote a natural or cultural locality by comparison

The specifiers in the following names which Jakobsen and/or Stewart interpret as a personal name, are better interpreted as common nouns:

A. Common interpretation as a personal name (by Jakobsen and Stewart)

- Ballista/Baliasta, *bolli* m., 'bowl, cup', may denote a concave shape of the landscape.
- Basta, *bessi* m. = *bersi* m. = *bassi* m., 'bear', may denote a rounded hill in the landscape.
- Oddsta, *oddr* m., 'point, spear, needle', may denote a tongue-shaped feature of the landscape.

- Ringasta, *hringr* m., 'ring, circle, bay, gulf, bend', may denote a curved shape in the landscape.
- Skellister, *skjöldr* m., 'shield, defence, bulwark', may denote a brink or a edge in the landscape.
- Ullsta, *ulfr* m., 'wolf, enemy', may denote a shape of the landscape which may resemble a wolf.

B. Different interpretation of specifiers (by Jakobsen and Stewart)

- Hoversta (Bressay), *hafr* m., 'he-goat', may denote a shape of the landscape. The specifier may also denote a place where there are he-goats.
- Klusta, *kló* f., 'claw, nail, ring, hook, curl', may denote a curved shape of the landscape.

C. Unclear interpretation of specifiers by Jakobsen

- Brinnister/Brindister, *brandr* m., 'fire, burning; trunk, firelog', may denote something of woodwork in the landscape.
- Skatsta/Scatsta, *skati* m., 'trunk without branches, man', may denote shape of the landscape or treetrunks.
- Tresta (Fetlar), *tré* n., 'tree, woodwork', may denote trees in the landscape or something of woodenwork.
- Tresta (Aithsting, Mainland), see above.

D. Jakobsen's interpretation of specifiers in doubtful *staðir* names

- Pundsta, Gaelic *pund*, 'pound', may denote wet, marshy ground.

E. Stewart's interpretation of specifiers in additional names

- Bailister, *balli* m., *bolli* m., 'bowl, cup'. See Ballista/ Balliasta above.
- Bardister, *barði* m., 'sort of ship, sort of whale', may denote a shape of the landscape or a place with connection to the sea.
- Benston, *beini* m., 'benefit, advantage; bone, knuckle, leg', may denote a favourable place or a shape of the landscape.
- Hoversta (Unst), *hafr* m., 'he-goat'. See Hoversta above.
- Lumbister, *lambi* m., 'lamb', may denote a shape of the landscape or a place where there are lambs

– Oxensta, *oxi* m. = *uxi* m., 'oxen', may denote a height in the landscape or a place where there are oxen.

4.4.2. Appellatives which directly are denoting a natural or cultural locality

The specifiers in the following names which Jakobsen and/or Stewart interpret as an appellative, may be interpreted as an appellative:

A. Common interpretation as an appellative (by Jakobsen and Stewart)

– Bøsta/Busta, *bœr/býr* m., 'farm, town', may denote a farm.
– Grista, *grið* n., 'sanctuary, refuge', may denote a place where people may be in security.

These are the only two names where Jakobsen and Stewart agree about a common noun interpretation.

B. Different interpretation of specifiers (by Jakobsen and Stewart)

– Kalsta, *kaldr* adj., 'cold, ill, hostile', may denote a climatically cold place.

C. Unclear interpretation of specifiers by Jakobsen

– Asta, derivative of *á* f., 'stream', or *áss* m., 'ridge'. Stewart writes: 'A derivation from á, a stream, and áss, a ridge, is ruled out, as there are no such geographic features here, and long 'a' in Shetland becomes 'o'. There is, however, considerable laxity between a and á in personal names' (256). This may be correct for the common noun *áss*, but not definitively for *á*. The significance of the laxity between *a* and *á* in appellatives should not, however, be exaggerated.
– Flamister/Flamaster, derivative of *flá* f., 'level part on a hillside'. This occurs elsewhere in Shetland. Stewart writes: 'Staðir does not combine with hill names' (254), but he offers no plausible argument for this.
– Quendista, *kvern* f., 'mill', may be a place where there is a mill.

4.4.3. Specifiers which may be a personal name

The specifier in the following names is probably a personal name:

A. Common interpretation as a personal name

– Elvister, man's name *Ölvir* m.

- Girlsta, woman's name *Geirhildr* f.
- Grimista (Lerwick, Mainland), man's name *Grímr* m.
- Grimista (Quarff), woman's name *Gríma*, see *Grimista* above.
- Gunnista, man's name *Gunnar* or woman's name *Gunnhildr* f.

B. Unclear interpretation of specifiers by Jakobsen

- Hagersta/Haggersta, man's name *Hallgeirr* m., or woman's name *Hallgerðr* f.
- Ongersta/Ungirsta, woman's name *Una*, *Unn* or *Unna* f.

C. Stewart's interpretation of specifiers in additional names

- Ancesti, man's name *Øysteinn* m.
- Vollister, man's name *Vali* m.
- Wethersta, man's name *Viðarr* m., son of Odin
- Yugasta, man's name *Jóðgeirr* m. or *Jólgeirr* m. (Stewart 253).

The specifier in 24 *staðir* names may be interpreted as a common noun. In 11 names the specifier is arguably to be interpreted as a personal name.

5. Results and conclusion

This analysis shows us that as far as *staðir* names are concerned there is a continuity between Shetland and (Western) Norway on no less than four levels:

1.: Name elements: Many of the specifiers which are found in Shetland may also be interpreted in the way place name elements are interpreted in Norway.

2.: Many of the *staðir* name constructions we find in Shetland, are also found in Norway.

3.: Many Norwegian *staðir*-farms are situated in or near a central part of a local district. Compare for instance the 'church farms'. This is also the case in Shetland, where some of the *staðir*-farms have a geographic, cultural and administrative prominent position.

4.a.: Last, but not least, the mental continuity is important. As W.F.H. Nicolaisen has told us on several occasions from the 1970s and onwards, and which he argued so brilliantly in the Lerwick Theatre during the conference, the Norse settlers brought with them a mental onomasticon when they left

Norway (Denmark and Sweden). When they came to the Northern Isles, this was to them a virgin onomastic landscape, so they could just open their onomasticon bags and throw names, generics and specifiers out over the landscape. For that reason we may find both 'old' names and 'new' *staðir* name constructions here.

4.b.: But there is also another type of continuity according to the onomasticon, namely the *onomast's onomasticon*, represented in this case by Jakob Jakobsen and John Stewart. They are both heavily influenced by the tradition from Oluf Rygh (1987, 1898a, 1898b, 1900, 1901) and Magnus Olsen (1910), two Norwegian scholars who wished to interpret the specifier in *staðir* names as personal names (Akselberg 1984, 2000a, 2000b). Jakobsen does so too, but he is nevertheless very cautious in his interpretations, while Stewart rarely has any reservations. Stewart puts a heavy pressure on all first elements so they can be interpreted as a personal name.

From the 1950s scholars like the Swedish Linde (1946), and not least the Danish John Kousgård Sørensen (1958) and the Icelandic Þorhallur Vilmundarson (1971, 1980, 1983), have demonstrated that in many cases we are not dealing with personal names as specifiers in *staðir* names, but rather with common nouns telling us something about the landscape, vegetation, animal life and cultural conditions (Akselberg 1984, 2000a, 2002b).

My opinion is that many of the specifiers in Shetland *staðir* names are common nouns, cf. 4.4. above, not personal names as Jakobsen and Stewart tell us – and there are linguistic, toponymic and cultural reasons for this.

According to what Richard Coates tells us in his article, the entire story of names has by no means been told so far. During the conference I visited a local Co-Op supermarket in Lerwick, and on the the the bag I got there it says: 'Our packaging tells you the whole truth'.

Jakobsen and Stewart have not told us the whole truth about the *staðir* names in Shetland. Somebody should tell us more about it.

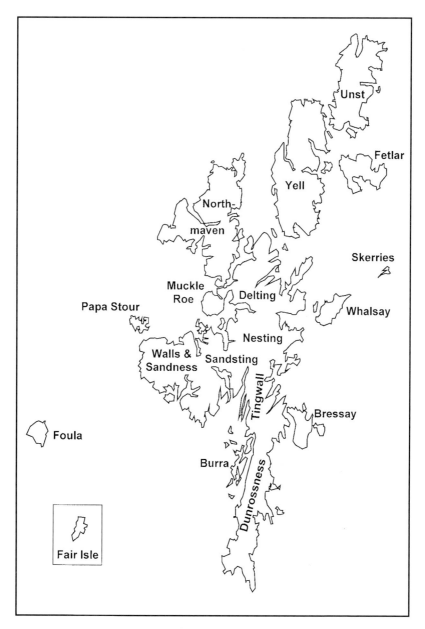

Figure 4. A map of Shetland with major districts.

Gunnstein Akselberg

Literature

Akselberg, G., 1984: 'Vikingtidsindividualisme eller naturnemne-relasjonar? Om utmerkingslekken i staðir-namn på Voss og i grannebygdene i indre Hordaland sett på bakgrunn av eldre og nyare nordisk forsking', *Namn og Nemne* 1, 51-82.

Akselberg, G., 2000a: 'Tolkingsmetodane til Oluf Rygh som mønster for norsk og nordisk gardsnamntolking. Eit faghistorisk og vitskapsteoretisk perspektiv', *Nordica Bergensia* 22, 201-221.

Akselberg, G., 2000b: 'Gardsnamntydingar – standardtolking og modelltolking hjå Oluf Rygh. Ei metodisk drøfting av gardsnamntolkingane til Oluf Rygh'. In: B. Sandnes *et al.* (eds), *Oluf Rygh. Artikler om en foregangsmann i humanistisk forsking*. Uppsala, 65-85.

Akselberg, G., 2002. 'Det kristne onomastikonet – utvikling, samansetjing og struktur. Om kristningsprosessen i mellomalderen og stadnamn på Voss'. In: S. Sigmundsson (ed.), *Rapport fra NORNAs 28. symposium i Skálholt 25.-28. mai 2000*. Uppsala, 67-101.

Bagge, S., 2001: *Norsk idéhistorie. 1. Da boken kom til Norge*. Oslo.

Berg, A., 1995: *Norske tømmerhus frå mellomalderen. Band 5. Hus for hus i Aust-Agder, Vest-Agder, Rogaland, Hordaland, Færøyane, Sogn og Fjordane, Møre og Romsdal, Sør-Trøndelag*. Oslo.

Bindloss, J. & Lucas C., 2002: *Scotland's Highlands & Islands*. Melbourne/Oakland/London/Paris.

Birkeli, F., 1973: *Norske steinkors i tidlig middelalder. Et bidrag til belysning av overgangen fra norrøn religion til kristendom*. Oslo.

Gunnes, E., 1976: 'Rikssamling og kristning 800-1177'. In: K. Mykland (ed.), *Norges historie*, vol. 3. Oslo.

Helle, K., 1982: *Bergen bys historie. Bind 1. Kongssete og kjøpstad. Fra opphavet til 1536*. Bergen/Oslo/Tromsø.

Hovda, P., 1971: '-stad. Noreg', *Kulturhistorisk leksikon for nordisk middelalder fra vikingtid til reformasjonstid*. 16. Oslo, cols 574-578.

Jakobsen, J., 1936: *The Place-Names of Shetland*. London/Copenhagen.

Johnsen, A.O., 1977: *De norske cistercienserklostre 1147-1264: sett i europeisk sammenheng*. Afhandlinger utg. Av Det Norske Vitenskaps-Akademi, 2. Oslo/Bergen/Tromsø.

Krag, C., 1995b: 'Kirkens forkynnelse i tidlig middelalder og nordmennenes kristendom'. In: H.-E. Lidén (ed.), *Møtet mellom hedendom og kristendom i Norge*. Oslo, 28-57.

Langstrøm, R., *et al.*, 1981: *Kystruta Oslo-Bergen*. Oslo.

Linde, G., 1946: 'Namnen på -sta och -inge', *Namn och Bygd* 34, 98-127.

Linde, G., 1951: *Studier över de svenska sta-namnen*. Uppsala.

Olsen, M., 1910: *Søndre Bergenhus Amt. Norske Gaardnavne* 11. Kristiania.

Rindal, M., 1996: 'Frå heidendom til kristendom'. In: M. Rindal (ed.), *Fra hedendom til kristendom*. Oslo, 9-19.

Rygh, O., 1897: *Smaalenenes Amt. Norske Gaardnavne* 1. Kristiania.

Names Composed in -staðir in Shetland and Western Norway.

Rygh, O., 1898a: *Akershus Amt. Norske Gaardnavne* 2. Kristiania.

Rygh, O., 1898b: *Forord og Indledning. Norske Gaardnavne.* Kristiania.

Rygh, O., 1900: *Hedmarks Amt. Norske Gaardnavne* 3. Kristiania.

Rygh, O., 1901: *Gamle personnavne i norske gaardnavne.* Kristiania.

Sandred, K.I., 1963: *English place-names in "-stead".* Uppsala.

Soga om Håkon Håkonsson = S. Tordsson: *Soga om Håkon Håkonsson. Norrøne bokverk* 22. Translated by K. Audne. 2nd edition by K. Helle. Oslo, 1963.

Stemshaug, O., 1985: *Namn i Noreg. Ei innføringsbok i norsk stadnamngransking.* 3. utg. Oslo.

Stewart, J., 1987: *Shetland Place-Names.* Lerwick.

Sørensen, J.K., 1958a: *Danske bebyggelsesnavne på -sted.* København.

Sørensen, J.K., 1958b: *Danmarks Stednavne.* 13. *Svendborg Amts bebyggelsesnavne.* København.

Sørensen, J.K., 1967: 'Indledningsföredrag'. In: G. Holm (ed.), *En diskussion om sta-namnen. Förhandlingar vid symposium i Lund 1963.* [Lund], 62-64.

Vilmundarson, Þ., 1971: '-stad. Island', *Kulturhistorisk leksikon for nordisk middelalder fra vikingtid til reformasjonstid.* 16. Oslo, cols 578-584.

Vilmundarson, Þ., 1980: 'Safn til íslenzkrar örnefnabókar 1'. In: *Grímnir* 1. Reykjavík, 57-143.

Vilmundarson, Þ., 1983: 'Safn til íslenzkrar örnefnabókar 2'. In: *Grímnir* 3. Reykjavík, 54-144.

Notes

[1] Cp. MLat *bucie*, 'sailing-ship for transport'.

[2] The bishop in Bergen had his *bússa* – and the royal chapels in Bergen, Apostelkirken and Katarinakirken, had their boats for overseas trading, Apostelsuden and Katarinasuden (Helle 1982: 361).

[3] The trade with Eastern England was in particular connected to King's Lynn (Helle 1982: 369). The bishop in Bergen also had trading relations with England, as had many wealthy private persons in Sogn, Bergen and Hordaland in the 13th century (Helle op.cit: loc.cit).

[4] *Kongsbóndi*, m., 'the king's farmer', a farmer who leases a farm from the king. This family also had close ties to the rural Milde district 15 km south of Bergen.

[5] The large timber hall at Kirkjubœr consists of two mediaeval buildings, the Roykstovan and the Stokkstovan. 'In the old bishop's residence at Kirkjubö there are two dwelling houses, or parts of houses, that have a form of notching, Findal laft, exactly corresponding to the Norwegian type from before 1350', writes Berg (1995: 249), and he especially finds many corresponding structures between "Storastovo" at Aga and the houses in the old Faroese bishop's residence.

[6] The steamboat from Bergen to Christiania used 111 hours in 1927, 60 hours in 1884 and 54 hours in 1924 (Langstrøm 1981: 22, 39, 64).

[7] This interest is reflected in different traveller's guides like Binloss & Lucas (2003: 347): 'There were still over 10,000 Norse words in common usage here [Shetland] at the start of the 20th century and most place names have Viking rather than Celtic origin'.

[8] Scholars claim that the bulk of *staðir* names were productive in the period 800-1000 AD., but many of them may date as far back as from 400-800 AD.

[9] In this paper I will not be questioning the interpretation of the generic, only the interpretation of the specifier. Because of this I will not problematize if any of the traditional written and oral forms used by Jakobsen and Stewart represent a *staðir* name or not.

[10] References to Jakobsen and Stewart in the text below concern Jakobsen (1936) and Stewart (1987) only.

[11] For Shetland regions, see map 2 at the end of this paper.

[12] Girlsta is not mentioned in Jakobsen's overview of *staðir* names (100-101), but he categorizes the name as a *staðir* name elsewhere (150).

[13] This section is structured in this way: Jakobsen's and Stewart's normalized forms, oldest written form, Jakobsen's and Stewart's reconstructed form(s), and Stewart's and Jakobsen's interpretations.

[14] *Longer Magnus' Saga* dates from the 14th century.

[15] *Longer Magnus' Saga*. See note 15.

[16] In section 4.4. I mainly discuss Jakobsen's and Stewart's linguistic interpretations. I am generally not qualified to ascertain whether the denotata (localities) fit the interpretations of the common nouns which is linguistically and culturally relevant. I hope that I sometime in future will have the opportunity to examine all the *staðir* localities in *situ*.

Names Around *Da Burn a Ham* and its Catchment, Foula

John R. Baldwin

1. Introduction

Foula is a small but mountainous island some 3.5 miles north/south and approximately 2.5 miles east/west (5.6 x 4 kms). It has three peaks over 1,000 ft. (305 m), the highest rising to nearly 1,380 ft. (420 m) and the western sea-cliffs to some 1,220 ft. (372 m). Once ashore, it never feels much like an island, largely because the hills tower steeply and immediately above the relatively narrow eastern lowlands and suggest a never-ending landmass reaching far out into an invisible Atlantic.

It has two main valleys. The great glacial trough referred to simply as Da Dal at the southern end of the island is the deep, vastly truncated, gently curving remnant of a far more extensive system that, once upon a geological time, did indeed stretch way out west. Its catchment has all but vanished and it has virtually no surviving tributaries. The other is a total contrast. It winds and twists its shallow, sluggish, inconsequential way along a route that rarely suggests a single, dominant valley; and unlike Da Dal its catchment resembles a considerable, albeit somewhat tattered, spidery web. It drains the northern slopes of the main island ridge, supplemented by an even more modest flow off the largely flat and low-lying eastern moorland. As a result, it has many but mainly tiny tributaries and a variety of generally tiny lochs, pools and springs, complemented by a number of significant bogs and mires.

2. Stream names

For those hoping to find a selection of good Norse names, Scots *burn* and Shetland Scots *da* (for English *the*) are ubiquitous. Virtually every watercourse on Foula with an identifiable name is called 'da ... Burn'; sometimes 'da Burn a ...'. If the name is associated with a landscape feature, it is often referred to as belonging to it – hence da Burn a Ou(v)rafandal can alternate with da Ou(v)rafandal Burn. However, Yelpers Burn is never 'da Burn a Yelpers' (J. and S. Gear 2003). In other words, some burns are often (but not necessarily always) found with a 'burn of ...' name; but this only applies to certain burns. (For discussion of this type of construction, see Nicolaisen 1976: 57-64.)

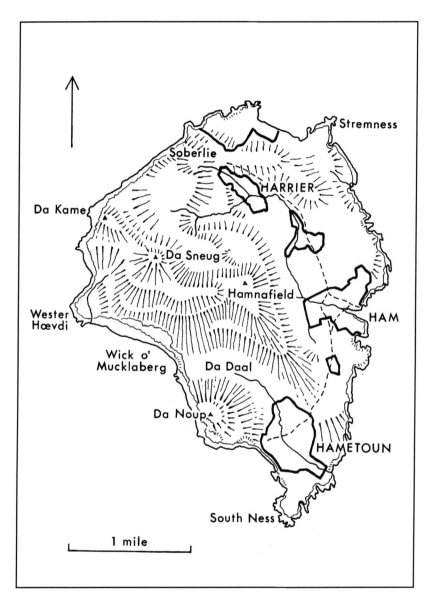

Figure 1. Foula's settlement areas. Da Burn a Ham flows down through da tun a Harrier, past Gossamüdo and da Burns, to da tun a Ham and into Ham Voe.

The main burn is known as da Burn a Ham. Nowadays, the section running through or alongside a particular croft might be referred to by the croft name, e.g.: da Ham Burn, da Leraback Burn, da Mogle Burn, da Loch Burn, da Burns Burn, da Wilse Burn, da Harrier Burn and da Bloburn Burn. Between the tuns or townships, however, names tend to betray other aspects of a burn's geographical location or its physical or other characteristics, e.g.: da Wast Burn (between Mogle and Burns), da Crookit Burn (between Burns and Harrier), da Mill Burn or da Loch Burn (named after da Mill Loch), da Peerie Burn (north side of Ham Voe) (Shetland *peerie* 'small') and Ross's Burn (south side of Ham Voe).

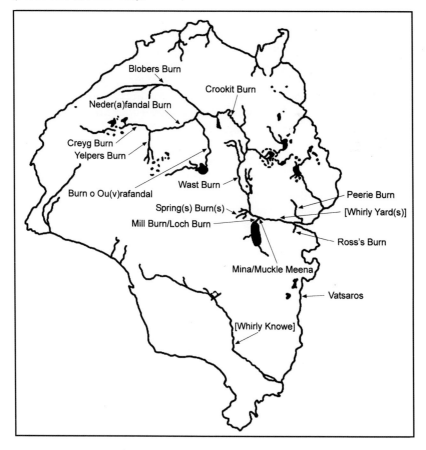

Figure 2. Burn names associated with da Burn a Ham, Foula.

Finally, beyond the uppermost parts of the tuns, tributaries display names reflecting either the valleys they run through or some distinctive feature associated with their environment, e.g.: da Neder(a)fandal Burn, da Ou(v)rafandal Burn, da Creyg Burn, Yelpers Burn and da Blobers Burn (which gave the croft name now generally shortened to Bloburn). Any traces of a surviving Norse element are generally found within names for these higher tributaries or those incorporating a croft name (which mainly reflect a geographical feature). Even so, they are set within an entirely Scots/English linguistic framework.

2.1. Around Da Tun a Harrier

Da Crookit Burn refers to the section of burn between da tun a Harrier and da Burns. It is probably the straightforward English description for a burn that twists tightly and meanders in multiple loops across flat marshy ground, but it may reflect ON *krókr* 'a corner, bend or nook', subsequently assimilated with or replaced by Scots *crookit*, English *crooked*. At the foot of the Leraback croft, (da) Kruk is the name of a small arable rig in the bend of the Ham Burn (Jakobsen 1993: 73, 141).

(Da) Blobers Burn. The last occupants of Bloburn, Peter Manson and his sister Katie, related it to the colour of the rock that the burn passes through in the higher ground just a little above the hill dyke (ON *bló-berg* 'blue rock'). The core name is also found in da Nebb a Blobrekk (Seim 1938), a clifftop point 0.5 ml. (800 m.) or so to the west on the sheer 700 ft. (213 m.) high Nort Bank.

Da Creyg Burn is sometimes referred to as da Burn a da Creyg (- Krig). ON *kríkr* or *kriki* 'a bend, curve or corner', is an apt term for the point at which two tributaries high up in the hills come together and turn sharply before descending towards da tun a Harrier. At some point, however, da Creyg has undergone locational transfer and maybe assimilated with Scots *craig*, for on the late-19th century Ordnance Survey 6 Inch map it refers to the rough ridge or tongue of land coming steeply down between the burns.

In current usage, however, the slope west of da Creyg Burn (i.e. between the two burns) is known as da Peerie Hill (stretching up to the corner that the side of da Sneug makes with the edge of da Fleck). Da Creyg, meantime, refers to the slope immediately east of the burn, reaching upwards until it becomes Cudlafield (M. Gear, per J. and S. Gear 2003).

Yelpers Burn, the second of these two tributaries, is more difficult. A *hjelpersten* or *hjilpersten* (*jalpersten* on Foula) was the 'flat lintel stone covering the mouth of a small kiln, the innermost edge of which projected a little into the kiln' (Jakobsen 1985: 317). The fire was lit within the short tunnel, and the projecting lintel helped protect the drying corn nearest the fire from catching fire.

What is distinctive about this burn 'is the way it suddenly appears out of a hole in the ground at the top of the slope. After heavy rain it actually bubbles up like a small fountain, making a lot of froth' (J. and S. Gear 2003). The kiln analogy would seem quite apt, therefore, whether echoing the mouth of the tunnel or the bowl of the kiln. Jakobsen suggested ON **hylpr* 'a hump or knot', maybe echoing the projecting lintel over the kiln flue.

2.2. Around Da Tun a Ham

In their various permutations, da Spring(s) Burn(s) (at the foot of Hamnafeld, a little north of the Mill Loch) are relatively recent, descriptive names. So too, is da Peerie Burn, a tiny stream or ditch that threads its way through the upper section of the Ham croft and into Ham Voe beside Tooshkarigg (Brownrigg 1970), one of 'two small, rocky headlands ... about 10-20 ft. high [3-7 m.]' (E. Isbister 1984).

Mina has been recorded only by Seim (1938). It is difficult to locate precisely, but his map suggests the flattish land on the south side of da Mogle Burn, either side of its junction with the short burn flowing out of the Mill Loch. As Da Muckle Meena, it lies more or less opposite to, albeit a little further west than, da Muggie Skins – a piece of land shaped like a 'muggie': any kind of stomach, often that of a fish (J. and S. Gear 2003) or a sheep (E. Isbister 1984) and originating in ON **maga-skinn* 'the belly skin of a slaughtered sheep' (Jakobsen 1993: 140).

ON *mynni, minni* 'a mouth or opening into which a stream disgorges', was generally associated with a burn or river entering the sea. As it survives, Da Muckle Meena applies not to a place where one burn empties into another, but to a small *brug* (steep slope) and deep pool on the south side of the Mogle Burn (J. and S. Gear 2003). A lot can happen to a stream over several hundred years, so that it would not be surprising if confluence, pool and name had shifted.

Whirly Yard(s). There is no obvious survival of ON *á* 'river', in any stream name on Foula. It is not at all unusual for it to have disappeared as the old language became increasingly influenced and replaced by Scots. It is a short element, easily lost at the end of a name, and where it survives it is more generally the first element in a compound. On Foula there are two occurrences of Whirly. Whirly Knowe is a burnt mound in the Hametoun, adjacent to a ruinous horizontal watermill and the present-day bridge. The field name Whirly Yard(s) (-Yat) (A. Umphray 1974) lies along the north side of da Ham Burn, next to the Leraback march (J. and S. Gear 2003) and just upstream from the Ham croft kailyard (E. Isbister 1984).

ON *ár-hlið* 'burn-gate', referred to an opening in the bottom of a dyke or fence through which a burn flowed (Jakobsen 1985: 1066). It could maybe have referred to an opening under a small bridge, but as at da Hametoun, the core definition is most likely. It would pre-date the taking in of the Brae and Groups crofts and relate to a time when the shore and the land below the Haa were still part of the skattald (probably late-18th century, but according to Harry Gear, possibly mid-19th century: J. and S. Gear 2003). This area included da Kwis (Jakobsen 1993: 74; J Gray 1974), cattle enclosures or pastures sited between the house of Ham and the old shop, just below the track leading down to the harbour (Baldwin 1984: 37).

Vatsaros. The name is preserved in several written forms: Vatsaros (Jakobsen 1993: 90; also Møkkel Vatsros: Seim 1938), Vats(a)ros (also Mikill Vastros and Piri Vatsross) (Stewart 1970: 314, 318), da Vats Ross (E. Isbister 1984), Vats a Ross (D.A. Brownrigg 1970) and Burn a Vatsros (Stewart 1970: 308). Most mid-20th century and later forms point to the name having lost its original meaning, whether metathesised Vastros, tautological Burn a Vatsros, or folk etymology that has steered the spelling in two quite different directions – the common Scots forename *Ross*, or the ordinary noun *vat*, 'a tub or cask'.

From ON *vatn* 'water' + ON *rás* 'path', *vatns-rás* 'water course', refers to a 'steep cliff with small grassy "toogs"' or ledges (E. Isbister 1984), and also to an extent of land around the clifftop (Seim 1938). The name is still occasionally current (as Vatsaros) for the land next to the clifftop. However, it no longer applies exclusively to where the tiny burns draining swampy ground between the cliff edge and Mornington trickle out from two small lochans (da Pools a Heedlicliv) and drop over the cliff. The name has shifted a little south, perhaps a result of its use as a fishing mede (Stewart 1970: 318). Whether fishermen continued to understand its underlying meaning is unclear, but being higher, the southern end of this stretch of cliff shows up better from the sea (J. and S. Gear 2003).

John R. Baldwin

By way of contrast, Ross's Burn, on the south side of Ham Voe, underlines both the importance of local knowledge and the dangers of expecting to see a Viking under every stone! It has no known association with ON *rás* (or ON *hross*). Referring to a short burn or ditch just east of the nurse's house (with a small waterfall in winter), it was named after the husband of the first nurse to live in the house, built at the beginning of World War II (J. and S. Gear 2003).

3. Lochs and pools

The very occasional 'pool' would generally reflect English *pool* – e.g. da Clay Pool/Clay Pødl, high up on da North Bank, on the edge of da Fleck. Otherwise, like *burn*, Scots *loch* is found almost everywhere, whether added to a word of Norse origin, to a word occasionally maybe replacing a former Norse specific, or to a purely Scots or Scots English creation, e.g.: Dry Loch, Figure Eicht Loch, Limey Loch, Mill Loch, Bottle Loch, Flick Lochs/Lochs a da Fleck, Gossa Loch, Rossie('s) Loch, Sandvatten (Loch), Ou(v)rafandal Loch.

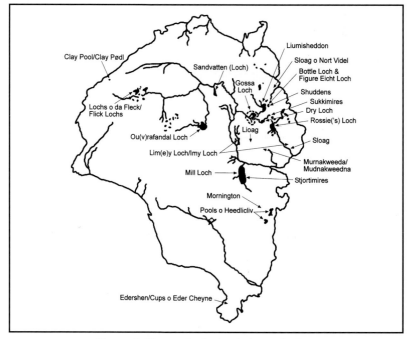

Figure 3. Names for lochs, bogs and mires.

31

Dry Loch; **Figure Eicht Loch**; **(da) Bottle Loch**. Such names mean simply what they say – a loch that is dry for part or much of the year (recorded on the OS 6 Inch map, 1877); one shaped like a figure 8; another resembling a bulbous old skin bottle (E. Isbister 1984; J. and S. Gear 2003).

The two latter well illustrate the vagaries of oral tradition. According to one source, Figure Eicht Loch was first noted from crofters in the Burns, Loch, Gravins and Ham around the mid-20th century (J. Holbourn 2003). According to others, 'John is the only person I have ever heard to use the name ...'. He used this name when he was a boy. All the islanders of the generation older than us who are still alive, call it the Bottle Loch, as do we. Mima, Tom a Gravins and Harry all called it this too' (J. and S. Gear 2003). Different families have different suggested origins and traditions. Ideally all need to be followed up.

Flick Lochs (OS 6 Inch map) has been changed on late-20th century Ordnance Survey metric maps to Lochs o' da Fleck, presumably to be more in line with local usage. The ON specific *flek* is 'a piece of ground' generally seen as significantly different from surrounding land – in this instance, a swampy area surrounded by a combination of good grassy grazing and tussocky hill grazing (Jakobsen 1993: 41).

Gossa Loch was drained in the early-19th century to create new croft land. A tiny bit survives, forms a pool in wet weather and retains its name (J. and S. Gear 2003). Like Gossamüdo (a croft taken in at much the same time) and the apparently nearby (if not identical?) Goster (Valuation Roll 1836; Holbourn 1938: 174), it contains ON *gás* 'goose', and reflects a one-time use of much of this extensive area as grazings for da tun a Ham.

Rossie('s) Loch. Over the past 130 or so years this has been variously spelt, not least by the Ordnance Survey. 'Horse loch', however, stands within an area once referred to as da Rossarentals, an outfield pasture where ponies grazed and maybe sought (relative) shelter.

'Russi' has been heard on Foula in the later-20th century 'as a rather disparaging endearment for a horse' (J. and S. Gear 2003). Otherwise, ON *(h)ross* survived only as a fisherman's tabu-term, recorded both on Foula and at Clousta (Westside) (Jakobsen 1985: 730). It also survived in Rossi-heog, a fishing ground a little off the north-east coast of the island (Seim 1938) presumably found by lining the boat up with 'horse-hill', probably present-day Heog (ON *haugr* 'a mound, cairn'), a modest rise most likely within or close to da Rossarentals (Jakobsen 1993: 51, 204).

Lim(e)y Loch/Imy Loch was considered 'very small to be called a loch' (E. Isbister 1984). It is a small round pool in da Bitten, said by some to have 'a limey deposit', by others to have been used for dyeing clothes (P. Gray, per J. Holbourn 2003) and for the soaking of cow skins to remove the hair (J. and S. Gear 2003).

Although Stewart (1970: 313) suggests ON *lím* 'lime', a more likely root is ON *ím* '(a coating of) dust or dirt'. In Shetland (*äim*), as in the Faroes, *im* is '(a layer of) fine black soot, especially on the underside of a pot', or 'black discolouring forming round the bottom of a kettle' (cf. Jakobsen 1985: 376). Used for dyeing cloth, it could also be found on the inside of the glass of an oil lamp or deposited by a candle (A. Gear 2003). There 'was another Imy/Limy Loch near the Sloag', thought to dye a blackish colour (E. Wiseman/ Holbourn, per J. and S. Gear 2003). It is described as 'an uprising of water associated with bog iron just to the east of the NE corner of the Sloag croft that was used for dying [*sic*] clothes' (J. Umphray, per J. Holbourn 2003).

Sandvadden/Sandvatten means sandy loch (ON *sandr* 'sand' + ON *vatn* 'water, loch'). The Ordnance Survey 6 Inch map gives a tautological Sandvadden Loch (and credited Sandvadden/-vatten to an adjacent area of gently-rising hill ground to the south-east). Whether Sandvadden had lost sufficient of its meaning by the later-19th century as to require 'clarification' is unclear, but Sandvatten remains current for the loch itself.

Liumisheddon, (da) Sjuddens, Edershun. ON *tjörn* referred to 'a small loch', though on Foula there seems to be no significant difference between Sandvatten and the largest of the *sjøns* – except that the former lies in the valley bottom, whereas the *sjøns/sødns* lie a little higher up on the skattald (*sjødns* in Foula: /n/ > /dn/) (see Figure 3).

Both Liumisheddon (Lommi-skjödn, Seim 1938; Lumishudn, Stewart 1970: 317) and Rossie Loch seasonally host a breeding pair of 'loons' (ON *lómr* + ON *tjørn* 'red-throated diver tarn'). Skjödden (Seim 1938) or the Sjuddens (Stewart 1970: 317) lie just east of Liumisheddon, atop the wet, slightly elevated but nonetheless low-lying watershed that leads over east to Sloag a Nort Videl (Seim 1938). Da Shuddens is an area 'full of very soft boggy bits that are hard to get across' (J. and S. Gear 2003); Sloag suggests comparison with Nor./Faer. *sloka*, Nor. *slage/slaagaa* and Sw. *slage* – all with the general sense of 'a low-lying, frequently damp but relatively wide, longitudinal hollow' (Jakobsen 1993: 99).

By contrast, Edershøn/Edersjen (Jakobsen 1993: 71, 108, 146; Stewart 1970: 317) is on the western edge of the South Ness, down past the Hametoun and a little outside the ruinous dykes once separating off the headland. It contains ON *æðr* 'eider' – and eiders still breed thereabouts. There may have been clear water when the name was first given, but simply 'a wettish area' had become widespread in Shetland by the 19th century (Jakobsen 1985: 768). The name survives only as Da Cups a Eder Cheyne, 'small grassy hollows or "cups" near cliff top' (E. Isbister 1984).

4. Swamps and mires

It takes very little for a small lochan or tarn gradually to infill with peat and vegetation and turn into a bog or swamp (see Figure 3). Those who visit Foula only in summer can be misled by the extensive tracts of springy, peaty moorland – mainly along the east side of the island, but also in da Dal (Hametoun) and to a lesser extent in the small, higher valleys of Ou(v)rafandal and Neder(a)fandal. Even so, with a climate where rainfall is not scarce, some of this skattald may still be saturated in high summer. Only after weeks of drying winds and sunshine, can tractors and trailers venture down amongst the peat banks close to the burn in da Bitten.

Mires; Stjortimires. The former croft of Mires (further anglicised from Mäirs, from ON *mýrr* 'bog or swamp', was a late-19th century intake, presumably named after da Stjortimires(-mørs). Jakobsen (1993: 241) glosses the latter as 'a swamp (lake)' and links it to the Norwegian river 'Stertelven'. He suggests a possible ON **stjartr-*, probably from *stertr* 'a tail', and noted *stjort* as an Aithsting fishermen's tabu term for the tail of a large fish (Jakobsen 1985: 898). In Foula, *styurt* has survived as a dialect word ('the place you urinate from'), and has been heard used for 'the end of a gutter, between two roofs, where water "pisses" out from' (J. and S. Gear 2003).

Seim (1938) seems to have associated the name with a long narrow stretch of boggy land flanking virtually the entire south side of the Mill Loch and extending along the south side of its feeder burn into da Hamnastou(r)s (ON *stúfr* 'a stump') – the 'valley bottom, [an] area roughly from Mill-loch to Mornington croft area' (E. Isbister 1984). It is unclear, however, whether Seim saw the piece of land as resembling a tail, or whether the name referred to trickles of water seeping out of the mire and into the loch.

Mornington is a house on the slight, southern/south-easterly slope of Hamnabreck, above da Hamnastou(r)s. Built as a manse, it subsequently became the croft house for the 19th-century intake registered as Mornington – whose original house (long-ruinous) was known locally as Hamnabreck in the same way as the croft registered officially as Magdala is known as da Groups (J. and S. Gear 2003).

Three points stand out. Manses in out-of-the-way places were rarely allocated particularly good land; there is barely a 30 ft. (10 m.) height variation between the nearby coastal cliff top and Mornington; and the area immediately to the east and south, encompassing da Pools a Heedlicliv (see Vatsaros above), is one of the wettest areas on the island. Rather than the very English name that Mornington suggests, therefore, it might well originate in ON *mýrrin/*mýrarnar* + ON *tún* 'fenced plot of the bog(s)'.

Sukkamires/Sukkimires. We are on surer ground with names such as Sukkamires (Sökkamørs: Seim 1938; anglicised as Sukkimires) – quite simply a quagmire (Nor. *søkkjemyr* 'a bog or swamp into which you sink') (Jakobsen 1993: 84). North of da tun a Ham, it describes 'an essentially flat area cut up with long, thin bits of bog, wriggling across it, that are difficult to cross' (J. and S. Gear 2003). Much of it dries out in summer 'except for a few swampy patches which are crossed by means of miniature turf bridges' (Holbourn 1938: 144).

Da Sukkamires are all-but surrounded by five or so lochans (Rossie Loch, Dry Loch, Gossa Loch, Liumishedden and da Sjuddens). They are also closed off to the north by the gentle slopes of Crougar, and to the east and west by the barely-perceptible Heog (ON *haugr* 'mound, cairn') and Scots Bred Knowe respectively. The latter is the 'highest' area east of da Leug, another marshy area (J. Holbourn 2003). Given also as Lioag (OS; J. and S. Gear 2003) and Ljug (Seim 1938), this may be ON *lögr* 'water, liquid', or more likely ON *lækr* 'a wet, grassy hollow or deep channel through which water flows quietly' (Jakobsen 1993: 79-81, 160).

Murnakweeda/Mudnakweedna. A little south from da Sukka-mires, just outwith the present township dyke (much extended in the 19th century to accommodate da New Tuns), a further area of bog has been described as 'a slight valley area running north from the Ham croft dyke towards the braid knowe' ... from which flows the tiny Peerie Burn (J. Holbourn 2003). It also runs along the back of the Gravins dyke.

This time the bog is defined by its colour: ON *mýrrin hvíta (*mýrina hvítu)* 'white mire' (Jakobsen 1993: 84). It is too wet for cotton grass, and is mainly sphagnum – which dries white in summer. The name shows transposition of the normal word order, *hvíta mýrrin* – for which there is an exact parallel across the valley at Leraback, where *Velta kodna kwida* substitutes for *kweeda kudna velta* (ON *hvítakorna-velta* 'corn rig'). (Jakobsen 1985: 1040; 1993:115; Stewart 1970: 318; J Holbourn 2003).

5. Conclusion

Today's winter-time population approaches 25. Excluding the current generation of children, around 10 of Foula's present-day inhabitants came to the island as teenagers or adults. Several settled in the 1950s-1960s, most within the last 20 or so years – some from elsewhere in Shetland, another from Orkney, others from lowland Scotland, and others from England and further afield.

The island was bought by the late I.B.S. Holbourn (from southern England) in 1901; one of his sons lived on the island for the latter part of his life, after some years as its teacher/missionary; all four of his grandchildren have lived on Foula for much or most of their lives and two still do, married into island families. Of the present adult population, therefore, three are half-island/half-Holbourn, and just four are from families where both parents were from older-established island families – the Gears arriving from Nesting in the later-19th century, the Isbisters from Quarff (and earlier Papa Stour) in the early-19th century and the Grays from Westside in the early/mid-18th century.

This does not necessarily mean that there have been clear-cut cultural breaks. In the nature of things, and given a mind to integrate, incomers assimilate a significant amount of a host community's culture. There comes a point in the evolution of a small, remote island, however, where 'critical mass' is reached and breached, and traditions, language and names vanish more rapidly than in less remote areas where a larger overall population can better accommodate a greater number of incomers yet still retain a strong (albeit changing) local culture. In this respect, Foula has long been more precarious than, say, Unst.

Such a point may have been reached in Foula on two earlier occasions. From around the 1570s, and perhaps more extensively by the mid-17th century, Scots were taking over from the old Norwegian landowners and steadily infiltrating the island and its culture. At this point it is likely that the indigenous Norn-speaking population remained numerous and cohesive enough to withstand what was probably fairly insignificant cultural and economic change. In the earlier-18th century, however, following a change of ownership and the ravages of smallpox, much of the island was repopulated from the Shetland mainland – primarily, it would seem, from Westside (Baldwin 1984: 55; 1999: 205-206). Their impact on the island's place-names is unclear. Were they Norn-speakers, or maybe first- or second-generation speakers of Shetland Scots? Families such as the Umphrays (originally brought in as weavers) and the Grays (originally blacksmiths) may never have been truly Norn-speakers, but rather the descendants (in part at least) of Scots skilled or professional families who lost part of their competitive edge or cultural identity over a couple of generations or so and assimilated into the wider prevailing culture. At the time (or in other circumstances), 'going native' would have implied adopting the 'native' language, but in 17th-century and later Shetland (very much as in the 20th- and 21st-century Gaeltacht), the incoming language was increasingly influencing and becoming the language of the 'native'.

Though in many ways life continued much as it ever had, the overlordship of the Scotts of Melby led to (or more likely accelerated) the breakdown of the old language. William Henry, a descendant if not survivor of the pre-smallpox population, was an old man when he provided Low with the *Hildina Ballad* in 1774. He was able to recite it, but quite unable to explain what it meant. This does not necessarily mean that Norn was extinct by that date, though it would suggest that very few islanders were still able to speak it (perhaps only descendants of the pre-smallpox population?), that the language of the ballad was by now significantly different from the spoken language, and that native speakers probably died out by around 1800 (Low 1879: 105; Barnes 1998: 26).

That is not to say that Foula Scots did not continue to be heavily laced with Norn – particularly in the lexicon. That said, given that most of the 18th-century settlers seem to have come from Scott's Westside lands just west of Waas (mainly Elvister and Setter?: Holbourn 1938: 74), and according to the Censuses most 19th-century settlers came from e.g. Papa Stour and Vaila (all still part of the Melby estates), may there have been a specifically Westside impact on the subsequent form of Foula's place-names and dialect? And might this help in explaining such parallel forms as *-f(j)eld/-fella*; *-gill/-gyell*; *shun/shudden*; *quivri-/k(w)ervi-*; *murnakweeda/mudnakweedna*?

There is a further factor. In times when everyday life took people out of their houses and townships on a daily and seasonal basis, activities required a detailed knowledge of the landscape and all the many little features within it (Baldwin 1978: 121-126). In particular, these activities required a knowledge of e.g.: the best grazings at different times of the year, the routes taken by livestock and where they would likely take shelter in bad weather, the location of the best supplies of peat, the location of dangerous (or difficult and unpleasant) bogholes and swamps, places where burns and bogs were most easily crossed, the best bird cliffs and rock fishing seats, the location of the fishing grounds. This required a detailed system of naming that would be known and clearly understood by all involved.

During the 18th and 19th centuries this traditional subsistence economy intensified, largely as a result of the proprietorial development of commercial fisheries and encouragement of a greater population to work the boats and cure the fish. Given a decidedly finite extent of cultivable land on Foula, the artifically-enlarged population was thrown back on an ever-more intensive and subsistence-level exploitation of traditional activities – which required an ever-more detailed knowledge of the landscape, environment and its resource potential. In such circumstances, and given a broadly-defined cultural continuity, the old names are likely to have survived (albeit through Scots, later English) and new, primarily Scots (later English) names given where older names had been forgotten or maybe never existed.

Today these traditional lifestyles have all but gone. Where it survives, modern crofting focuses mainly on the grazing of sheep (and preferably on enclosed infields and apportionments where a much-reduced population can more easily manage them). The cattle have gone, there is virtually no field cultivation, fowling in any significant sense disappeared long since, the inshore fisheries are largely exhausted and the need for myriad names for the tiniest of places in a landscape has largely evaporated. This process accelerated hugely in the second half of the 20th century, particularly over the past 30 or so years. And it is over these past three or four decades that almost the entire 'older' generation has passed away – those maybe in their 60s in the 1960s and 1970s, but still actively pursuing and conversant with the old ways. With them has gone so much (but certainly not yet all) of their detailed, first-hand knowledge of the natural environment, traditional crofting, dialect and place-names.

Additionally, large numbers of islanders (especially younger islanders) emigrated during the 20th century. Those of the (post-) World War II generation who stayed or returned retain much of the dialect, many of the names and are hugely knowledgeable. But they are few in number, their way of life has changed out of all recognition, and those who have married necessarily have non-Foula partners. What is true for that generation is even more true for their children (generally in their 30s). And it is yet more so for their children's children, the great-grandchildren of some of those still alive in the 1970s – three or four generations squeezed into a mere 30 years. It is these young children, and the children of more recent incomers, whose knowledge of the names is so scanty.

Even were they to follow traditional patterns of crofting, current generations are so influenced by television, video, mobile phones and the internet that they would be unlikely to focus so single-mindedly on the restricted world and once-plentiful place-names of the Foula tuns and skattald. Because place-names represent an innately conservative dimension in the life of a community, they often survive when other aspects of a local culture, whether social, economic or linguistic, have weakened or changed more rapidly. But change they have and change they will. Once rescued and recorded, many if not most of Foula's names, particularly the minor names, will be little more than entries on a page. Even where actively used or taught to others, they can never again be as they were. The much reduced number of names still used (as opposed to remembered or recognised), and the preponderance of essentially Scots and English names along da Burn a Ham should come as no surprise. None of this is a criticism. It is a fact of life – sad but inevitable. People and generations come and go. Life and cultures change. Dialect and place-names change likewise.

Acknowledgement

Sheila Gear and Isobel Holbourn co-ordinate the work of 'Foula Heritage', a small, hard-pressed but quite invaluable voluntary group seeking to secure Foula's natural and cultural heritage. It was a conversation on Foula in July 2002 that became the catalyst for this paper, a conversation during which Isobel Holbourn happened to mention how few names the present primary schoolchildren appeared to know.

Many islanders have assisted in gathering names these past 35 years. Particular thanks go to Eric Isbister and his late parents (South Biggins) for their enormous knowledge, patience and interest, and to many others who have now sadly passed away. Much was gathered initially by leaders of Brathay expeditions to the island, especially Ian Tulip (1969) and Donald and Dilys Brownrigg (1969-1970). More recently, Jim and Sheila Gear (Magdala/Groups) and John Holbourn (now away from Foula) have been particularly painstaking in helping assemble material more especially in the vicinity of da Burn a Ham in use in the 20th and early-21st centuries. Their listings include names from the late Mima Gear, Harry Gear, Tom Umphray, Elizabeth Wiseman and Peter Ratter (per J. and S. Gear) and the late Peter Gray, Peter Ratter, Tom Umphray and Joanna Umphray (per J Holbourn). In addition, the writer gratefully acknowledges the contribution of other islanders, all but one of whom are now deceased:

Ken Gear, Niggards	1969
John Thomas Ratter, North Biggins	1969
Bobbie Isbister, South Biggins	1969-74
Andrew Umphray, Leraback	1974
Joanna Umphray, Ham	1974
Tom Umphray, Gravins	1974
James Andrew Gray, ex-Dykes	1974-84

This paper is an abridged version of that given in Lerwick in 2003. No attempt has been made to standardise spellings as between different collectors/collections, and differing forms have frequently been given. At the conference, Tom Schmidt (Oslo) and Andy Gear (Yell, formerly Foula) offered a number of stimulating comments; I am most grateful to David Baldwin for improving and computerising the base map and adding the names; Jim and Sheila Gear, along with Andy Gear and Doreen Waugh, very kindly read a draft of this paper and have made further invaluable suggestions.

Literature

Baldwin, J.R., 1978: 'Norse Influences in Sheep Husbandry on Foula, Shetland'. In: J.R. Baldwin (ed.), *Scandinavian Shetland: An Ongoing Tradition?* Edinburgh, 97-127.

Baldwin, J.R., 1984: 'Hogin and Hametoun: Thoughts on the Stratrification of a Foula *Tun*'. In: B.E. Crawford (ed.), *Essays in Shetland History*. Lerwick, 33-64.

Baldwin, J.R., 1996: 'Heaps, Humps and Hollows on the Foula Skattald'. In: D.J. Waugh (ed.), *Shetland's Northern Links: Language and History*. Edinburgh, 205-229.

Barnes, M.P., 1998: *The Norn Language of Orkney and Shetland*. Lerwick.

Brownrigg, D.A. & D., nd [1969]: *Place Names of Foula: Key to Preliminary Maps* [+ maps]. Brathay Exploration Group, Ambleside. Unpublished ms.

Brownrigg, D.A. & D., nd [1970]: *The Place Names of Foula: Key to Maps* [+ maps]. Brathay Exploration Group, Ambleside. Unpublished ms.

Gear, J. & S., 2003: *Names along da Burn o Ham, Foula*. Unpublished ms.

Gear, S., 1963: *Foula: Island West of the Sun*. London.

Holbourn, I.B.S., 1938: *The Isle of Foula*. Lerwick.

Holbourn, J., 2003: *Ham Burn*. Unpublished ms.

Isbister, E., 1983-1984: *Foula Place-Names*. Unpublished ms.

Jakobsen, J., [1928-1932] 1985: *An Etymological Dictionary of the Norn Language in Shetland*, 1-2. Lerwick.

Jakobsen, J., [1936] 1993: *The Place Names of Shetland*. Kirkwall.

Low, G., 1879: *A Tour through the Islands of Orkney and Schetland, Containing Hints Relative to their Ancient, Modern and Natural History – Collected in 1774 by George Low*. Kirkwall.

Nicolaisen, W.F.H., 1976: *Scottish Place-Names: Their Study and Significance*. London.

Ordnance Survey, 1877-1896: *Six Inch Name Book of the Island of Foula* (including material added in 1878, 1881 and up to 1896).

Ordnance Survey, [1877] 1900: *6 Inch Map, Zetland, Sheet LIV*. Southampton.

Ordnance Survey, 1972: *1:10,000 Map; Foula*. Southampton.

Ordnance Survey, 1978: *1:25,000 Map; Foula*. Pathfinder 18. Southampton.

Seim, E., 1938: *Place-Name Map of Foula* (names collected during fieldwork in 1938 and superimposed on OS 6 Inch map). Unpublished ms.

Stewart, J., 1970: 'Place-Names of Foula'. *Fróðskaparrit* 18. Tórshavn, 307-319.

Stewart, J., 1987: *Shetland Place-Names*. Lerwick.

Tulip, I.F., 1969: *Place Names of Foula (A Preliminary Draft)*. Brathay Exploration Group, Ambleside. Unpublished ms.

Valuation Roll, 1836: hand-written copy per R. and E. Isbister, Foula. Unpublished ms.

Shetland Place Names Project

Eileen Brooke-Freeman

1. Introduction

The Shetland Place Names Project received inaugural funding from the Heritage Lottery Fund, Shetland Islands Council, Shetland Enterprise Company and Shetland Amenity Trust, and aims systematically to record all available information on Shetland's place-names, collecting previously unrecorded information from people throughout Shetland and beyond. A comprehensive database of Shetland place-names will be established, and linked to digital maps so that users can relate the names precisely to their locations. The Project will promote the collection, understanding and use of place-names through establishing links with schools and community groups and involving volunteers in the collection of new material. We will explore methods of making information available in various formats to a range of users.

This project builds on the extensive work of individuals such as Jakob Jakobsen and John Stewart who dedicated years to recording and interpreting Shetland place-names. Both men tended to arrange names by linguistic elements rather than geographically, and this causes difficulties when relating the names precisely to their locations. Hence one of our key aims is to locate all the names on maps. We therefore want to build on the work already undertaken and to make it more accessible both within Shetland and beyond.

2. Implementation Strategy

What became very apparent in the early stages of the project was the sheer volume of material that is available. Therefore, having secured three years' funding to collect names and set up the database, priority had to be given to collecting names from oral sources before those names which do not appear on maps or survive in documents die out altogether. Many names relate to fishing and crofting, with individual rigs, geos and rocks all carrying names, which were passed down between generations who lived in the same area. Additionally, many names have been written down, but not plotted on maps, so again there is an urgency to talk to the older folk who remember these names and can help us locate them before this information is lost forever. The project concentrates on collecting these names first, before moving on to check documentary sources and undertake linguistic analysis. Emphasis has to be much more on collection rather than interpretation and preparing material for publication in the first three years.

The project has generated a high level of public interest and support. Our place-names are of interest to people with a wide range of pursuits – academics, linguists, people carrying out house name searches (including naming new houses), school studies, local history projects, locating archaeological, biological and forestry remains, and official purposes, such as updating maps and road signs. The names can tell us a great deal about Shetland's history and geography and about the people who lived here – where did they come from, what language did they speak, what were their occupations, what was the land used for, what types of building were here in the past, where did they catch fish and what were their beliefs and taboos?

3. Existing material

The project aimed initially to conduct an audit of all existing sources of place-name information. I have pulled together for the first time a list of all potential sources including tapes, maps, lists of names and documents available in the deposit of museums and archives, local history groups and key individuals. Many articles or lists of names have also appeared in print, and these too need to be collated. I have been checking these sources and, where appropriate, making copies.

A significant source deposited in the Shetland Archives is the papers of John Stewart, only a fraction of his work having been in a suitable state to be published in his book *Shetland Place-Names* (1987). Most local history groups and local heritage centres have collected lists and maps of names in their local area. The detail varies from short lists of names to detailed maps showing all the coastal names.

A wealth of material remains in private hands. As a result of local publicity and contacts made through Local History Groups and Heritage Centres, I have located very detailed maps and lists of names from throughout the isles. More information continues to come to light as the project progresses. It is only through meeting people that you discover lists of names, maps or documents, which have been carefully preserved in private homes. In the same way that Shetlanders are very modest about their knowledge of place-names, 'I dunna keen very much, you wid be better aff spaekin tae...', they are often also unaware of the sheer value of the list of names, maps or documents which they hold. It is often just at the end of your visit that you happen to come across the real gem – something perhaps hidden away in the loft and almost forgotten.

4. Volunteer recorders and informants

Our project aims to achieve coverage for the whole of Shetland and its success is dependent on recruiting enthusiastic volunteer recorders throughout the isles.

I have identified volunteer recorders and potential informants for all parishes in Shetland. This complete coverage is much more desirable than having very detailed information for just a few areas. The list of potential informants needed organising to ensure we attempted to reach certain older residents as a matter of priority. Since starting the project, we have already seen potential informants die or become incapacitated before we had a chance to talk to them.

I have tapped into the network of Local History Groups and the Shetland Heritage Association. There are currently 18 local history groups, mainly meeting through the winter months, but some continuing through the year. Local History Groups and Heritage Centres have proved to be a very good starting point. These groups have been instrumental in identifying the potential informants for each local community and a focus for commencing the current recording project. Many of them have at some point started to record place-names, but often abandoned their efforts when they encountered a problem such as the difficulty of writing down names on maps. I have been visiting groups to explain the project and show them how to record names for their areas. Half of these are already helping with the project.

Other groups that have become involved include the staff and day care residents at Wastview Care Centre in Walls. Staff acted as recorders, helping to note names on maps and recording sheets. I have visited Local Women's Rural Institutes and the Women's Royal Voluntary Service to show group members how to record and to furnish them with maps, guidelines and recording sheets.

Interested individuals have volunteered as a result of publicity; both volunteering to help record names and suggesting names of people that we should talk to.

This year I have been exploring ways of working with primary school children. Place-name studies fits well within the school 5-14 Environmental Studies plan. Currently two primary schools, Uyeasound in Unst and Hamnavoe in Burra, are commencing place-name projects, using our copy maps, recording sheets and guidelines.

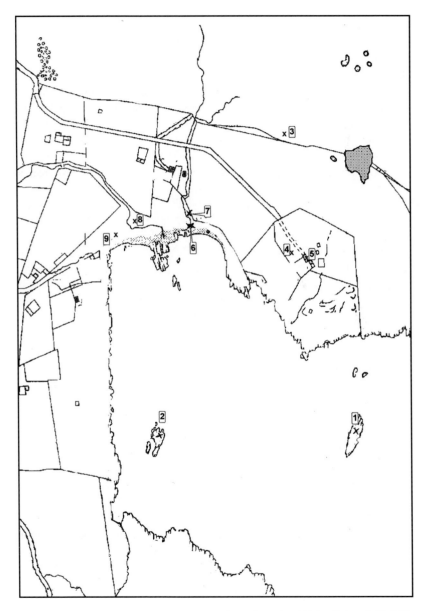

Figure 1. Example of a recording map based on the 1973 edition 1:10,000 Ordnance Survey maps.

5. Recording method

Various techniques are being employed to record place-names. Volunteer recorders have been supplied with recording guidelines, pro-forma recording sheets and copies of the 1973 edition 1:10,000 Ordnance Survey maps for their locality. They have been trained how to record each place-name on the map with a running number and to add the details about the feature on the recording sheet, including how to take grid references and spell out names (see Figures 1 and 2). We try to record all names including such features as tracks, wells, 'crös' (sheep-folds), outbuildings, 'broos' (brows of hills or slopes), 'noosts' (places where boats are drawn up), and rocks, whether named on the map or not.

The recording sheet comprises three parts, allowing for details about the informant and recorder to be noted on the cover, with a notes section at the back. The main part of the sheet is for recording detailed information about each place-name, spelling it as it sounds; recording the grid reference; noting any other names it is known by; details of what the feature is, e.g.: rig, burn, ruined house, craig seat (fishing rock); and information about the name or suggested interpretations, e.g. named after an individual. Names that are mis-positioned or mis-spelt on the maps are also being corrected.

NO. ON MAP	NAME (Listen to how it is pronounced and spell it as it sounds)	GRID REF (e.g. 192574)	NAME GIVEN ON OS MAP	OTHER NAME KNOWN BY	FEATURE (e.g. house, croft, rig, burn, stack)	NAME OF LAST OCCUPANT/ APPROX. DATE	SUGGESTED MEANING AND/OR INFORMATION ABOUT SITE (eg marshy area, named after ----, thought to have been church site)
1	Da Black Skerry	530850	Black Skerry	Swarta Skerry	Skerry		Old Norse svartr - black
2	Klubba Skerry	524850	Swarta Skerry		Skerry		Incorrectly named on OS maps
3	Firzils	528858		Grindypoil	Ruined house	Thomas R Fraser (Taamie Firzil) June 1902	Hermit who lived in felly-roofed house outside hill dykes (on his own after his mother's death.) Father drowned in Da Poil, Aywick.
4	Da Hwaes	528855			Park		
5	Wheein	529855	Queyon		Croft and House	Currently occupied	
6	Gilsa Burn	525856			Burn		
7		52388565			Site of old water mill		Grass grown over remaining stones
8	Da Fids	524856			Flat marshy area by Otterswick Burn		Old Norse fit meaning fertile meadow alongside river or lake
9	Da Carvel	523856			Flat grassy area above beach		Said to be wide enough to play "da baa" on New Year's Day

Figure 2. Example of a recording sheet.

We are using tape or minidisc recorders where possible to determine pronunciation and therefore spelling. Recording conversations also helps yield further background information about the locality.

Part of the recording process involves using existing lists to try and pinpoint the exact location of each place-name. Some locations in the field are being recorded using Geographic Positioning Systems (GPS) and these locations can then be transferred to the digital maps. We are also studying the features and taking photographs of some of them.

Various tools are acting as memory triggers. These include the Ordnance Survey maps themselves (particularly the 1973, 1902 and 1878 editions), photographs and aerial photographs; and names that have already been recorded, particularly the lists of names that appear on the John Stewart recording sheets, compiled in 1951. Figures 3-6 show how layers of data collected over 50 years can be overlaid on maps for verification of locations, pronunciation and spelling of names, prior to entering them into the database.

We are also extracting information from documentary and printed sources, deposited in the local museums, library and archives. It is also very important to crosscheck written evidence with current local knowledge to avoid mistakes in suggested origins of names. This is demonstrated by the following example. Stewart (1987: 317) lists Fersills originating from Forsoela (a shady place). Firsills is listed on an original record sheet, and current local knowledge confirms the name, but gives the origin as the house being named after Tammy Firsil or Fraser, who died there in 1902. A 95 year-old woman recited the following poem, which verified the link with the name Grindypoil (also recorded by Stewart 1987: 220):

> Thomas R Fraser is my name and England is my nation.
> Grindypoil is my domain and it is my possession
> And when I'm dead and in my grave
>   and all my bones are rotten
> Look at this and think of me and say he's quite forgotten.

I have visited the site to determine the precise grid reference and to photograph the remnants of this former turf-roofed house.

Data collected by volunteer recorders is now being returned, in the form of completed record sheets and marked up maps, and these need to be crosschecked and the names verified before entering details into the database.

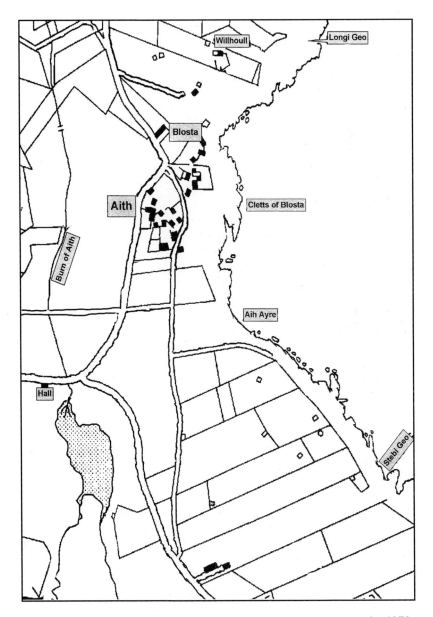

Figure 3. Aith, Cunningsburgh, showing names which appear on the 1973 edition 1:10,000 Ordnance Survey map.

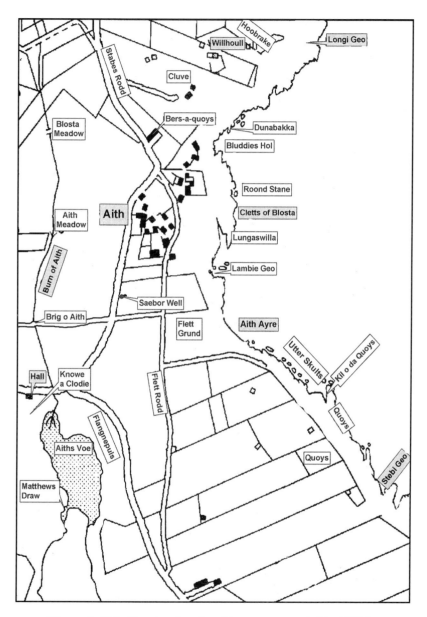

*Figure 4. Aith, Cunningsburgh, with names recorded in 1977 by
Cunningsburgh Scottish Women's Rural Institute.*

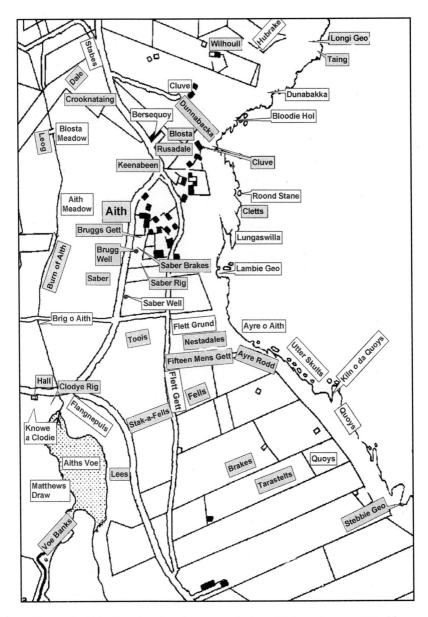

Figure 5. Aith, Cunningsburgh, now with the addition of names listed by Stewart's informants in 1951, pinpointed by current residents.

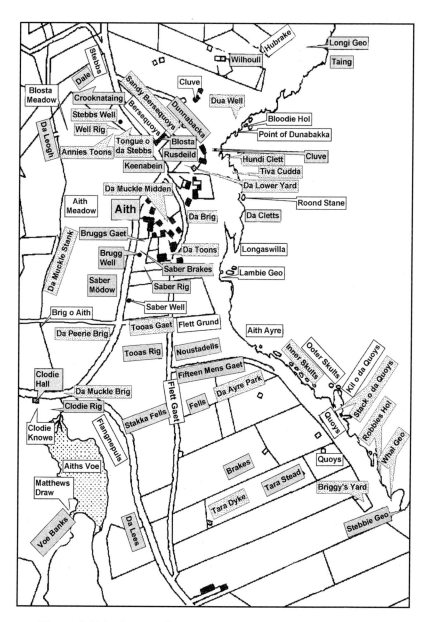

Figure 6. Aith, Cunningsburgh, showing further names added by the History Group members.

6. Database

We have a copy of the Scottish Place-Name Database for recording data. This is being modified for our own needs and linked to digital maps and other local databases e.g. the Sites and Monuments Record. It includes fields for linguistic, historical, geographical and geological analysis of place-names in their environment. The Scottish Place-Name Database is based in the Department of Celtic and Scottish Studies in Edinburgh. The database features an automatic numbering field and in order to avoid duplication or having to re-enter data to be incorporated in the national database, we have adopted the simple approach of starting at a much higher number. Thus the Shetland database entries carry numbers higher than 50,000.

7. Digital mapping

The key to recording and presenting the data is the use of digital mapping. I have worked together with other Amenity Trust Projects – Archaeology, Biological Records and Woodlands – to obtain a digital map package, which can be linked to the Place Names and other databases. We have purchased the 1973 edition 1:10,000 Ordnance Survey maps and can already see the scope for presenting data and verifying names and locations.

8. Access to the information we record

I have been talking to people and looking at projects elsewhere in the United Kingdom and worldwide to assess the best means of making information available. We need to employ various methods to accommodate the wide range of interests mentioned earlier. The database and digital mapping will form the basis, but they will need to be developed to allow easier access for users. Local people do want to be able to access the data for their community locally and we will therefore explore methods of supplying data to local museums, history groups and schools.

9. Fishing meids

I have developed a parallel project to record Shetland's fishing meids, in conjunction with the Shetland Biological Records Centre. Before the advent of navigation with radar and Geographic Positioning Systems (GPS), fishing grounds around Shetland were located by taking the transect of two meids (each meid involves lining up two landmarks).

Meids have both biological and historical significance. In biological terms they are used to locate fishing grounds that yielded particular species of fish. Historically, many of the meid names will soon be lost; many features not seen from the land are recorded from the sea; and many place-names having an alternative name in fishing terms – either a descriptive name (its appearance from the sea) or a taboo name (because of the superstition of not using certain names when in a boat).

Our objectives are to collect information on meids and the fishing grounds that they were used to locate; gather information on place-names relating to meids and the wider coastline; and collect an oral history relating to the contemporary environment, fishing and culture. The main focus of this pilot is interviewing retired fishermen. What is already appearing is a detailed history of the fishing industry, comprising information about fishing and also place-names and dialect.

10. John Stewart

I have commenced a programme of extensive research on the previously un-accessed archive of John Stewart. Born in Whalsay in 1903, Stewart went on to Aberdeen University and became a teacher in Aberdeen. He devoted his leisure time to the study of Shetland's history, archaeology, place-names and language.

Back in 1941 he had identified the value of working with local schools to help compile the place-names for the whole of Shetland. By 1950 he had devised a comprehensive project to record the place-names of Shetland and secured funding to help with his project through a grant from the Carnegie Trust.

Stewart's method followed the model of similar projects in Western Norway. In 1951 he issued almost 5,000 numbered questionnaires to schoolchildren to take home to their parents and grandparents, and also to other houses in the district. The questionnaires asked respondents to:

> Write every name you know near your home. Spell the names as you say them; for example Soombra ... Saanis ... If you know any story about a name, or its meaning, or when it was given, say so. Group the names as follows:

> 1. Names on your Croft
> 2. Names in the Hill
> 3. Names at the Shore
> 4. Names in the Sea.

The response was overwhelming. By May of 1951 the pupils, their relatives and neighbours had returned large numbers of the folded record sheets with many thousands of names. Almost 1,200 original sheets are now deposited in Shetland Archives, some listing up to 250 names. From the record sheets, Stewart extracted lists of names for his own field notes, which he added to and amended on his trips. He also traced every six-inch Ordnance Survey map for the whole of Shetland, copying all the names as they appeared on the map. He then stuck these in books and gradually annotated and amended them. These annotated maps cover the areas Stewart appears to have visited during his annual field trips. During subsequent summer holidays, Stewart came to Shetland and travelled to various districts to carry out his fieldwork. He went from house to house talking to older people, verifying names and noting down new ones.

Evidence appears in the form of lists of names, notes of possible contacts, lists of houses, rigs and meids on scraps of paper, occasionally in notebooks, and sometimes annotations in his map books. He then proceeded to make alphabetical lists of names for each parish and give them reference numbers, which relate back to the original recording sheets. These lists are estimated to contain over 30,000 different place-names.

For the next 10 years Stewart worked on his study of Shetland island- and farm-names, plotting them on maps, checking for early forms of the names, suggesting the meaning of each name, and making comparisons with names in Norway, Faroe, Iceland, Orkney and the North of Scotland. He wrote a detailed introduction to his study of farm names, which he presented as a paper to the Fourth Viking Congress in 1965. Sadly, he did not live to see his main work published as he died, in 1977. However, Brian Smith's careful editing of the typescript island- and farm-names resulted in the publication of *Shetland Place-Names* in May 1987.

Stewart's remaining work has remained fairly inaccessible until recently, when all his original papers became available in Shetland Archives. The greatest shortcoming of the collection as it stands today is the difficulty of locating many of the place-names on the map. I am now trying to pinpoint these names on maps, adding information about these and other known place-names. I am currently extracting names from these original sheets to take out to people in each community to try and verify the names and, more importantly, locate them on the map. It is a slow process, as many of the sheets are difficult to read as a result of Stewart's work method. When he had copied names from the original record sheets onto his subsequent lists, he crossed them off, often almost com-pletely obliterating the name. These lists are working in the same way as the Ordnance Survey maps – acting as triggers to people's memories and resulting in names on these sheets (as on the Ordnance Survey record) being corrected and added to. Figure 5 (see above) shows the names from Aith in Cunningsburgh listed by Stewart's informants, but pinpointed by current residents. Figure 6 shows further names added by the History Group members (see above).

11. Progress of project

The second half of the project will involve maintaining regular data collection and inputting using the existing framework, and providing ongoing training and support to new and existing volunteers. A web page will be established, and there will be increased publicity through school and group visits and public talks. We will undertake an in-depth study of one or more areas, and commence the linguistic analysis.

We will ensure that information is accessible through Shetland Amenity Trust, the new Shetland Museum and Archives and the Scottish Place-Name Database.

12. Future of the project

Shetland Amenity Trust is already looking into ways of securing further funding for the Project. The next phase of the project needs to concentrate on making the information available to all through developing the database and website, also linking in digital images and sound recordings. There is much more work to be undertaken collecting and verifying new information, inputting data, checking documentary sources for earliest reference to names, and undertaking detailed linguistic analysis.

13. Conclusion

Two key messages recur throughout the Shetland Place Names Project – the urgency to record, and access. In 1893 Jakob Jakobsen tried to record remnants of Norn through words and place-names before they went out of use. In 1951 John Stewart wrote:

> With every new generation the names diverge farther and farther from their original form. Our maps are almost completely full of such corrupted names.
>
> Thousands of our names are suffering the worse fate of being forgotten ... the present is a belated attempt to recover and record what remains. (Stewart 1951: 7)

We have already seen potential informants die before we had a chance to talk to them. Never has there been such urgency. The schoolchildren who helped record 30,000 names 50 years ago, need to be contacted, and their names plotted on the map before we see another passing generation.

The other key is accessibility. Again turning to Stewart, his intention was that the place-names were to be published so as to be accessible to all Shetlanders. Interestingly, one Stewart informant recently commented that he did not think of contacting me to help with the Project because he had done it all before (in 1951) and had never seen results of his contribution. We cannot allow this to happen again, and therefore need to be very focused and ensure the unwritten record is recorded and all written sources are identifiable to future scholars.

Stewart succeeded with the recording and we must not pass up the opportunity to locate the names and make the information available to Shetlanders, linguists and any interested parties in a range of useable formats. The writers in this volume need to be able to continue their research using the new material. Once recorded and accessible there will be plenty of opportunity in the future to study and analyse the names, no doubt at great length!

Literature

Brooke-Freeman, E.L, 2003: 'John Stewart's Shetland Place Name Survey'. In: L. Johnson & B. Smith (eds), *The New Shetlander* No 223. Lerwick, 4-8.

Jakobsen, J., [1936] 1993: *The Place-Names of Shetland*. Kirkwall.

Shetland Archives, D.27/1-6: *Papers of John Stewart*.

Stewart, J., 1951: 'The Shetland Place-Name Collection'. In: *The New Shetlander* No 28. Lerwick, 7-8.

Stewart, J., 1987: *Shetland Place-Names*. Lerwick.

Trowie Names

Katherine Campbell

1. Introduction

In July 2002 I visited the Shetland Isles to take photographs of locations that are mentioned in trowie stories which include reference to the fiddle.[1] The trows or fairy people form an important part of the culture of Shetland and have a long history there. The earliest reference to them given in the *Dictionary of the Older Scottish Tongue* is to a Sheriff Court trial in Shetland of 1616, where Katherine Jonesdochter is reprimanded:

> for art and part of witchcraft and sorcery 'in hanting and seing the trowis ryse out of the kirkyeard of Hildiswick and Holiecross Kirk of Eschenes and that she saw thame on the hill callit Greinfaill at monie sindrie tymes and that they come to ony hous quhair thair wes feasting or great mirrines, and speciallie at Yule;' ... (Donaldson 1991: 39).

One aspect of the stories concerning the trows – certainly in the case of those which mention the fiddle – is that they normally give fairly precise locations where the trows were said to have been seen or where music connected with them was said to have been heard. In addition, these places are invariably real rather than imaginary, and would have been known to people living locally to them at the time, although knowledge of some of them is now beginning to fade from folk memory.

In this paper, I offer a selection of the stories concerning these locations derived from both oral and literate sources.[2] I have included several visual illustrations since these offer the individual unfamiliar with the landscape a much greater sense of place and of context.[3] In addition, by gathering together such images we can potentially compare and contrast the landscapes with those of fairy locations in other geographical areas of the British Isles and further afield.

Figure 1. Klodi Knowe, Cunningsburgh

2. Klodi Knowe, Cunningsburgh

The settlement of Cunningsburgh lies in the south part of mainland Shetland. John Stewart and Peter Moar in their article 'When the Trows Danced' in *The Shetland Folk Book* (1951) give a story that is placed in the eighteenth century of a carpenter who witnessed trows dancing accompanied by their fiddler. The story goes:

About the year 1790, a Cunningsburgh carpenter, who had been celebrating the completion of a newly-built sixareen, was staggering home in the early hours of the morning. After he had progressed some distance along the seashore towards the head of Aiths Voe, he was suddenly aware of the sound of strange music coming from the green mound at the side of the burn which runs into the voe. Being a noted fiddler, he began to pay what attention he could to the music, while, full of Dutch courage he cautiously slipped forward in the direction of the mound. On reaching it, he discovered that the music came from inside. Groping around the side by the light of the moon, he

discovered a door. Quietly edging it ajar with the adze he was
carrying, he was amazed to behold a trows' dance in full swing,
their fiddler playing a lively melody in six-eight measure. How
long he listened he did not reveal but it may be that the trows'
dancing tune, which he named Aith's Rant, has in it the clink
of seam and røv, the splashing of the burn, and the pleasant
little sounds which one hears in the ebb on a still night all
metamorphosed into a vivacious magic by the fumes of good
aqua vitae (Stewart and Moar 1951: 23-24).[4]

Mrs Mimie Malcolmson who was born in the Cunningsburgh area in
1917, gave me a version of the story that had come down her mother's side
of the family and that she had learned from her grandparents, which identifies
the carpenter as 'a Donald Jamieson ... [who] lived in a place called Ukinster'
near Fladdabister. The knowe mentioned in the story is known locally as the
'Klodi Knowe' (HU 4429).[5]

MM: This was what they called the trowie knowe or the
fairies' knowe. And you see this man, I think he was my great-
great-grandfather, he was a carpenter and he went to a place
called Greenmow. ... And he was coming back, it was a dark
night, he was coming back and he saw this side of the knowe
seemed to be the light, and he saw a small door, and he went
up, you see, to see it. An he said as long as he – he had an axe
wi him, as long as he had the axe and you stuck it in the door,
then they wouldna come after you. This was his version. And
he heard this most beautiful music and he said he saw all this
ladies and men dressed up dancing; small folk, so he stood
there as long as he could and he catched the tune that they were
playing. So he come home and he didna forget it, he just played
it and he remembered it. So that was that.
KC: And is that tune still going nowadays?
MM: It's still going ... 'Aid's Rant'.

3. Hollanders' Knowe, Gulberwick

John Nicolson in *Some Folk-Tales and Legends of Shetland*, 1920, gives a
story about the Hollanders' Knowe (HU 4339) at Gulberwick, also in the
south of mainland Shetland. A Gulberwick woman collecting peat was:

arrested by the sound of low, soft music when near the Hollanders' Knowe. She was satisfied that the sound came from within, and stood entranced until she knew every note of the tune being played. The woman never forgot the melody that she had learned in so strange a fashion, but although she sang it over to several well-known fiddlers, not one of them had heard it before, but all were struck with the charm and beauty of the composition. (Nicolson 1920: 10)

The name of the tune is not mentioned in the story. Mr Tommy Goudie who lives at Gulberwick told me that the Hollanders' Knowe is apparently so-called because it was a trading point for Dutchmen pre 1700 before a harbour was built in Lerwick. The knowe is identified with a marker.

Not far from the Hollanders' Knowe, 'The Trowie Burn' (HU 4139) runs near to the road between Gulberwick and the road connecting Scalloway to Lerwick. Here it was said that you could hear the sound of fiddles playing, but Tommy Goudie explained that 'mainly it was the water running over stones and making a nice tinkling sound.' This was meant to be the fiddles. He continued:

Quite often, I think, people, well I know my mother said once that coming from a wedding, walking home, and they went past there and of course the music was still in their ears, as you might say, the fiddle music, and they sat down there and they thought they could hear the fiddles playing.

4. Hill of Wormidale

John Spence in *Shetland Folk-Lore* (1899) mentions how a fiddler was taken to the home of the trows where he played for two days, in the following story set at the Hill of Wormidale (HU 4046) on mainland Shetland. The taking of a mortal musician by the trows who is made to play for them at a dance or at a wedding is a common theme:

A noted fiddler named John Herculeson had been invited to a wedding at Whiteness, where he was supposed to arrive early on the bridal e'en. The company waited long and patiently, but John did not turn up, and it was only on the eve of the 'sindering day' that he reached the festive dwelling. Now, it turned out that John, while crossing the Hill of Wormidale, had been taken into a *trowie* abode, and had been kept playing the fiddle for two whole days. It was deemed imprudent to accept any reward from the *trows*, or to partake of their food. (Spence 1899: 151)

Figure 2. Broch a Houlland, Aithsting

5. The West Side

A tune called the 'West Side Trows Reel' is heard at the Broch a Houlland in the west side of Shetland (HU 4455):

Hakki Johnson lived at Tumlin, Aithsting, in the early days of the 19th century. He was an excellent fiddler, but rather weakminded when the moon was full. His neighbours said he was 'no aa dere'. One winter night he called on a neighbouring fiddler and played a weird tune, asking, when he had finished, 'Kens du yon tøn?' On getting a negative reply he told the following story, 'Twa nights ago I was playin at yon rant at Aith an left for hame my lane some time after tree in da moarnin. When I was below da Broch a Houlland I tocht I hard a fiddle playin'. I stopped and listened and hard da reel goin on for some time. When it stopped I gaed on my way. Yon was hit I played een-noo.' (Stewart and Moar 1951: 24)

The following tale from Nicolson's *Some Folk-Tales and Legends of
Shetland* mentions a place called Lunklet (HU 3657), a now unpopulated
settlement in the Aithsting area which has a burn that is popular with tourists.
The story takes place at Yule, and sightings of trows were particularly
common at this time as well as at Hallowe'en:

> It was Yule morning, and Magnie o' Lunklet and his wife were
> having breakfast in the *ben* end to mark the occasion. It was
> still quite dark outside, but, of course, no one cared to lie abed
> on Yule morn. Breakfast over, the guidwife fetched a bottle
> from the corner press, and proceeded to pour out two glasses,
> one for Magnie and one for herself. The guidman, however,
> interposed with the remark that she need not pour out his glass
> meantime. He had decided to take his fiddle, for Magnie was
> no mean performer, and visit their next neighbours for a few
> minutes, and give them a *spring* or two to enliven them. He
> would get his glass when he returned.
>
> He took his departure, but no sooner had he set foot on the
> *brig-stanes* than he was requisitioned by the Trows, who
> hurried him regardless of protests to the Trowie Knowe outside
> the hill-dykes. There Magnie fiddled with vigour, and the little
> folk danced to his music until dawn-day. When the dance
> ceased, Magnie hurried home, and his first remark as he
> entered the door, was: – 'So lass, I'll tak' da gless o' whisky
> noo.' 'It's no afore da time,' remarked his wife, 'what i' da
> Loard's name is come ower dee?' Then to Magnie's surprise,
> he learned that he had been missing for a week. (Nicolson
> 1920: 16)

Another tale from Aithsting tells of Tirvil o' Stivva who was on his
way to Klusta to play at a *yule-rant* (ball). He hears music at the Knowe of
Görwill (HU 3257; also spelt Guerawill):

> When he came to Görwill, he heard the strains of music
> proceeding from within that Trowie knowe. He stopped to
> listen, and having a very musical ear, soon mastered the tune.
> When Tirvil arrived at his destination he played it as the first
> *spring* (reel) that night, and the company was charmed with the
> quaint melody. The young folks quickly learned the tune, and
> it became known as the *Trowie spring* ever after. (Nicolson
> 1920: 9)

Figure 3. Knowe of Görwill

The settlement of Gord (HU 2057) on the West Side of mainland Shetland forms the location of the story called 'The Fiddler of Gord'. It is told by George P. S. Peterson, a well-known fiddler and story-teller from Papa Stour, and is also found in a printed source: an article entitled 'Sigurd o' Gord' by 'J.P.S.J', who has been identified as Dr J.P.S. Jamieson of Nelson, New Zealand, a native of Sandness – in *The Shetland News*, January 1963. The newspaper version opens by telling us that Sigurd o' Gord was coming back from fishing sillicks at the craigs at Bousta on Toylisha Eve, and continues:

> It was just dark when he reached the rock which is now known as the Packman's Stane. He was astonished as he drew near to hear sounds of music and revelry. When he arrived at the rock, he was amazed to find the face of it open. It was hollow and brightly lit inside with high festival. A Trow stepped out to meet him and very civilly enquired if he were not Sigurd o' Gord. Sigurd admitted, and the Trow expressed pleasure, for he said, 'We know of you as a fine fiddler, and we would have you play for us at our Yule festival.

Figure 4. The Packman's Stane

Sigurd took a drink of the trows' liquor, and so put himself in their power for a hundred years. When Sigurd returned to Gord he found that his house was full of strangers. He went outside, followed by a young man of the house, and 'took the fiddle and played over and over again the refrain he had picked up in the rock, till the listening young man also caught it.' Then Sigurd and his fiddle crumbled to dust. The story ends: 'If you go, by yourself, at midnight, on Toylisha Eve, to the Well of Gord, you will hear the tune played on the fiddle.' (*Shetland News* 1963: 6)

6. Collafirth, Delting

A long walk up a steeply sided voe in the north of mainland Shetland in very boggy conditions – certainly when I was there – brings one to what is known as 'The Thieves' Knowes' (HU 3867). Arthur (Ertie) Cooper from Collafirth, told this story about the place that was collected by Alan Bruford in 1974:

> Well me grandfather used to tell me about a knowe that the thieves bade in. An a fellow goin till a weddin and carried his fiddle, and the trows took him. An they keepit him and he played to them for days and nights, and then they ran short o food. And he said that this people [at] home hed a fat animal that they could get and he also had a jar o fresh butter. And if they would come wi him he wid ... go, put them in the byre and

[they could] spot the animal that they wanted. And he would go in and get this churn oot, and so he went in an awakened the people of the house, and they all rushed oot and catched the whole lot of them before they got the cow oot.

7. The Hill of Skellister, Nesting

The Hill of Skellister (HU 4655) in the Nesting area of mainland Shetland is the setting for a story printed in *The Scotsman* newspaper in 1893.

They [the fairies] preferred Shetland fiddlers to their own musicians, and good fiddlers on going and returning from evening parties had always to be accompanied by one or two friends. Magnus of Brough was a genius in his own way. He could build a boat and make a spoon, was a good mason, and a better tailor, and as a fiddler he was far superior to any in the whole islands. His love of music was intense, and the whole of his leisure time was devoted to it. He was a tall, easy-going, dreamy sort of man, and his wife, a small, dark-complexioned, energetic, quick-tempered person, scolded him heartily for his inattention. When she was in her highest moods, he would listen till his patience became exhausted, and then he would betake himself to the fiddle. He drew from it the sharpest, scolding notes, which intensified her indignation, and then he would suddenly break out into the most violent sobbing strains of weeping, which either subdued her on the spot or made her fly. He continued thus all his life. Age did not abate his musical ardour. He passed away listening to the melody of his own fiddle, and it is said that his warbling powers have been transmitted to his descendents. After his death it was discovered that he was not really dead, but had been removed by the good folk. His family acting on the advice of persons intimately acquainted with the most successful methods of working in such cases, did everything in their power to effect his recovery, and at last called in the aid of a doctor whose skill in similar cases had been, it was said, often proved. He told them that Magnus of Brough's skill as a fiddler and his resistance to control rendered his rescue extremely difficult; but if they paid his fee at once, and returned to him at the end of three days, and after sunset, he would let them know how he had succeeded. They came, and he told them that Magnus was sitting in an iron-bound chair playing on a magnificent fiddle in a beautiful furnished house in the hill of Skellister, and his release was impossible. (*Scotsman* 1893)

8. The North Isles

The Voe o' Gloup (HP 5004) in North Yell is the setting of the story of how 'Spence's Reel' is learned from the trows. Brucie Henderson, a well-known storyteller from South Yell, related how music was heard at the knowe at the head of the voe. The tune in question is very likely to be 'Spence's Reel':

Da man wis gyan, at Christmas time, ta fitch his Christmas stocks; an he wis gyaan fae Gloup tae Nort Yell, aroon da voe. An he gied, an hit wis night whan he cam hem, an he wis quite aaright, he wis taen nae drink or nothin. An whan he cam tae da hed o da voe o' Gloup, he heard music, an he windered wha wis play-actin wi him. But he sed dat he wis niver heard dis fiddle tune before; an dan he luikit up an on da tap o da Knowe whar da reeds an dokkens wis, here wis peerie men, aafil peerie tings ... dancin on da taps o dis dokkens, an kerryin on. An dan dey cam doon an danced in a ring aroon dem; an dis wis gyaan on, an he wis a fiddler, an he got da tune. An he cam home an he played hit tae his wife dat Christmas Eve. An dat tune in Shetland is going on yat.

Figure 5. Hoose-a-Hooligarth

In the Westsandwick area of Yell there is another trowie knowe where fiddle music is said to be heard. Mrs Netta Inkster lives just next door to a knowe called the 'Hoose-a-Hooligarth' (HU 4589) and told me that when she and her husband built their house 'everybody said, now ... trows'll come in and live in the house and take everything, but we've never seen any trows yet!' They built the house about twenty years ago. She related a story about the knowe that had been handed down in her family:

> We were told when we were young that this knowe, there were fairies in this knowe, and if we went out at night we would hear this music played. Well we always, ... we'd maybe been in our teens, we'd sit there and listen ... hoping we would hear music or probably see the trows or the fairies, but we were so disappointed we never saw or heard anything.

The following story taken from the article by Stewart and Moar relates to Vallafield (HP 5908) on the west side of Unst and particularly to the rock called Gullahammar. I was able to locate the rock in the hillside with the help of Mr Smith who lives in Uyeasound:

> One November day, early in the 19th century, Sandy Winwick, of the Westing, Unst, set out four miles to Colvadale to pay a long-promised visit to his boyhood friend, Andrew Manson. Time passed pleasantly chatting about boyhood exploits, and in the afternoon of the following day Sandy thought it time to start for home. After mutual 'Blissins' they parted at the hill grind, and Sandy set out on his tramp over the hills. Dusk had fallen when he crossed the south end of Vallafield, but as he had only half a mile further to go he stopped to have a smoke in the shelter of Gullahammar, a steep rock face on the west side of the hill. He was about to produce his tinder-box when the sound of music was borne to his ears. He sat spellbound, and only when it dawned on him that this was unearthly music did a cold chill of fear creep down his spine. As he jumped to his feet he grabbed his pocket-knife, and as his fingers touched the steel the music ceased. He raced across the valley, his heart beating a rhythm as fast as that of the tune, and did not pause or look back till he came to the hill daek. Nothing could be seen or heard. Proceeding home at a more sober pace, he told

the story to his family as soon as he got in, and sang the tune to his daughter. It was she who played it on her fiddle and gave the Westing a new tune called Vallafield. (Stewart and Moar 1951: 21-22)

A place that is connected with the dancing of the trows and their music is Haltadance (HU 6292) on the island of Fetlar. Jakobsen (1936: 171-172) writes of it:

> On this spot there are three concentric circles formed of upright stones with two higher stones in the centre. An old local tradition says that the stones in the circle are trolls which, during a dance, were surprised by the rising sun and were thus turned into stones. ... Of the name Haltadans it may be mentioned that in old Shetland traditions about trolls and fairies it is commonly said that they limped when dancing. ... In the colloquial language in Fetlar and Yell the expression 'to had (hold) a haltadans', to rush about noisily, can still be heard.

He notes that the two stones in the centre are said to be the fiddler and his wife.

Stewart and Moar (1951: 19) state that the trows were said to have come out at this ring of stones 'on quiet nights and when the moon was full', and observe that it is a pity that only one of the trows' tunes from the place has survived. This is the tune 'Hyltadance' about which they have the following comments:

> It is ... remarkable that the tune 'Hyltadance' should have been handed down for 350 years, for it was that long ago that the indweller in Culbenstoft who was in the habit of going to the craigs at the Stucks, a craigseat at the seaward edge of Busta Hill, heard the trows singing and dancing when crossing the Fluddens. It may have been the father of John Robertson who was at Culbenstoft in 1642, or it may have been John himself.

Stewart and Moar publish a version of the tune, and it was also recorded from Jeemsie Laurenson of Fetlar who sang nonsense syllables to it.

9. Conclusion

In conclusion, stories linking the trows to the fiddle seem to be most frequently found around the middle of mainland Shetland, with locations also on the islands of Yell, Fetlar, Unst and Papa Stour. Knowes or knolls are the most common places where trows are seen or their music is heard, but fairy people are also associated with stone circles, valleys, mills, hills, brochs, crevices in rocks, and wells, and one of their tunes was heard at sea. With the exception of the last, these are places that stand out in the physical landscape and have the feeling of being set apart, particularly where the land surrounding them is relatively flat. MacInnes (1992: 10) gives an insight into the concept of the fairy hill:

> We could take the fairy knoll as a metaphor of the imagination, perhaps as an equivalent of the modern concept of the Unconscious. From this shadowy realm comes the creative power of mankind. An old friend of mine used to say, when he produced songs or legends that I did not realise he knew: *Bha mi sa Chnoc o chunnaic mi thu*: 'I was in the [fairy] Hill since I saw you.' And others had similar vivid expressions. None of them was to be taken literally but there was a system of belief behind the expression.

Locating trowie stories at particular places would have had the effect of creating a degree of fascination amongst people with the places but no doubt also a degree of fear and apprehension. This could have been used as a way of local control to deter people from visiting them, particularly in the case of children.

Literature

Campbell, K., 2005: *The Fiddle in Scottish Culture*. East Linton.

Donaldson, G., 1991: *Court Book of Shetland, 1615-29*. Lerwick.

Craigie W.A., *et al.*, 1937-2002: *A Dictionary of the Older Scottish Tongue, from the Twelfth Century to the End of the Seventeenth*. Chicago/London.

Jakobsen, J., [1936] 1993: *The Place Names of Shetland*. Kirkwall.

MacInnes, J., 1992: 'Looking at Legends of the Supernatural', *Transactions of the Gaelic Society of Inverness* 59, 1-20.

Nicolson, J., 1920: *Some Folk-Tales and Legends of Shetland*. Edinburgh.

Scotsman, 1893: 'The Trows in Shetland', *The Scotsman*, 19 January 1893, p. 7, col. 3-4 (no author given).

Shetland News, 1963: 'Sigurd o' Gord' by J.P.S.J, 8 January 1963, p. 6.

Spence, J., 1899: *Shetland Folk-Lore*. Lerwick.

Stewart, J. & Moar, P., 1951: 'When the Trows Danced'. In: E.S. Reid Tait (ed.), *Shetland Folk Book*, II. Lerwick, 17-20.

Notes

[1] I would like to thank everyone who helped me with my research on the trows in Shetland, and extend special thanks to Angus Johnson and Brian Smith of Shetland Archives and to Dr Doreen Waugh for assisting me in identifying certain of the locations.

[2] For further trowie stories see Campbell (2005), chapter 4, 'The Fiddler and the Trows'.

[3] The photographs from my fieldwork in Shetland are held in the School of Scottish Studies Archives, department of Celtic and Scottish Studies, University of Edinburgh.

[4] The tune is given in Stewart and Moar and in Campbell (2005).

[5] Interview 4 July 2002, School of Scottish Studies Archives, University of Edinburgh, SA2002.071.

[6] Interview 11 July 2002, SA2002.070.

[7] SA1974.197.A1.

[8] SA1954.113.3, collected by Calum Maclean in 1954. Transcription from Patrick Shuldham-Shaw in the Tale Archive of the School of Scottish Studies.

[9] Interview 8 July 2002, SA2002.072.

[10] See Shetland Archives TA 80B.

The Grammar of Place-Names in Scandinavian England: a Preliminary Commentary

Richard Coates

1. Introduction

This paper shares the conference theme of culture and language contact and replacement with those of Bill Nicolaisen, Gillian Fellows-Jensen, Arne Kruse and Barbara Crawford; it links with Gillian Fellows-Jensen's interest in the significance of place-names in *-by*, and with Berit Sandnes's exposition of the problem of how difficult it may be to identify the language in which a name is formulated. The focus of this brief preparatory study is personal habitative compounds, defined here as *compound place-names with a personal name as the first element and a habitative term as the second*, irrespective of the language out of whose material they were created. Examples of this structure are *Alvaston*, *Grimsby* and *Theddlethorpe*. Most are what toponymists consider to be either major places, i.e. parishes, townships or manors, or secondary settlements which are recorded early.

A regional sample was taken. The areas investigated were those covered by the following EPNS volumes available in early 2003: *PN L* II-VI, *PN Db* II, *PN YWR* I, *PN Lei* II, *PN Nf* II & III. The rationale for this was firstly, of course, that the areas are known, on the basis of historical and of place-name and dialect vocabulary evidence, to have been settled by Scandinavians, with varying degrees of density, and secondly, that the EPNS surveys for these areas are done to an acceptable modern standard, at least as regards the major names which feature most prominently in the discussion. The early documentary record for Yorkshire is thinner than for the other counties, on the whole, which may lead to greater etymological uncertainty there than in the other counties. All spellings recorded before 1400 for the names identified as relevant were counted. This date was chosen as the cut-off point because it was ascertained that by that date the crucial issues of spelling-variation had very largely been resolved in favour of one of the variants.

The goal of the present work is the modest one of showing that there are issues unresolved about personal habitative compounds that are sufficiently interesting to warrant extensive further study.

2. Languages and sociolinguistics of the Danelaw

The names which are considered may be classified according to two criteria, namely language of origin and morphology: (1) they may be etymologically fully Scandinavian or fully English, or have one element from each language; and (2) since both languages have similar morphological systems, the names may illustrate either stem-compounding or genitival compounding irrespective of the historical source of the elements of the name. The personal names may be linguistically Scandinavian (Sc.) or (mainly Old) English (Eng.), and should not be thought of as reliably indicating the ethnicity of the bearer unless the identity of the bearer is known and s/he can therefore be dated with confidence – and even then there is room for doubt on the grounds of parental exogamy or fashion. Purely for the purposes of this brief paper, such caution has been thrown to the winds, and I speak provisionally in a way which equates Sc. lexis and Sc. personal names as "Sc." objects. If this is thought to be bad policy for names, it should also be thought bad policy for ordinary lexemes, as the eventual full development of this work will show; lexemes may be equally problematic when one tries to assign them to a particular language in a bilingual situation. As food for thought, consider Driby (L; Cameron 1998: 39), where the unambiguously Eng. specifier could suggest that the language in which the coiner was coining it was Eng., and that *by* here must therefore be an Eng. word though borrowed from Sc. Recall that my purpose is to indicate some matters which are unresolved; the question of which language(s) a lexical or onomastic item may belong to is one of them.

The county editor's judgement about what the first element is – i.e. about whether it is a personal name or not – has been followed for the purpose of establishing a dataset for this paper: for alternative views on some of the names see Fellows Jensen (1978). The habitative element of the names is mainly expressed by one of the following: the historically Eng. *tūn*, *worð*, *hām*, *stōw*, *mynster*, *wīc*, *burh*, *cotu/cote* and *þorp*, and the historically Sc. *bȳ*, *thorp* and *bōth*. Overwhelmingly, the cases of interest involve *tūn*, *worð*, *bȳ* and *thorp*. Although the possible presence of the English counter-part of *thorp* must be acknowledged, in my view the later spellings of the form <thorp> in this area can usually safely be taken as the originally Sc. word, which always had more onomastic vitality than its Eng. counterpart, as the thin evidence for *þorp* outside the Danelaw suggests. As we know, assigning a particular place-name to speakers of one language or the other can be very problematic, and not just because of the historical ambiguity of <thorp>. Little enough is known about the sociolinguistics of the Danelaw to make it uncertain what vocabulary was borrowed by either speech-community from the other. The evidence we have is available solely from writers with literacy in Eng., which displays well-known lexical and grammatical borrowings from Sc.; we have not the slightest idea what if anything went in the other direction, because there was no literacy in Sc., or at any rate no evidence for any has survived with the exception of a tiny number of inscriptions (13 runic ones in England; Haugen 1976: 141; cf. the discussion in Parsons 2001: 302-303). We have evidence for the borrowing of *bȳ* into Eng., but none for the borrowing of *dry* into Sc. Nor is it even certain whether it is appropriate to think in terms of two speech-communities. Surely it is thinkable that there was one bilingual one for some of the period that interests us most, say 865-1100 C.E., i.e. that there was in at least some of the region a group of people, many of whom were bilingual and who shared linguistic attitudes and usage-patterns in a way which defines a speech-community (as originally defined by Gumperz 1968). This issue of the relationship between the two languages, which is usually presented from a somewhat different perspective as being about the survival and eventual demise of Sc., has been addressed before, notably by Ekwall (1924: esp. 90-92; 1930), Page (1971), Fellows Jensen (1975: 201-204) and Parsons (2001), and implicitly Fellows-Jensen (2000: 140). But, to push the matter further, it could be argued that in some senses (which will need to be spelt out properly on a different occasion, but cf. Hines 1991 and the survey and discussion by Kastovsky 1992: 327-332) the two languages merged, and some basic lexis and some basic grammatical features which may be of Sc. origin have been mediated by the northern dialects into what eventually became Standard English.

3. A key linguistic issue: the status(es) of schwa and <e>

For this paper, the focus is on a narrow range of phenomena. The most serious problem in interpreting the data collected is what to make of an <e> which appears between the two elements, and which I assume to represent, exclusively, [ə] (schwa) in an unstressed syllable in the period from which most of the evidence comes, namely after 1085. Firstly, in many names it is only variably present. That might mean that it was only variably present in pronunciation. If that is the case, then it might appear for phonological reasons: epenthesis, i.e. insertion to ease consonant clusters that were difficult for at least some speakers, or elision, i.e. deletion as a rapid-speech phenomenon, which might result ultimately in its systematic loss (and did in later Middle English). Alternatively, the presence or absence of <e> might be a scribal phenomenon. Languages have constraints on sequences of letters just as they do on sequences of sounds. The breaking-up of sequences of consonants by means of an <e> might be due to scribal convention within the language (just as, overwhelmingly, in modern Eng. a word-final /v/ is conventionally written <ve>), or due to the importation of conventions from the scribal tradition of another language, and the conventions in use in England after 1066 were those which stabilized at the Carolingian court for writing Latin and, in due course, French (in England firstly Norman and then Parisian). Yet another alternative is that the variable presence of <e> might be neither phonological nor graphological, but morphological. A particular name might be variably formed by genitival compounding, where the <e> expresses the genitive case of the first element, or by stem-compounding, where this material would be absent (unless the stem itself ended in <e>, of course). Or, at least in theory, the <e> might be a morphological expression of compound status, i.e. what German scholars call a *Fugenvokal* or what is now usually called an *interfix* (Bauer 2003: 29-30). Such a thing developed sporadically in OE (Campbell 1959: 152-153), but I know of no discussion of its appearance in place-names.

4. Point of departure: the medial elements found in the dataset

The appearance of many of the names studied is one of great structural inconsistency, *whether they are apparently of hybrid, of Scandinavian or of English origin*. In detail, the material found which related the two elements of the names exhibits either genitival composition or stem-composition as follows:

4.1. Names showing genitival compounding

4.1.1. Strong inflection

4.1.1.1. Eng. <-es> vs. Sc. <-s>

Strong inflection with an <s> may be of (1) either the Eng. type in <-es> or the Sc. <-es> genitive of nouns in <-ir>, or (2) the Sc. type in <-s> proper to other declensional classes.

4.1.1.2. Sc. <-ar>

Strong inflection with Sc. <-ar> is occasionally found intact in names in England, as in *Osmotherley* or *Amounderness*, but the <r> is regularly lost in East Sc. As a result of this process, rather than <er>, forms in <-e> may be found which are indistinguishable from forms containing reflexes of weak inflection.

4.1.2. Weak inflection

Where medial <-e> represents an inflection rather than being due to phonological or graphological epenthesis, it might in principle reflect OE weak masculine or feminine <-an>, or Sc. weak <-a> of whatever gender.

This situation is complicated by the fact that during the ME period unstressed schwa was generally lost under most conditions, firstly in the north, with the phenomenon later spreading to the south. Accordingly, the regular mark of the difference between Eng. and Sc. strong inflections in <s> could be lost, and the difference between weak genitival elements and elements in a bare-stem form could be obliterated. There is usually a discernible progression in the record of individual names from earlier forms with <e> to later forms without it. Interpretation of the key names is affected by this process and its consequences; scribal traditionalism might give the impression that the change had been delayed or even that the loss of schwa had been aborted (Pinxton *Db* II: 291; Pillsbury *Db* II: 370; Williamthorpe *Db* II: 333-334). In a few instances, one has the distinct impression that scribal inconsistency may be due to cloth ears and/or Chinese whispers between the locality and the Exchequer and Chancery in Westminster (Gunthorpe *Nf* III: 125-126).

4.2. Names showing stem-compounding

This is self-explanatory; such names show from the outset no compositional material (Booton *Nf* III: 64; Thealby *L* VI: 44-45, in which medial <e> appears only after the time of its progressive elision). I shall not dwell on this here, except to emphasize that personal names are not infrequently found in such structures.

4.3. Element-identical names which differ in morphological type

Some names which etymologically contain the same elements may be structurally different; compare Alby (*Nf* III: 48) and Aylesby (*L* V: 1-2), or Ketsby (*L*; Cameron 1998: 73) and Kettleby (*Lei* II: 157, 188). In these instances with a Sc. second element, as with Aylesby, apparent strong inflection of a Sc. weak masculine personal name is generally attributed to ME so-called "secondary inflection", i.e. where genitival material appropriate to English is used irrespective of the original language of coining, which suggests continuing transparency of the place-name to its users (or at least a perception that it contains two elements, as one finds genitival composition also in non-personal compounds (Tengstrand 1940).

5. The consistency of form hypothesis

For whatever reason, scattered strong forms are sometimes found in a record otherwise of weak forms or apparent stem-compounds, or vice versa (Tealby *L* III: 131-136; Thurlow Booth *Db* II: 438). Place-name scholars tend to argue such difficult cases out of existence on the grounds that names must be (or must have been on coining) structurally unique, and that one must be able in principle to identify THE original grammar of a name. Following this approach, scribal inconsistency must demonstrate error rather than endemic variation, and the form in the majority in the record is normally taken as representing the original structure. Such a view is of course supported by the fact that some names show something close to total consistency in this respect (Grimsby *L* V: 46-48; Thorganby *L* III: 157-158; or Beckham *Nf* III: 8, 59, after the 11th century). But in the end, the *consistency of form hypothesis* should at least be interrogated.

6. Selected results in some detail, and discussion

In accordance with the time-honoured technique, I tried to establish the dominant, and therefore arguably original, compositional type for each personal habitative compound. This was not always a straightforward matter methodologically. But I shall focus on results here and then return to the methodological implications. What emerged from my survey?

6.1. Strong genitival compounding

As would be expected, where both elements are Eng., <-es> prevails (21, with 2 in <-s>). But there were problematic findings in three categories.

- <-s> might have been expected to prevail in names with both a Sc. first and a Sc. second element. In fact it dominated in names with a Sc. first and an Eng. second element (8 names, with 5 in <-es>, but mainly because of 6 in *Lei*, suggesting a local scribal tradition, a matter which so far as I know has not previously been subject to systematic investigation, and which remains to be investigated).

- <-es> might have been expected to prevail at least where the second element, and therefore the grammar of the expression, was Eng., whereas it also proved to be general in certain names where both elements were Sc. (21 names, with 6 in <-s> and 3 ambiguous), including Grimsby (*L* IV: 22), Ormsby (*L* IV: 46-48), Grainsby (*L* IV: 98-99), Grimesthorpe (*YWR*

I: 210), Grimethorpe (*YWR* I: 268) and Rollesby (*Nf* II: 73-74). Exceptionally, one form in <-s> was found for Grimsby, but only in *Orkneyinga saga*, which of course is written entirely in Old Norse. However, the modern pronunciation requires there to have been pre-cluster shortening of the first vowel, which means at a time when the pronunciation used by Eng.-speakers had a consonant directly after /m/, which must mean either in a hypothetical period before "secondary" ME <-es> had been adopted or one after medial <e> which this morpheme contained had disappeared.

– A large number of names with strong masculine first elements showed stem-composition rather than genitival inflection (a typical one: Usselby, *L* III: 168-169, with an anglicized ESc. first element).

Even where Sc. <-s> is expected and found, there are interpretational problems. Phonologically, Ulceby (*L* II: 291-292) sounds a cast-iron case of Sc. strong -*s* because it has modern /s/ not /z/; but, with only four exceptions in a brief tradition from 1294 onwards, the record always shows <-es>/<-se> (later <-ce>). This might be a case of an epenthetic vowel in the spelling, and evidence for cluster-breaking in a French pronunciation- or spelling-tradition.

Thoresway (*L* II: 150-151) is a Sc. name with a Sc. personal name as first element, which Cameron argues to be the theonym *Thor* as opposed to the human *Thóri-* (against Cox 1994: 42, fn. 20). If that is so, one would not expect <-es> at all, but it is well-nigh universal in this name. One might be tempted to conclude that the personal name involved is after all *Thórir* with its etymologically expected genitive in <-es>, but that would be bad policy. Other names expected to have <-s> in fact have frequent <-es> or <se>:Claxby (*L* III: 17-18), Croxby (*L* II: 26-27), Clippesby (*Nf* II: 51-52).

The data on which these findings are based are summarized numerically in Figure 1 (see below). All this suggests the need for *a reappraisal of the entire question of the way the strong genitive is rendered* in the spelling of the ME period, founded in an understanding of the sociolinguistics of bilingualism.

	L	Lei	YWR	Nf	Db
	-es / -s	-es / -s	-es / -s	-es / -s	-es / -s
Sc + E	1 / 0	0 / 6	2 / 2	1 / 0	1 / 0
Sc + Sc	15 / 5	1 / 4	3 / 0	4 / 0	1 / 0
E + Sc	0 / 0	1 / 0	0 / 0	2 / 0	0 / 0
E + E	3 / 0	1 / 0	6 / 0	3 / 1	9 / 1

Figure 1. The rendering of the strong genitive according to compound-type

6.2. The vowel <e>

Gillian Fellows Jensen (1969) has advanced an argument for epenthesis as a characteristic feature of the names found in the 12th-century Lindsey Survey, where previously the relevant letters had been treated as having morphosyntactic significance, but we need to consider whether the phenomenon of epenthesis is not more widely represented in the historical record. An <e> could represent a phonological phenomenon breaking clusters of the type *CCC* or *C#C* (where <#> represents a morpheme boundary); it could be an orthographical one protecting <v> as in Kniveton (*Db* II: 383-384), or a device for guaranteeing the pronunciation of <c> as /ts/ as in Ulceby (*L* II: 291-292). But the apparently fully English name of Buxton (*Nf* III: 67) normally shows no <e> in its genitive first element, which therefore has the appearance of a Sc. strong noun.

The spelling <e> is generally understood to be the norm for genitival compounding with several categories of first element, mainly weak genitives in both Sc. and Eng. The principal interest in <e> for this paper is to compare two-element structures where the first is a personal name with those in which it is a common noun. The latter category does not automatically consist of stem-compounds, as we have known since the rich and full analyses of Tengstrand (1940). It is more surprising, perhaps, to discover that in such structures personal names may show (largely, as explained earlier) zero inflection (Usselby *L*, Beckham *Nf*), and that what are apparently common nouns in names with Sc. second elements may show regular or even consistent <e> (Risby *L* III: 173 'brushwood farm', Keelby *L* II: 174-175, Saltby *Lei* II: 250-251, Maltby *YWR* I: 137, Mautby *Nf* II: 10, among which only Keelby might reasonably be suspected of having a first element ('keel; ridge') in the genitive singular). Names with two Eng. elements of which the first is non-personal, such as Plumstead (*Nf* III: 127) and Gresham (*Nf* III:

18), are almost always without <e>. Mackworth (*Db* II: 479-480), with a personal first element, varies between <e> and zero. Despite this variety, scholars have used the presence or absence (dominance or paucity) of an <e> as critical evidence in deciding whether the first element is a personal name or not. Besthorpe (*L* III: 164-165) is explained by Cameron as including OE *bēos* 'coarse grass' rather than the Sc. personal name *Besi* because the record, with no medial <e>, suggests to him that the first element cannot be a personal name; he is thereby probably committed to explaining (away) a hybrid name. By contrast, Risby (*L* III: 173) and Risley (*Db* II: 496) have dominant <e> despite the fact that the most plausible candidate for the first element is either the Sc. or the Eng. word for 'brushwood'. Extremely problematic is the case of the various *Ashbys* which, formally at least, are of the type Eng. + Sc., but which without exception among the six instances in Lincolnshire (Cameron 1998: 4) have medieval forms where the first element is phonologically Sc. and contains a medial <e> (type: <Askebi>). What then is this <e>? Must they all be taken as containing the Sc. weak personal name *Aski* or does the first element *ask-* 'ash-tree', unusually, always appear in the genitive plural? It is clear that *questions about the interpretation of this <e> in a range of names need to be asked afresh.*

6.3. Stem-compounding

More problematic still is what happens with stem-compounding. Numerous place-names of the region have what appears to be an OE personal name stem-compounded with a Sc. element. These include Barnetby (*L* II: 8-9), Audleby (*L* II: 88, except the earliest record), Worlaby (*L* II: 302-303, where early <-es> gives way to <-e> and then zero), Kingerby (*L* III: 47-49), Usselby (*L* III: 168-169), Yaddlethorpe (*L* VI: 23), Ringlethorpe (*Lei* II: 208-209) and Brentingby (*Lei* II: 132-133, where the discussion may overrate the significance of the three early instances of <e> in the record). This may also occur when the second element is Eng., as with Alfreton (*Db* II: 187-188) and with most of the record of Thurgarton (*Nf* II: 43-44). All the personal names in these names are polysyllabic and bimorphemic, but the absence of an explicit genitive marker is not a phonological or morphological matter: Autby (*L* IV: 166-168) and Wartnaby (*Lei* II: 165-166) include a polysyllabic and bimorphemic OE personal name, yet have general <-e> in the record.

In post-Conquest place-names, we find significant inconsistency in this respect. Herringthorpe (*YWR* I: 185-186) shows stem-compounding whilst Baconsthorpe (*Nf* III: 54) has principally an <-es> genitive.

Names with OE second elements and first elements which may be masculine OE personal names have, expectedly, a first element with a strong genitive in <-es>: Brodsworth (*YWR* I: 71), Breaston (*Db* II: 430-431), Roxton (*L* II: 165). But other names with definitely OE first elements may appear with stem-compounding (Aylmerton *Nf* III: 4-5) or with stem-compounding and weak genitival formation in parallel (Wymondham *Lei* II: 286). It is clearly not appropriate to conclude that stem-compounding is simply a Sc. phenomenon unless we argue that such names as *Aylmerton* were of a structural type understood for what they were by Scandinavian-speakers and restructured by them. On the other hand, they are much more frequent in the Danelaw than are such similarly-structured names as *Edgarley* (So) outside it.

The conditions governing or (dis)favouring stem-compound-ing need a fresh look.

7. Conclusions

The main conclusions, a programme for action, occur in italicized form in the body of the paper.

Literature

Bauer, L., 2003: *Introducing Linguistic Morphology*, 2nd edition. Edinburgh.

Cameron, K., 1998: *A Dictionary of Lincolnshire Place-Names*. Nottingham.

Campbell, A., 1959: *Old English Grammar*. Oxford.

Cox, B., 1994: 'The Pattern of Old English *burh* in Early Lindsey', *Anglo-Saxon England* 23, 35-56.

Db = Cameron, K., 1959: *The Place-Names of Derbyshire*, 1-3. EPNS 27-29. Cambridge.

Ekwall, E., 1924. 'The Scandinavian Element'. In: A. Mawer & F.M. Stenton (eds), *Introduction to the Survey of English Place-Names*, part I. EPNS 1. Cambridge, 55-92.

Ekwall, E., 1930. 'How Long did the Scandinavian Language Survive in Britain?' In: N. Bøgholm *et al.* (eds), *A Grammatical Miscellany Offered to Otto Jespersen on his Seventieth Birthday*. Copenhagen/London, 17-30.

EPNS = English Place-Name Society county surveys.

Fellows Jensen, G., 1969: 'The Scribe of the Lindsey Survey', *Namn och Bygd* 57, 58-74.

Fellows Jensen, G., 1975: 'The Vikings in England: a Review', *Anglo-Saxon England* 4, 181-206.

Fellows Jensen, G., 1978: *Scandinavian Settlement Names in the East Midlands*. Navnestudier 16. Copenhagen.

Fellows-Jensen, G., 2000: 'Vikings in the British Isles: the Place-Name Evidence', *Acta Archaeologica* 71, 135-146.

Gumperz, J., 1968: 'The Speech Community'. In: *International Encyclopedia of the Social Sciences*. London, 381-386. Reprinted in: P.P. Giglioli (ed.), *Language and Social Context*. Harmondsworth 1972, 219-231.

Haugen, E., 1976: *The Scandinavian Languages*. London.

Hines, J., 1991: 'Scandinavian English: a Creole in Context'. In: P.S. Ureland & G. Broderick (eds), *Language Contact in the British Isles: Eighth International Symposium on Language Contact in Europe, Douglas, Isle of Man, 1988*. Tübingen, 403-427.

Kastovsky, D., 1992: 'Semantics and Vocabulary'. In: R.M. Hogg (ed.), *The Cambridge History of the English Language*, vol. I. Cambridge, 290-408.

L = Cameron, K., 1984-2001: *The Place-Names of Lincolnshire* 1-6. EPNS 58, 64/65, 66, 71, 73, 77. Cambridge/Nottingham.

Lei = Cox, B., 1998-2002: *The Place-Names of Leicestershire* 1-2. EPNS 75, 78. Nottingham.

Nf = Sandred, K.I., 1989-2002: *The Place-Names of Norfolk* 1-3. EPNS 61, 72, 79. Nottingham.

Page, R.I., 1971: 'How Long did the Scandinavian Language Survive in England? The Epigraphical Evidence'. In: P. Clemoes & K. Hughes (eds), *England before the Conquest: Studies in Primary Sources Presented to Dorothy Whitelock*. Cambridge, 165-181.

Parsons, D.N., 2001: '"How Long did the Scandinavian Language Survive in England?" again'. In: J. Graham-Campbell *et al.* (eds), *Vikings and the Danelaw. Select Papers from the Proceedings of the Thirteenth Viking Congress, Nottingham and York, 21-30 August 1997*. Oxford, 299-312.

Tengstrand, E., 1940: *A Contribution to the Study of Genitival Composition in Old English Place-Names*. Uppsala.

YWR = Smith, A.H., 1961-1963: *The Place-Names of the West Riding of Yorkshire*, 1-8. EPNS 30-37. Cambridge.

The *Papar*: Viking Reality or Twelfth-Century Myth?

Barbara E. Crawford

1. Introduction

The Carnegie Trust for the Universities of Scotland is currently funding a project on the *papar* – the name given by the Norse settlers in the North Atlantic to the Celtic holy men (monks or priests) whom they encountered on their voyages to the Northern and Western Isles of Scotland and further north to the Faeroes and Iceland. This name underlies the island name Papay (Pabbay in the Western Isles, 'island of the priests'), and the district or local name Papil (Payble in the Western Isles, 'settlement of the priests'). The project is led by Professor Ian Simpson of the Dept. of Environmental Science, University of Stirling, Beverley Ballin Smith of Glasgow University Archaeological Research Division and myself, and the grants have been given to pursue these historical and scientific objectives:

1. To acquire a better understanding of geographical, environmental and cultural factors underlying Papay/Pabbay/ Papil/Payble locations.

    Do the islands and other places with the Papil name in the Northern Isles differ from those in the Western Isles? What is the geographical relationship of the Papay/Pabbay islands with neighbouring islands or coastal communities? Do the Papil/Bayble locations have any distinctive features?

2. What was the nature of the presumed ecclesiastical establishments of Celtic priests or monks in these places?

    Were they monastic communities living a coenobitic lifestyle on the best land and most favourable situations? Or were they primarily individual hermit retreats in remote locations and on isolated rock stacks? Or was there a combination of the two?

3. What was the nature of the Norse impact on the *papar*?

    Can the survival of these names reveal anything about the Vikings' attitude towards the Celtic ecclesiastical communities in particular and the Christian religion in general?

4. The environmental element is a continuation of a Research Programme into Anthropogenic Soil Structures which has been pursued by the University of Stirling in the Northern Isles. The long-term objective is to understand better the dating of the apparent change in manuring systems from the prehistoric human manure (as analysed at Tofts Ness, Sanday), to the medieval animal manures found in the West Mainland of Orkney and on Papa Stour, Shetland. The change-over is in the late Iron Age.

   Could the ecclesiastical/monastic element provided by the *papar* communities provide an explanation for the change in manuring systems?

   Can we find these soil structures associated particularly with *papar* sites? What was the 'land-management' of the *papar* communities?

5. It is planned to make a comparison of Hebridean Pabbay/Payble anthropogenic soil structures with those already examined in the Northern Isles.

   Were they different, as a result of natural conditions, chronological gaps or system management, or are there similarities in the soil morphological properties and in the datable changes of manuring strategies?

6. The first phase of the Carnegie Trust project was completed in the year 2001-2002. It consisted of:

   i) The collection of historical and archaeological evidence relevant to every *papar* place-name location in the North and West of Scotland.[1]

   ii) A compilation of place-names recorded in Pabbay islands and around Payble locations in the Western Isles.[2] This aspect of the research programme was confined to the Hebrides because there had been no linguistic surveys done in any of these specific locations previously. Compared with the Northern Isles there was a great dearth of studies of the Norse place-names of the Western Isles, explained by the problematical linguistic complexities arising from a two-language situation.[3]

   iii) Field survey of two *papar* locations in the Outer Hebrides, Paible on Taransay and Pabbay in the Sound of Harris, where test borings were taken to assess the deep-soil formations near the main church sites in the two places.[4]

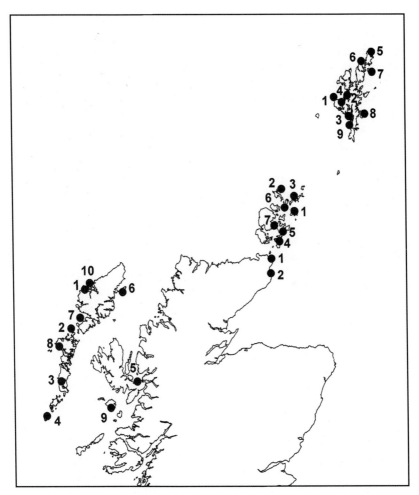

Figure 1. Map of papar *names in North and West Scotland (numbered according to the list of* papar *names in Appendix to MacDonald 2002).*

2. Discussion

If we look at a map of the distribution of the *papar* names in the Northern and Western Isles we can get the best impression of the scale of the task confronting us and the geographical nature of the problem. There are other problems apart from geographical ones. This is a 'place-name driven project' (quote from Dr Simon Taylor), and it is the names which are our main body of 'historical' evidence. How these names are interpreted is therefore all-important for our understanding of the historical situation. But place-names are not easy historical evidence to work with, and the questions we ask of them and the conclusions we draw out of them have to be carefully constructed. Moreover the issues we are raising are very big ones in the early history of the Celtic and Scandinavian worlds. What do these names indicate about the nature of the Celtic religious communities in the islands? And, as mentioned above, can we learn anything from them about the meeting of Scandinavian pagans with the Christian Celtic west? These are very difficult questions to pose of toponymic evidence and we should not expect to get immediate historical information or certain results from our study of the names. The simple fact that we are looking at the totality of these names, and the places where they have survived throughout the Scottish islands (and on the north mainland) is achieving something which has not been attempted before. Too often academic studies of the Vikings and the history of the Norse impact on north Britain focus on either the Western Isles, or, more frequently, on the Northern Isles.[5] The history of the two groups of islands diverges in the late Viking period and throughout later medieval and modern history so that there are conceptual problems about taking a holistic view of the whole insular 'thalassocracy' in the early Viking Age. We need to break the mind-set of looking at either the Northern Isles or the Western Isles, and we have to try to encompass the insular world from Unst in the north to Pabbay (Barra) in the Outer Hebrides, and Rum in the Inner Hebrides. This maritime zone is vast (360 miles) and we struggle to emulate the Vikings, and indeed the *papar* themselves, who ranged over this maritime world and left a visible linguistic record of their presence in the place-names.

3. Historical Evidence

First of all I want to look at the historical evidence for the *papar*, such as it is. There are two later sources which mention them, showing that they were remembered in north Atlantic tradition, although not without strange legendary accretions. The first is from the *Historia Norvegiae* (History of Norway), one of the earliest Norwegian chronicles, which however survives only in a late medieval copy in Scotland. Despite a recent modern edition it is still not clear what the cultural environment of the History of Norway was, where it was written or where the author had got his information from.[6] The extract below is from Chapter VI – *De Orcadibus Insulis* (Concerning the Orkney Islands) – and relates what was known or remembered in the 12th century of the pre-Norse inhabitants of Orkney (and of course Shetland although Shetland is not mentioned), the Picts and the Papar (*Peti* and *Papae*):

> These islands were at first inhabited by the Picts (*Peti*) and Papae. Of these, the one race, the Picts, little exceeded pigmies in stature; they did marvels, in the morning and in the evening, in building [walled] towns, but at mid-day they entirely lost all their strength, and lurked, through fear, in little underground houses. But at that time [the islands] were not called Orchades, but Pictland (*terra Petorum*) . . . And the Papae have been named from their white robes, which they wore like priests; whence priests are all called papae in the Teutonic tongue (*Papae vero propter albas, quibus ut clerici induebantur, vocati sunt, unde in Theutonica lingua omnes clerici papae dicuntur*). An island is still called, after them, Papey (*Adhuc quaedam insula Papey ab illis denomi-natur*). But, as is observed from their habit and the writings of their books abandoned there, they were Africans, adhering to Judaism (*Sed ut per habitum et apices librorum eorum ibidem derelictorum notatur, Africani fuerunt, judaismo adhaerentes*). In the days of Harold Fairhair, King of Norway, certain pirates, of the family of the most vigorous prince Ronald, set out with a great fleet, and crossed the Solundic sea; and stripped these races of their ancient settlements, destroyed them wholly, and subdued the islands to themselves.[7]

It should be stressed that this is the only information that we have about the Picts and the Papar in the Northern Isles from the medieval period, and most likely came from local insular tradition, telling us how the previous inhabitants were remembered in 12th-century Orkney.

Better known is the information in *Íslendingabók* and *Landnámabók*, two of the most famous medieval Icelandic accounts of the settlement of Iceland, about the *papar* in Iceland (dating slightly earlier than *Historia Norvegiae*):

> *Íslendingabók*:
> Iceland was first settled from Norway in the days of Harold Fairhair... At that time Iceland was wooded between the

87

mountains and the coast. At that time, Christian men were here, whom the Norwegians call *papar*; but they departed afterwards, because they would not be here with heathen men; and they left behind them Irish books, and bells, and croziers. Therefore one could perceive that they were Irish men' (Anderson 1922: I, 337-340; and cf. 338 n.4. Icelandic text in Benediktsson 1968: 3-28, at 4-5).

Landnámabók:
But before Iceland was settled from Norway there were other people there, called *Papar* by the Norwegians. They were Christians and were thought to have come overseas from the west, because people found Irish books, bells, croziers, and lots of other things, so it was clear they must have been Irish (Pálsson and Edwards 1972: 15. Their translation is based on the standard edition of the *Sturlubók* text of *Landnámabók* by Benediktsson, 1968: 31-397, at 31-32).

In later texts the information is given about two places named after the *papar* in eastern Iceland, Papey and Papyli.

Taken at first sight these two very different documentary sources appear to provide independent evidence corroborating the existence of Celtic monastic communities, or ecclesiastical settlement of some kind in very different parts of the north Atlantic world. There is currently a historical approach which would regard these as sharing 'elements of a common tradition' (historical or literary), i.e. a learned tradition circulating in Norse-speaking ecclesiastical circles in the 12th century. In a paper published from the *papar* Conference held in St. Andrews in 2001 Aidan MacDonald would see the information about Irish books, bells and croziers left behind when the *papar* are supposed to have fled on the arrival of the Norse in Iceland as a 'learned elaboration'. He suggests that:

'we may ... have in these details, evidence of a learned (and so partly literary?) knowledge of the Irish church of (probably) the later tenth, eleventh or early twelfth centuries ... rather than an essentially uninformed and purely oral tradition stemming from the ninth or early tenth centuries'.[8]

Indeed there may be both, as Aidan MacDonald continues: 'some elements may be broadly traditional but elaborated eventually in a learned milieu'. We can note that there is some independence in these two traditions (Orcadian/Icelandic), in that the former mentions that the writings were Jewish, while the latter stresses the Irish character of the ecclesiastical impedimenta.

What sort of 'learned milieu' might it have been in which this traditional information was elaborated? Mortensen, in his recent discussion of the date and transmission of the text of *Historia Norvegiae* favoured a centre in eastern Norway rather than the west coast (Ekrem and Mortensen 2003: 22-23). He suggests that the author could have spent time in Iceland or Orkney, which would explain his access to Icelandic sources and his interest in the islands (there are sections describing not only Orkney but also Faeroe and Iceland). If the *Historia* was conceived as a consequence of the creation of Norway's own archbishopric in 1152-53 then it was likely to have been produced in an ecclesiastical or royal scriptorium: indeed, it can hardly have been produced anywhere else. The mid-12th century was a time when there was much contact between literate clerics of the episcopal establishments in Norway and the islands. Somewhere in this maritime world the author of the *Historia* had heard about the previous inhabitants of the Orkney islands, and we can be sure that it must have been in Orkney or from an Orcadian, possibly a cleric like Bishop William. This 'first' bishop of the Orkneys had a long episcopacy (1102-68) (Crawford 1996: 9-10), throughout the period when the archbishopric of Nidaros was created and when the *Historia* was being compiled. He would have been the first person to whom an author of such a work would have referred for information about his island see. He would also have been present at the events surrounding the creation of the archdiocese by Cardinal Nicholas Breakspear, in Trondheim in 1152-53,[9] and there are one or two references in *Orkneyinga saga* to his visits to Norway, although quite unspecific as to exactly where he went.

4. Linguistic Evidence

The ON term *papi* which underlies the place-names, and which is used as a name for the pre-Norse clerics in the islands is usually understood as a borrowing from Irish *pápa*, itself borrowed from Latin. Aidan MacDonald's discussion (2002: 15) cites the Irish uses of the term, which are not very numerous but seem to be associated with ecclesiastics of a monastic or anchoritic calling, although it could perhaps be used in secular contexts too – as an honorific term. We should perhaps take seriously the comment in the

Historia that 'all priests are called papae in the Teutonic tongue' which points to a Germanic context for the term.[10]

If we turn to the place-names which incorporate this term *papi* we have to acknowledge the fact that this was a term which the Norse encountered when they moved into the coasts and islands around north Britain, and which they then took up and incorporated into their names for some of these islands. As Aidan McDonald stresses these are linguistically Old Norse names and they were coined by speakers of Old Norse: 'They reflect directly the interests and activities of Norsemen and only indirectly the activities of Celtic ecclesiastics' (2002: 21). This is a cautionary note for those of us involved in the *papar* project and pursuing the research objectives already outlined. A body of toponymic evidence is directing our research parameters, and what that evidence means, and how it is interpreted, is of vital significance for the right direction of the research programme.

We will now have a closer look at that toponymic evidence. The range of forms is very limited, and this standardisation in the use of the element *papi* must be telling us something about the Norse use of the term although it is difficult to know exactly what. There are the non-habitative names, referring to topographical features of which the most prominent is Papa (N. Isles), Pab(b)ay (W. Isles) – **Papa-ey*, 'island of papar'; but there are also a few others, such as Papdale, Papadil – **Papa-dalr*, 'valley of papar'; Papa Geo and Papigoe (probably) – **Papa-gjá, -gjó*, 'ravine of papar'; Pabanish (W. Isles) – **Papa-nes*, 'promontory of papar'.

Then there is the problematical habitative name Papi(e)l, Paple(a)y (N. Isles), Paible (Bayble) (W. Isles) which appears to refer to a specific settlement rather than a generalised geographical area in some ways associated with the *papar*:

> It is taken to be the same as the Icelandic Papyli, which has been derived from an original **Papa-býli*, or **Papa-bœli*, '? settlement of papar' (e.g. Marwick 1923: 262-263; Jakobsen 1936: 172-173; Wainwright 1962: 100). *Býli* seems more likely as an original second element than the by-form *bœli*. Hermann Pálsson has, however, objected, with Einar Ólafur Sveinsson, that **Papabýli* is unlikely to give *Papyli*; and that *Papyli* is in fact the original form (1955: 118). Benediktsson's *Papbýli* (1968: 32 n. 2) may have been intended to try to resolve this problem (*-pb- > -pp- > -p-*). Whatever the connotation(s) generally of this place-name, however, it seems that it could be

Barbara E. Crawford

a district name embracing other named places: the *Hauksbók* version of *Landnámabók* mentions Breidabólstadur and Hof in *Papyli* in Iceland (Pálsson 1955: 115). (MacDonald 2002: 20)

These names still appear on the maps of today and are the current names for the places, but the earliest recorded forms are from both the *Historia Norvegiae* (12th century) and *Hauksbók* version of *Landnámabók* (early-14th century). The island called *Papey* referred to in the section on the Orkney Islands in the Historia might be the same as the *Papey* in *Landnámabók*, that is the *Papey* in S.E. Iceland. One would assume that it is one of the Orkney Papays, but the fact that the Historia says that there is an island named after the *papar* (when there is clearly more than one in both Orkney and Shetland) suggests that he might have been thinking of the single *Papey* in Iceland .[11]

There are eight main *papar* place-names in Shetland, five (or six) in Orkney, eight in the Hebrides, with a few extra topographical ones throughout this zone, including Caithness.[12] What do these names tell us? Precious little in hard evidence. Their significance is in their geographical extent and topographical location. The name of an island signifies that the whole island was so closely connected with the *papar* that their presence was the most remarkable feature about it, but whether that signifies an actual community of *papar* residing on the land, or small numbers of anchorites on the remoter coastal fringes is quite unclear. We cannot even be sure that it might not indicate merely ownership of the island and not actual presence, although it seems unlikely that the Norse would bestow a name as a record of land ownership.

Perhaps there is more potential for illumination in the Papil/Payble form. This seems to suggest a settlement on the ground, but what is the connotation of the *býli* element? The very use of this term indicates that the settlement was of a different order from a secular farming unit, for which there were many different elements such as *bý*, *staðir*, *tún*. If we could develop a better understanding of this element it seems to me to have some potential for increasing our knowledge of what an actual *papar* community was. Was it merely suggesting a non-agricultural settlement, i.e. a community of monks or priests which did not till the ground or earn their own bread, but were supported by the secular communities around them? It must be of some significance that there are Papil/Payble place-names on islands which in other respects might have been called Papay/Pabbay (such as Yell or Taransay). Or are the Papil/Payble places to be understood in connection with nearby islands called Papa/Pabbay? i.e. were they off-shoots of a larger community on the islands, which were established to minister to the nearby

91

secular population? It is questions like this which we must ask before we have a closer look at the geographical, archaeological and historical evidence for these places, and attempt to get some answers.

5. Norse attitudes

If we turn to the other element of the research project, we have to ask more questions. What do these names reveal about the Norse exploration and settlement of the north Atlantic in the Viking Age? Do they reflect the 'actual historical experience of encounters between Norsemen and insular ecclesiastics ... during the early phases of Norse expansion' (MacDonald 2002: 21)? We have contemporary evidence from Dicuil the Geographer about Celtic ascetics in the North Atlantic islands and this 'provides us with a certainty' (Dumville 2002: 128) that they were living there c.800 and had been (probably in the Faeroes) for about a century before that.

So can we use these *papar* names as evidence of Norse tolerance of such Christian ecclesiastical communities or individuals, or perhaps indeed reverence of them, as a result of which they enshrined the *papar* in the toponymy which they gave? Why otherwise would they bestow such names?[13] As indicated above the suspicion has been voiced that the whole batch of information about the *papar* in the medieval written sources may derive from a later period than that of the early Viking encounter. Aidan MacDonald is also positing that the place-names themselves may also have been given at a later date, which is certainly a novel suggestion, and a rather devastating one. He is saying that a tradition develops and the names were 'coined and applied retrospectively'. He argues that 'the unspecific nature of the names', 'the restricted range of forms common to all areas' suggests this was a process of retrospective naming (2002: 21). So here is a challenge for all toponymists of Norse naming practices. How can we know at what date such names were given in the Northern and Western Isles? Certainly the previous chronologies of habitative names have been much loosened in recent discussions (Crawford 1987: 108; Thomson, 2001: 51-54). How do the *papar* names fit into this structure? Island names are usually considered to be of early coining, but the Papil/Payble names with the *býli* element defy any attempts to date them according to current understanding. This fraught issue needs further consideration.

Aidan MacDonald was driven to his position also by the currently growing historical opinion which sees the initial Viking raids as being exceedingly devastating for Christian ecclesiastical communities. How could we imagine that the *papar* would be left in peace in these exposed locations long enough for their name to be applied permanently to those places which they had occupied? Alternatively the names may have been given to abandoned *papar* sites. The destruction of the insular ecclesiastical communities would have left many ruined churches. So was it these ruins which had the *papar* name applied to them after a certain lapse of time and in relatively more settled conditions? Aidan does not suggest that they were given in conjunction with the general conversion of the Norse settlers to Christianity (whenever that may have been and it was not necessarily at the same time in the Northern and Western Isles). But he would prefer to see these names being applied in the second half of the 9th or during the 10th centuries (a period about which we know very little indeed especially in the Hebrides).[14]

The situation on the ground is confused of course by the fact that the majority, if not all of the pre-Norse church sites were eventually re-occupied after the Norse populations were converted and a parish structure developed. This pattern of re-occupation is being appreciated more and more as excavation proves that medieval churches were built on top of Celtic ecclesiastical sites – St Ninian's Isle in Shetland being the best-known and most dramatic example (Crawford 1987: 166). There is much need of a holistic examination of all church sites in the Northern and Western Isles to try and draw some general conclusions about this aspect of what has been termed 'continuity of resort' (Goudie 1904: 57).[15]

As well as the actual church sites there is the body of early Christian sculptural evidence which is so important for the visual images which it provides of the cross, clerics, Pictish symbols and sometimes inscriptions (Fisher 2002). Some of this evidence is certainly associated with important *papar* sites, telling us clearly that there had been Christian activity in these places. But there are also plenty of early Christian memorial stones in locations without *papar* names, as Ian Fisher's map of *papar* sites and early Christian sculpture in the Hebrides shows, cf. Figure 2 (based on Fisher 2002: Figure 3.1). The survival of these wondrous pieces of Christian art is so random that we can hardly rely on the known evidence for providing a hard and fast indicator of *papar* sites. This situation, along with his suggestion that the names may have been given in a later century leads Aidan MacDonald to warn us that progressive application of *papar* names by the Norse 'could have been largely capricious' (2002: 21-22). If so, this would undermine the whole validity of the *papar* project which is using the names themselves as an important pointer to locations particularly associated with the *papar*!

6. Situation in the Hebrides

It is a very curious and possibly significant factor that the *papar* names in the west are confined to the Hebrides north of Ardnamurchan Point (see Figure 1), although, as is well-known, the greatest centre of Celtic ecclesiastical activity was located in Iona. Why did the Norse not apply *papar* names (contemporaneously or retrospectively) in the southern Hebrides?

Is it a simple reflection of the greater density of Norse names in the north Hebrides? Those working on place-names in the S. Hebrides would be able to answer that question, but the impression is that recent work on the toponymy of the Inner Hebrides is beginning to show that there is not such a great distinction in this respect as has been postulated in the past.[16]

Or the answer may lie in the pre-Norse political/ecclesiastical situation. A simplistic suggestion might be that the *papar* names reflect a Pictish ecclesiastical pattern, in the northern Hebrides (and of course in the Northern Isles), as opposed to the Columban Church zone in the southern Hebrides, where the *papar* did not operate, or the term was inappropriate. That sounds a tidy explanation but I suspect that there will be some central objections to it!

The differentiation may also reflect a difference in the Norse impact on the church, so that the greater destruction in the N. Hebrides meant the need to name islands where Celtic priests had once been dominant, whereas the survival factor of religious communities in the southern Hebrides resulted in less need to record former church lands or possessions.

Or, if we go for retrospective naming does it reflect a greater number of devastated church sites in the northern Hebrides and Northern Isles, whereas there was less disruption in the southern Hebrides and therefore fewer abandoned church sites? All these postulated distinctions will have to be tested.

Another possible hypothesis looks to the political situation in the late 10th century when there may have been some links developing between the Northern Isles and north Hebrides. This is the period when Earl Sigurd II of Orkney was expanding his power to the Hebrides (Crawford 1987: 66 and forthcoming) at a time when Christianity was becoming accepted among the earls of Orkney, and Sigurd was forcibly converted to Christianity by Olaf Tryggvason in 995. Can we look to him and his sons as being responsible for the implementation of the *papar* names throughout the area under their control?

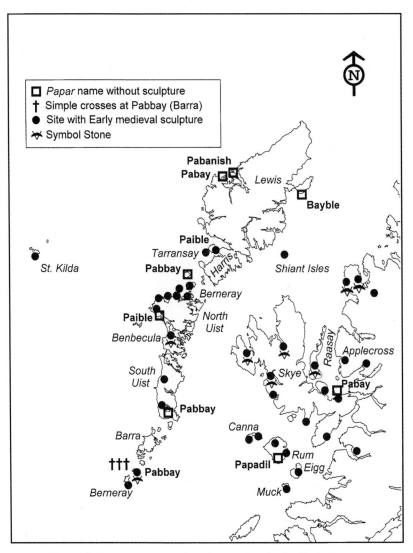

Figure 2. Papar *names and sculpture sites in the Hebrides*
(map by Kevin MacLeod).

These are some of the multi-disciplinary problems which face us in a project which is trying to throw light on a murky historical situation by means of slippery toponymic evidence.

7. Geographical situation

It is essential that we encompass geographical factors in our search for common denominators among all these places which have been given names incorporating the *papar* element, as well as the material evidence.

i) We have to look at the *papar* locations on the ground to see if they have common features of locality which are significant in any way, and what sort of agricultural potential they might have had.[17]

ii) We have to bring together surviving sculptural remains and archaeological evidence, including church sites, currently in use or abandoned or remembered only in tradition.

We need to illuminate the potential living circumstances of the monastic communities, or indeed of the single anchorite living in an isolated location on a headland or rock stack.[18]

This is to get some insight into the nature of all *papar* locations in the Northern and Western Isles, and of the monuments which can still be associated with these places. Only then might we be able to draw some conclusions about the nature of the *papar* places and increase our better understanding of why these places were chosen for settlement by the Celtic priests, and when they were abandoned to the Norse.

Acknowledgements

Without generous financial support this project would never have got off the ground, and we would like to acknowledge our gratitude for two awards from the Carnegie Trust for the Universities of Scotland.

[A recent study by Peder Gammeltoft (2004: 31-50) suggests that the most obvious explanation for the *papar* names is that the Norse incomers into the Northern and Western Isles lived long enough alongside the *papar*, actually encountering them, for these names to be given by them. BEC]

Literature

Anderson, A.O. (ed.), 1922: *Early Sources of Scottish History*, vol. 1. Edinburgh.

Benediktsson, J. (ed.), 1968: *Íslendingabók. Landnámabók*. Íslensk Fornrit 1. Reykjavík.

Crawford, B.E., 1987: *Scandinavian Scotland*. Leicester.

Crawford, B.E., 1996: 'Bishops of Orkney in the Eleventh and Twelfth Centuries: Bibliography and Biographical List', *The Innes Review* 47, 1-13.

Crawford, B.E. (ed.), 2002: *The* Papar *in the North Atlantic: Environment and History*, *Proceedings of a Day Conference*. St. John's House Papers No.10. St. Andrews.

Crawford, B.E., forthcoming: 'The Earls of Orkney and the Hebrides' In: C. Batey & M. Macleod (eds), *Gall-Gaedheil. The Western Isles in the Viking World*.

Dumville, D., 2002: 'The North Atlantic Monastic Thalassocracy: Sailing to the Desert in early medieval Insular Spirituality'. In: B.E. Crawford (ed.), *The* Papar *in the North Atlantic*. St Andrews, 121-132.

Ekrem, I. & Mortensen, L.B. (eds), 2003: *Historia Norvegiae*. Museum Tusculanum Press, Copenhagen.

Fisher, I., 2002: 'Crosses in the Ocean: Some *Papar* Sites and their Sculpture'. In: B. E. Crawford (ed.), *The* Papar *in the North Atlantic*. St Andrews, 39-58.

Gammeltoft, P., 2004: 'Among *Dímons* and *Papeys*: What Kind of Contact do the Names Really Point to?', *Northern Studies* 38, 31-49.

Goudie, G., 1904: *The Celtic and Scandinavian Antiquities of Shetland*. Edinburgh.

Jennings, A. 1994: *An Historical Study of the Gael and Norse in Western Scotland from c.795 to c.1000*. Unpublished Ph.D. thesis, University of Edinburgh. Edinburgh.

Jørgensen, K.R., 1992: *Series Episcoporum Ecclesiae Catholicae Occidentalis, series VI, Britanniae etc. ii Episcopatus Lundensis*. Stuttgart.

Lamb, R.G., 1973: 'Coastal settlements of the north', *Scottish Archaeological Forum* 5, 76-98.

Lamb, R.G., 1976: 'The Burri Stacks of Culswick, Shetland and other paired-stack settlements', *Proceedings of the Society of Antiquaries of Scotland* 107, 144-154.

MacDonald, A., 2002: 'The *Papar* and Some Problems. A Brief Review'. In: B.E. Crawford (ed.), *The* Papar *in the North Atlantic*. St Andrews, 13-30.

Olson, D., 1983: *Norse Settlement in the Hebrides. An Interdisciplinary Project*. Unpublished dissertation, University of Oslo. Oslo.

Pálsson, H., 1955: 'Minnisgreinar um Papa'. *Saga, Tímarit sögufélags* 5, 112-122.

Pálsson, H. & Edwards, P. (trans.), 1972: *The Book of Settlements. Landnamabók*. University of Manitoba Icelandic Studies 1. Winnipeg.

Phelpstead, C. (ed.), D. Kunin (trans.), 2001: *A History of Norway and the Passion and Miracles of the Blessed Óláfr*. The Viking Society for Northern Research. London.

Sawyer, P. (ed.), 1997: *The Oxford Illustrated History of the Vikings*. Oxford.

Stahl, A-B., 1999: *Place-Names of Barra in the Outer Hebrides.* Unpublished Ph.D. thesis, University of Edinburgh. Edinburgh

Thomson, W.P.L., 2001: *The New History of Orkney.* 2nd edition. Edinburgh.

Notes

[1] This desk-based survey was carried out by Dr Janet Hooper and Lorna Johnston.

[2] This collection of toponymic material was carried out by Kristjan Ahronson and Dr Anke-Beate Stahl.

[3] Recent exceptions to this are the doctoral studies of the place-names of Barra completed by Anke-Beate Stahl in 1999 and by Andrew Jennings (1994) on the chronological pattern of Norse habitative place-names throughout the Hebrides. Previous pioneering studies of Norse place-names in the Hebrides were carried out by Oftedal and more recently in an unpublished thesis by Olson, 1983.

[4] A successful application for further funding from the Carnegie Trust means that some archaeological assessment will be carried out at these two sites in the summer of 2004.

[5] As in Sawyer (ed.) 1997, where there is one chapter (4) on 'Ireland, Wales, Man and the Hebrides' and another (5) on 'The Atlantic Islands' which includes the Northern Isles!

[6] *Historia Norvegiae*, I. Ekrem and L.B. Mortensen (eds) (2003), where it is dated to the time of the erection of the archdiocese of Trondheim (1152-53) by Ekrem, and to the decades after that event by Mortensen (1160-75).

[7] The translation used here is from A.O. Anderson, *Early Sources of Scottish History*, vol.I, 330-332. There is also a new translation by Devra Kunin in an edition by C. Phelpstead published by the Viking Society for Northern Research (*A History of Norway and the Passion and Miracles of the Blessed Óláfr*, 2001). The translation by Christenson in the Ekrem and Mortenson edition (2003) has unfortunately translated the Latin 'Peti' as 'Pents'.

[8] A. MacDonald, 'The *papar* and some problems. A Brief Review'. In: B.E. Crawford (ed.), *The* Papar *in the North Atlantic. Environment and History*, St Andrews, 19. This was the considered view of Aidan MacDonald in his published paper although he did not take this definite line at the Conference itself. Much of my present discussion is focused on issues raised at that Conference and published in the Conference papers (which are available for purchase from The Committee for Dark-Age Studies, Dept. of Medieval History, University of St. Andrews, 71, South St., St. Andrews KY16 9SH. Price £14).

[9] Between 1103 and 1152-53 the diocese of Orkney would in theory have been subject to Lund which Bishop William might therefore have visited. Lund is a place which has been suggested as 'a strong Danish candidate' for the compilation of the Historia, being 'a leading centre of learning in the Nordic countries during this period' (Ekrem

and Mortensen 2003: 19). However there is absolutely no evidence for any connection between Orkney and Lund at this time and it is considered most unlikely that the dioceses of Orkney or Man were ever part of the Lund province (Crawford 1996: 3, quoting Jørgensen 1992).

[10] Phelpstead's comment.

[11] This raises the problem of why the author was so ignorant of the Orkney situation when he appears to be well-informed about the pre-Norse history of the Northern Isles. It could point to the author being in fact Icelandic and deriving his information about the Picts and Papar entirely from hearsay. Then one might ask: why did he not refer to the papar in his section on Iceland? All of which suggests that the author probably was Norwegian as suggested by Mortensen (2003).

[12] See MacDonald's list in the Appendix to his chapter in B.E. Crawford (ed.) (2002), 26-29.

[13] Questions posed in Scandinavian Scotland, 166.

[14] Aidan MacDonald initially extended this period of name-giving into the 11th century, but was persuaded by editorial intervention to restrict it to the 10th century!

[15] The Viking and Early Settlement Archaeological Research Project (VESARP) led by Professor Christopher Morris in the north isles of Shetland has made a very good start in examining the evidence on the ground, see annual reports produced by GUARD.

[16] Arne Kruse's paper to the Conference also touched on this aspect and referred to a possible boundary between the Pictish north Hebrides and the Gaelic south Hebrides: perhaps this boundary is reflected in the presence or absence of papar names, and relevant to my next point concerning the different ecclesiatical situations in the north and south Hebrides.

[17] This environmental element will be pursued by Professor Ian Simpson, during the second phase of the Carnegie Research Grant.

[18] Although this element is not the main focus of our ground work, see Raymond Lamb (1973, 1976) on some of the monastic promontory sites.

Extermination or Economic Exploitation?

Gillian Fellows-Jensen

1. Introduction

In a learned but provocative article in the journal *Northern Studies* entitled 'The Picts and the Martyrs or Did Vikings Kill the Native Population in Orkney and Shetland?', Brian Smith, who must know as much about the history of Shetland as anyone present at the Shetland conference and certainly much more than I do, has accused a number of earlier scholars, archaeologists and philologists alike and me included, of being too mealy-mouthed in refusing to expect the worst from the Viking settlers in the Northern Isles (Smith 2001). Ranging me in the *Peace School*, Smith quotes a remark that I made when I knew even less about Shetland than I do now, in a paper read 22 years ago at a conference to mark the Bicentenary of the National Museum of Antiquities of Scotland in 1981 (Fellows-Jensen 1984: 152). In that paper I did in fact offer two possible suggestions for the lack of survival of pre-Norse place-names in the Northern Isles, firstly reiterating the suggestion made by Ian Fraser with respect to Lewis that even if the native population continued to use their own names for places after the Viking aristocracy had replaced these with Scandinavian coinages, it would be the names used by the dominant class, the incoming Vikings, that would be most likely to survive (Fraser 1974: 18-19). I shall return to this comment later. Smith ignores it in his piece of propaganda and only mentions my alternative explanation for the lack of pre-Viking settlement names, i.e. 'that there was no communication between the Vikings and their predecessors'. Michael Barnes has thrown some doubt on this latter view, in part because the inscription on the Bressay stone has been thought to prove that there was linguistic communication, and Barnes argues that the pre-Norse names disappeared from Shetland because of the 'low regard by the incomers for the languages of the people they displaced', i.e. more or less the view expressed by Fraser and me (Barnes 1998: 9). The complications offered by the Bressay stone, unknown to me in 1981, had dawned upon me by 1994, when I suggested in a lecture that Pictish craftsmen must have survived into the period of Norse settlement in Shetland (Fellows-Jensen 1995). I assumed at that time with the archaeologists in the *Peace School* that the Norse adopted native artefacts and used the old grave enclosures and carried on farming in much the same way as their predecessors (Morris 1985: 216-221). I also accepted Kenneth Jackson's view that there must have been a very mixed language-situation in Shetland in the late 9th or early 10th century with Picts speaking a pre-Celtic non-Indo-European Language, a Gaelic-speaking minority and a Norse elite (Jackson 1955). The Bressay stone had been assigned to this late date partly on the basis of its obviously degenerate decoration with stylistic similarities to that of a more craftsmanlike Pictish stone found at Papil on Burra which had been dated by Robert Stevenson to the end of the 8th century (Stevenson 1955: 128; 1981: 285). More recently the Papil stone has been dated by Anna Ritchie to about 800 (1993: 28), while Michael Barnes has questioned whether the Bressay inscription really does show any traces of Norse influence (Barnes 1998: 8), and I am therefore reluctant to involve myself more deeply here in a discussion as to the age of this stone but shall return to it very briefly later. I do not intend to say more about the situation in Shetland here but shall instead discuss some other areas of Norse settlement where there has been no suggestion of an extermination of the pre-Viking inhabitants but where my own researches have shown that there is little remaining trace of the place-names these people must once have employed.

2. Case Study 1: The Isle of Man

I shall begin with the Isle of Man, on which I have been working on and off for the last quarter of a century and where the situation was in many ways similar to that in Shetland. The native inhabitants had originally spoken an insular Celtic language, namely Brythonic, of which no certain traces remain, while the settlement of the island by Goidelic incomers from Ireland had begun around 500 AD and the language in Man would seem to have been Goidelic when the Vikings settled there, although only three place-names of certain pre-Norse Celtic origin survive.

There is slightly more surviving written information about Man than about Shetland in the early period but the information can be difficult to exploit because it is often impossible to be absolutely certain whether the references in the foreign sources are to Man or to Anglesey, whose Welsh name is Môn. In Man itself there are a small number of pre-Norse inscriptions carved on stone (Wilson forthcoming a). The inscriptions are generally brief and often difficult to interpret but the fact that several different scripts are employed on them – the Latin alphabet, a few letters of the Greek alphabet, the Ogham script and the runic alphabet in its Anglo-Saxon form – reflects the strategically important situation of the island in the middle of the Irish Sea, while the content of the inscriptions, mainly of a memorial nature, shows that Christianity had been introduced to the island and that the people named were related by their script or language to other communities around the Irish Sea, while the comparatively large number of inscribed stones found at Maughold suggests that there must have been a literate Christian settlement at the site in the pre-Viking period, probably a monastery, a suggestion that is supported by the presence there of the foundations of three single-celled buildings, characteristic of the type of monastery familiar in the Irish Sea region in the early period. A few of the stones at Maughold bear designs of Pictish origin and Ross Trench-Jellicoe, who has studied the early crosses on the Isle of Man for many years, has recently argued that by the second half of the 9th century Maughold was probably working in concert with other centres, mostly in Scotland, with the aim of converting to Christianity the pagan incomers, that is the Vikings, partly with the aid of a range of shared iconography (Trench-Jellicoe 2002). The Bressay stone is perhaps also to be associated with this mission.

There is no doubt that the first Norse settlers in Man were still pagans on their arrival. For this there is abundant archaeological evidence in the form of pagan graves, stone sculpture including epigraphy and coin hoards that make it possible to erect a framework chronology for the Viking Age in Man (Wilson forthcoming b). No traces would seem to have been left of early raiding but as Wilson has pointed out, it is doubtful whether there can have been sufficient wealth on the island, even at the monastery of Maughold, to have attracted raiders, particularly since landing on the island, with its rocky coastline and the very changeable weather conditions, has always been a rather perilous undertaking. Nor is there any recognisable evidence for Viking settlement before – at the earliest – towards the end of the 9th century.

The earliest evidence for Viking settlement is provided by 24 Norse inhumation burials, which can be seen to be pagan because they are accompanied by grave-goods, in one case by a human sacrifice. There are no pagan burials later than the early 10th century and this fact, together with the survival of many carved stones with Christian iconography, both within Christian cemeteries and elsewhere, suggests that the Vikings in Man were soon converted to Christianity, possibly by the native inhabitants, possibly by the Pictish mission. David Wilson, presumably not wanting to be called mealy-mouthed, suggests that the native inhabitants must have been overwhelmed by initial force, 'otherwise the incomers would not have been able to sleep at night', and he assumes that a *modus vivendi* was achieved with the aid of brute force, threats or bribery, or all three. We know from the

Danelaw that some of the more nervous Danes who had acquired land in the Danelaw returned home to Denmark because, as they stated, they were afraid of being murdered by their labourers or otherwise inconvenienced (Fellows-Jensen 1995). The settlers in Man can perhaps be assumed to have been either braver or more cunning. At all events they allowed themselves to be converted to Christianity and adopted the native practice of erecting stone memorials over the graves. The style of ornament on these has made it possible to put them in a chronological sequence between about 925 and 1000. From the point of view of naming, the most significant feature about the memorial crosses is the inscriptions, some of which show that although the Norse formed a powerful elite in the island, they did not avoid contact with the native population and that intermarriage must have taken place between Celts and Vikings. The cross now known as Braddan 1, for example, is particularly interesting because it points to a probable example of intermarriage between a Gael and a Scandinavian. Its damaged inscription reveals that a man with a Scandinavian name whose first element is *Por-* had the cross raised over a man with a Scandinavian name *Ófeigr* who was the son of a man with the Celtic name *Crinan*, while the inscription on Braddan 4 commemorates a man called *Fiak* (Gælic *Fíacc*) who was the son of *Porleifr hnakki* and brother's son of *Hafr* (Wilson 1970). The long inscription in Norse runes on the slab bearing a Celtic cross on each broad face and now known as Michael 2, is interesting in the present context for two reasons. Firstly it tells us that the cross was raised by a man with a Celtic name and a Celtic father with a responsible position in society, namely 'Melbrigdi son of Athakán the smith'. Secondly it was carved by a man with the Norse name *Gautr*, who claims to have carved not only this stone but 'all in Man', perhaps suggesting that it must be one of the earliest Norse crosses to be erected there, and also revealing the Norse spelling of the pre-Norse name of the island *maun* (Wilson 1970: 2-4; Page 1983: 136). The very existence of such stones and inscriptions is a reflection of a fruitful combination of two traditions, the Anglo-Celtic one of raising crosses over the dead and the Norse one of raising runic memorial stones to them. The inscriptions also show that men and women of Manx origin and sympathies could achieve a reasonably high standing in the island and were not simply a semi-servile labour force.

Basil Megaw drew attention many years ago to the significant fact that several of the kings of the Norse dynasty on Man had Gaelic by-names such as Crovan (**crobh-bhán* 'white handed'), while none had Scandinavian by-names, although their forenames were always Scandinavian (Megaw 1978:

276). Since the Norse were willing to adopt Celtic personal names and by-names, there is no reason why they should not also have adopted place-names of Celtic origin, but this was very rarely done. As already mentioned, only three certainly pre-Norse place-names are generally accepted to have survived. The one is the name of the island itself, Man. The other two are the sheading- and parish-name Rushen, and the treen-name Douglas, while George Broderick has been able to point to a few extra names whose semantic content or structure suggests that they are likely to have arisen in the pre-Norse period (*PNIM* 1: xxiii).

It is significant that almost all of the more impressive natural features in the island bear Scandinavian names, since the pre-Norse names of mountains and rivers, for example, might have been expected to survive anything other than a massive Norse immigration. The names borne by natural features in Man are of the same types as the names of natural features in the homelands of the Viking settlers. A few of these are simplex names, for example *gnípa* 'steep rock, overhanging rock'. The first record of this name in Man is as the specific of a Manx Gaelic formation *Ballacgniba* in a 14th-century transcript of a charter from 1228 in which the Norse king of Man, Olaf II, grants an estate of this name to Whithorn priory in Galloway. The generic of the name is the Manx word *bollagh* 'gap, track between curragh and mountain land', which also lies behind the quarterland-name Bollagh in the neighbourhood of the prominent hill known as Greeba that probably marks the site of *Ballacgniba* (*PNIM* 1: 210). The simplex hill-name, however, must have been coined by the Norse settlers long before it was employed by Manx speakers to form the specific of the quarterland name. The element *gnípa* occurs as a mountain-name at several places in Norway, for example in the forms Nipa, Nipen and Knipen (Sandnes & Stemshaug 1976: 186, 233). An identical name occurs in England as Gnipe (Howe) in Yorkshire and (High and Low) Knipe in Westmorland, and also, perhaps surprisingly, in Denmark in the forms Gniben and Nibe, the first of which refers to a long, horizontal, horn-shaped projection, while the second denotes a settlement situated on the shore of Nibe Bredning beneath a, for Denmark, rather prominent ridge (Jørgensen 1994: 97, 206).

Most of the Scandinavian mountain-names in Man, however, are compound names in *fjall* and several of these are still very obviously Scandinavian at the present day, for example the name of the island's highest mountain, Snaefell, which causes the thoughts to fly across the Atlantic to Snæfell in Iceland. The form Snaefell, however, is a comparatively modern antiquarianising one, with its first record dating from 1733 (*PNIM* 3: 464).

The Manx form of the name, *Sniaul*, represents the normal Manx Gaelic development of Scandinavian **snæ-fjall* 'snow mountain', while the earliest recorded forms such as *Snawble* 1586 and *Snafeld* 1595 suggest that 16th-century English scribes associated the name with the English words *snāw* 'snow' and *feld* 'open land'.

Other compound names in *fjall* in Man are Lambefell/ Lambfell 'lamb mountain' in German (*PNIM* 1: 267) and Sartfell < **svart-fjall* 'black mountain' in Michael (*PNIM* 2: 95). Once again it should be noted that English scribes have been responsible for the easily recognisable Norse forms. Without their influence it would probably have been the gaelicised forms that survived, namely Lammell and Sartell. There are also two prominent mountains whose names do not appear on the surface to be of Norse origin, namely North and South Barrule. South Barrule, however, is recorded as *Worzefel'* in the description of the Abbeyland bounds from c. 1280 with the character *z* standing for the Norse voiced consonant *ð*, and as *Warthfel* in a late addition to the Manx Chronicle s.a. 1316. These spellings represent **varðar-fjall*, 'lookout mountain', or perhaps **vörðu-fjall*, 'cairn mountain' (*PNIM* 1: 53). South Barrule is mentioned in many other documents through the centuries, probably because of its function as a lookout place, but in all the late sources it appears with spellings reflecting the pronunciation Barrule. North Barrule, which is not recorded in writing until 1789, probably because it was not one of the official lookout places, only has records reflecting the modern form of the name (*PNIM* 3: 306-307). If it were not for the two early recorded forms of the name of South Barrule, it might not have been realised that the name shared by the two mountains is of Norse origin, for in all the other records the name appears in a form in which initial bilabial *v* has been radicalised to *b*, the intervocalic *th* has been lost and the element *fjall* has developed to - *ūl*, as a result of Manx voicing of /f/ to /v/ and the subsequent falling together with the Manx adjectival ending *amhail* '-like', which has attracted the main stress.

As Margaret Gelling has pointed out, it is a commonplace of toponymic studies that river-names have the highest survival rate and are least likely to be replaced by new names in the language of an invading race (Gelling 1991: 443-444). She therefore found it curious that Douglas is the only ancient river-name to have survived in Man and that the longest river on the island has no proper name at all, being generally referred to as the Sulby river and that the Silver Burn near Castletown has an English name which is first recorded in 1666. Several rivers did receive Norse names. Two of these go back to Norse **kvern-á*, namely *Corna* in Malew, now known as Santan

Burn, and the present Cornaa in Maughold, while two river-names recorded in 13th-century sources, *Ramsa* and *Laxa*, are now both spelt and pronounced with the ending *-ey*, perhaps reflecting the English river-name ending *ey* < *ēa*, as in the English name Mersey.

Most of the Norse names of natural features that have survived have been recorded in writing because they were transferred to neighbouring settlements. The settlement names which originated as Norse topographical names have a fairly general distribution over the island, only avoiding the high ground, the marshy area in Lezayre and the hinterland of Peel. Studies of settlement names in England, for example, have suggested that the first names bestowed on settlements by new waves of settlers were very often such transferred names. The Norse in Man would have begun by coining a name such as Bradda (**bratt-höfuð* 'steep headland') for the headland and subsequently transferred it to the neighbouring treen and quarterland, and a name such as Foxdale (**fors-dalr* 'waterfall valley') for the beautiful valley with a waterfall and then transferred it to the village and the lead-mines.

In England it was apparently only during expansions of settlement some time after the original arrivals of settlers that more stereotype settlement names containing habitative generics such as *hām* and *tūn* in the Anglo-Saxon period and *bý* and *þorp* in the Viking period came into use. Similarly in Man, the Norse coined about a dozen names in *staðir* for dependent secondary settlements of low status and often in inferior situations. None of these secondary settlements in Man developed into villages. They may well have been similar to the *staðir*-farms in Iceland which would certainly seem to have been of low status and looked upon merely as a source of income and power for their owners, who actually lived on primary farms with topographical names. The etymologies of the *staðir*-names in Man are often rather doubtful but in most cases the most likely specific is a personal name, for example *Hæringr* in *Herynstaze* c. 1280 (*PNIM* 6: 153). There is only one very doubtful instance of a name in *bólstaðr* in Man, namely Bravost (*PNIM* 3: 313), while this element denoting a secondary settlement is very common in place-names in the Northern and Western Isles and Caithness (Gammeltoft 2001: 96-162).

The Scandinavian habitative name-type that is borne most frequently by secondary settlements in Man is one that would seem to be typical of Denmark and the Danelaw rather than Norway, namely, the place-names in *bý* (Fellows-Jensen 2001). There are a total of 26 names in *bý* in Man. Eleanor Megaw pointed out to me on my first visit to the island, shortly before she died, that no fewer than 15 of these names have exact parallels in either north-west England or North Yorkshire. The 15 names are two Colbys, two Crosbys, Dalby, Jurby, Kirby, two Rabys, Regaby, Scholaby, Soulby, Surby and two Sulbys. There are several possible explanations for the presence of these names in Man and for the forms they take, all involving some form of influence from the Danelaw. Firstly, there would seem to have been an anticlockwise movement of Danish settlers in the Danelaw or their immediate descendants in the late 9th or early 10th century out westwards across the Pennines, particularly along the Eden valley. From Carlisle, some of these settlers moved northwards into Dumfriesshire and others southwards into the coastal plain of Cumberland, from where it seems likely that some made their way across the Irish Sea to Man. This anti-clockwise movement outwards from the Danelaw can be traced not only in a trail of settlement names in *bý* but also by the presence of pagan Viking burials along the routes followed, confirming that the movement must have begun before the settlers in England had been converted to Christianity. The reoccupation of northern Cumbria by the Strathclyde Britons at some date before 927 and the fact that English rule had been restored over Cheshire and southern Lancashire by 934 imply that most of the Scandinavian place-names in these areas must have been coined before these dates at least and the same must apply to the names in Man, if, as I have suggested elsewhere, the *bý*-names in Lancashire and Cheshire were in fact coined by settlers from Man (Fellows-Jensen 2001: 38). Secondly, the large silver hoard found in 1894 at Ballaquayle (Douglas) would seem originally to have contained a preponderance of coins from mints in north-west England and to have been deposited about 975 (Dolley 1969: 123), so we should perhaps reckon with a continuing influx of settlers from northern England into Man throughout the 10th century. Thirdly, the names in *bý* may be linked, as suggested by Marstrander (1932: 327), with Godred Crovan's partition of the island in 1079 after his victory at the battle of Sky Hill in which his own followers who wanted to stay on the island and who may have been recruited in England were granted large farms in the fertile south of the island, while the native Manxmen were allowed to retain the swampy northern part of Man. I have earlier been reluctant to accept this third suggestion, mainly because I found it unlikely that prosperous Norse estates that may have been in Scandinavian hands since about 900 would have been subjected to a change of name simply because they passed into the hands of new lords from the Danelaw in 1079. I have recently, however, become convinced that place-names in *bý* tended to be bestowed not, as earlier thought, on new settlements established on vacant land but on pre-existing settlements to mark some change in their administrative status, a subject to which I shall return later. Fourthly and lastly, there was a documented immigration to Man from England in the early 15th century, after the island had been granted by the English king, Henry IV, to Sir John Stanley in 1405, and English administrators probably came to Man even earlier than this. Michael Dolley has pointed out that over 500 surnames of an essentially non-Gaelic nature are recorded in Manx sources and that most of these are in fact English place-names functioning as surnames (Dolley 1983). To judge from these surnames, about two-thirds of the immigrants in the period down to 1540 came from Lancashire. This is natural enough, since this is where most of the Stanley estates were situated and the Stanleys would presumably have looked first to their tenantry when making appointments to the insular administration.

The situation in the Isle of Man is thus that a population of Celtic-speaking Christians was overrun in the period from about 900 to about 1080 by Scandinavian incomers who assumed positions of authority and changed many of the major place-names on the island, although they would not seem to have killed or enslaved the native population or to have refused to acknowledge their personal names. Since there is no systematic coverage of the place-names of Man earlier than the setting books or rent rolls in which the entries are grouped according to treens, parishes and sheadings and which date from 1506 for the administrative South side of the island and from 1515 for the North one, there is no way of knowing how many of the Manx names recorded in these books were coined or revivified in the Norse period or how many of the Norse names were given Manx alternative forms while the island was still under Norse dominion. There have been differing views as to the degree of survival of the Manx language in this period. When Basil Megaw demonstrated that the Abbeyland bounds, which had long been believed to date from the 14th century, must have been noted down at the end of the Manx Chronicle by one of the Rushen monks no later than about 1280, it became clear that many more Manx Gaelic names must have existed in the 13th century than had previously been thought and the reason for the small proportion of Gaelic names recorded in the 12th- and 13th-century charters is probably related to the fact that all the places they refer to lay in the South side of the island, many of them in the neighbourhood of the royal stronghold (Megaw 1978: 271-273). What does seem certain, however, is that the Scandinavians, some of whom would seem to have been Danish or Danelaw Danes, had been able to impose names of their own choice both on the majority of the natural features in the island and on most of the treens or major settlements, names that mostly survived in recognisable Nordic forms until they were recorded in writing by English administrators, whereas the names of quarterlands and intacks had been subjected to gaelicisation to a greater or lesser degree before they were recorded in writing at the beginning of the 18th century or later. Everything points to a survival of the Manx language throughout the period of Norse domination but even so there was an almost total loss of pre-Norse place-names. The not immediately recognisable Norse names are probably the best reflection we now have in Man of place-name survival in oral tradition. There is nothing to suggest that the place-names of Manx origin, with the exception of the handful of pre-Norse names mentioned earlier, can have survived from before the arrival of the Norse settlers. It was apparently much easier to exterminate the Celtic onomasticon than the Manx-speaking population. The explanation for this must be the role played by the administration, since there has never been a tradition for the use of Manx Gaelic for administrative purposes and the records would seem to have been kept by English scribes from soon after the end of Norse rule.

3. Case Study 2: La Hague in Normandy

There are different kinds of problem connected with the assessment of the situation in the district of La Hague, which takes its name from the promontory of the same name (Scandinavian *haki* 'chin, promontory', Ridel 2002: 35) which forms the north-western extremity of the Cotentin peninsula in Normandy. It is now delimited by two rivers with French names, La Diélette and La Divette and it was bounded in the Bronze Age by an earthen rampart long known as Hague-Dike and thought by the locals to have been built by the Vikings or at least re-exploited by them. The dike has, however, been shown by excavations in the 1950s to date from between 900 and 800 BC, with subsequent excavations in the 1980s revealing that the re-exploitation had not taken place until the twelfth or thirteenth centuries AD (Ridel 2002). The great mystery here, however, is the complete absence of archaeological evidence for a Viking presence, although place-names of Scandinavian origin or containing Scandinavian personal names lie thick on the ground. My attention was drawn to this area by an article on the possible occurrence here of a Scandinavian assembly site by the name of *Thingland* (Renaud & Ridel 2002). It is not surprising that little attention had been paid to this site earlier. It is apparently not indicated on any map and the name is not recorded in any early sources. The recorded forms were first noted by Françoise Girard in 1972 but she did not explain them (Girard 1972: 362). They are all found in early 20th-century real estate registers of the *commune* of *Jobourg*, whose own name would seem to be a reflex of Old English *eorðburh*, referring to an earthen rampart of some kind (de Beaurepaire 1986: 142-143), and which probably dates from the period when the Viking settlers arriving in Normandy were accompanied by men from the British Isles. The four recorded forms, *Le Tungland*, *Le Tengland*, *Le Tangland* and *Le Tanbland* can all be explained as reflexes of **Thingland* and the variation in the forms, all borne by small plots of land that must once have made up one larger holding, points to a name of some antiquity that had in the course of time become incomprehensible to the Norman officials. A modern name would hardly have been distorted in so many ways. The variant forms of the name can best be explained as the result of oral transmission.

The closest parallel to the situation in La Hague that is found in England seemed to me to be that at the northern end of the Wirral peninsula in Cheshire. This district, which is of similar extent to La Hague but squarish rather than triangular in shape, had certainly not been left vacant by early settlers (Fellows-Jensen 1985: 366-373 and map 22). It was already quite densely settled in Roman times and the Romans thought it worth their while to construct a branch road from Chester to the interior of the peninsula. There are also a number of place-names which reflect the presence of British settlers and many place-names of Old English origin. There are several names of Scandinavian origin, including Raby in the south (*rá-bý* 'boundary settlement') which marks the southern limit of Scandinavian settlement here. Of particular interest is the occurrence of the name Thingwall. This name is recorded in Domesday Book of c. 1086 and it is thus the earliest of all the Thingwalls in Scandinavia or the British Isles to be recorded in writing, although I am inclined to think that it is Tynwald in the Isle of Man, which is still the site of an annual ceremony of the reading of the laws, that is the model for the name in Cheshire (Fellows-Jensen 1993 & 1996).

A detailed study of the possible occurrence of the name **Thingland*, in the parish of Bowness in Cumberland, where it is now known as Fingland (Fellows-Jensen 2003), has brought me to the reluctant conclusion that I am unable to decide whether or not Fingland in Bowness is a name of Nordic origin, but it is at least not without significance that the Clerk of the Assize Roll in 1279 was willing to accept the presence of a surname *Thingland* in the district (Armstrong *et al.* 1950: 150).

The great puzzle about the district of La Hague, however, is not so much the question of whether or not there was a Viking assembly place here. It seems in fact most likely that they would have had one. What puzzles me most is how a mixed band of Viking settlers, including men who had come from the Viking colonies in England and the Celtic-speaking areas, were able to impose an almost blanket coverage of names reflecting the Scandinavian presence on an area that must have been French-speaking when they arrived and probably remained French-speaking throughout the period of Scandinavian domination. This is assuming, of course, that Frenchmen then refused to understand any language other than French, making it imperative for the first generation Scandinavian settlers to become French-speaking. It is not perhaps particularly strange that there should be so many Nordic place-names of maritime origin in the district of La Hague (Lepelley 2002). These names are those of skerries, stacks, underwater rocks, small islands, currents, headlands and bays and would have been of particular significance to the Vikings on their voyages.

It is stranger to find so many Nordic names for smallish inland settlements, for example a simplex *Le Tourp* in Omonville-la-Rogue, now Ferme du Tourps (Renaud 1989: 177), which presumably originated as the Nordic appellative *thorp*, which originally denoted a dependent, secondary settlement but which seems to have acquired the significance 'isolated farm' in Normandy.

Most characteristic of the district of La Hague, however, are the names in French *ville* (Latin *villa*), a generic which was popular in Normandy from the 8th century to the 12th. When, as in this district, the specific of these names is a personal name of Nordic origin, these are probably the forenames of the Vikings who took over the settlements or at least the rights and dues owing from them to their lords, or of their immediate descendants. There are purely Nordic forenames in such compounds, for example *Skúli* in Éculleville, *Ásmundr* (or an anglicised form *Osmund*) in Omonville-la-Rogue and Omonville-la-Petite, *Hnaki* in Naqueville, the by-name *Skjaldari* 'shieldmaker' in Équeurdeville (de Beaurepaire 1986: 113-114, 116, 171-172), while the specific of *Herqueville*, hitherto assumed to be an unrecorded Anglo-Scandinavian personal name, may well be a Nordic by-name *Herki*, *Herka* or *Herkia* 'lazy, listless person', 'weakling', which occurs in Domesday Book for Buckinghamshire and Hampshire (Feilitzen 1937: 289-290; de Beaurepaire 1986: 138). There are also some names in *ville* whose anthroponymic specifics would seem to be personal names introduced from the British Isles, namely *Auderville*, which seems likely to contain the Old English name *Aldhere* (de Beaurepaire 1986: 70-71), and *Digulleville*, containing the Celtic personal name *Dicuil* (Musset 1978: 112), as well as Flottemanville-Hague whose specific may be an English by-name 'pirate' (de Beaurepaire 1986: 119) or else the common noun that lies behind this and

111

which would seem to form the specific of the Yorkshire place-name Flotmanby (Fellows Jensen 1972: 28). I am inclined to assign the formation of all these names in *ville* to the Viking period. The most striking feature about the place names in the district of La Hague, however, is the almost complete absence of Gallo-Romance names (de Beaurepaire 1986: 38 carte 7). The site of a Roman camp is indicated on sheet 16 of the French Ordnance Survey map from 1910 at the southern end of the Baie d'Écalgrain, however, and it is unlikely that the rest of the district was left vacant until the arrival of the Vikings. It must therefore be assumed that the Vikings, in company with settlers from the Viking colonies in England and Gaelic-speaking areas, took over the earlier settlements and gave these new names of Nordic or partially Nordic origin.

Why so few of the earlier names survived the invasions is difficult to understand. Noting the absence of Gallo-Romance place-names in *(i)acum* from areas where Anglo-Scandinavian place-names are of frequent occurrence, François de Beaurepaire has offered two explanations: 1) that the Vikings eliminated all the pre-existing place-names or 2) that the Vikings preferred to settle in areas that had previously been depopulated (de Beaurepaire 1986: cartes 7, 9 and 11). There is some documentary support for both these explanations in the records. That the Vikings were indeed responsible for a toponymic upheaval in Normandy has been pointed out by Lucien Musset, who notes that the monks of the abbey of Saint-Florent near Saumur bemoaned in about 1055 the fact that the estates they had owned in the Cotentin had been deprived of their names as a result of Viking occupation of the area (Musset 1955: 52). One of the settlements with pre-Viking names that was lost in the district of La Hague is mentioned specifically in the chartulary of Saint-Florent as *Moucel* or *Muncel* and has been identified by Musset as the present Flottemanville-Hague (Adigard des Gautries 1951: 32). As mentioned above, this latter place-name is one that is likely to have been coined in the period of Viking settlement. Changes of name would naturally have made the administration of property extremely difficult for absentee landowners such as religious establishments and it is not impossible that the desire to make it difficult for former owners to lay legal claim to their property was one of the motives that led the Vikings both to substitute Scandinavian names for the existing names of some settlements and to destroy the records of the monasteries they attacked. That more destruction would seem to have been caused by the Vikings in Normandy than in the Danelaw is also indicated both by records such as an edict of Charles the Bald, which states that all those who were fleeing from the persecution of the Northmen should not be oppressed by any taxes, perhaps because it was considered that they were unlikely to have any possessions worth taxing (Wallace-Hadrill 1978: 17), and by the frequency of occurrence in Normandy of Scandinavian place-names in *toft*. This element originally had a meaning such as 'building plot' but would seem to have been employed in Normandy with the meaning 'site of deserted settlement', reflecting the destruction and desertion of settlements under the Viking invasions and subsequent occupation of the deserted sites by Viking settlers (Dauzat 1926: 147). The places with names in *toft* in La Hague include *Merquetot* in Jobourg,whose specific is perhaps Danish *mark* 'boundary' (Holmberg 1946: 261, 280), a farm near Digulleville called *Rantot* (Renaud 1989: 176), whose specific is possibly Danish *rand* 'border, ridge', Jalletot, whose specific is more likely to be a by-name *Jarl* than the Norse title, and Pénitot, whose specific is probably an English personal name *Penning*. It would seem that the situation was so chaotic in La Hague in the period of Viking settlement that it was impossible for the abbeys and the other former property owners to lay claim to their lands. The absentee landlords were not exterminated but they would seem to have been deprived of their lands and their rights, while the peasants who had worked on these lands fled before the Vikings, leaving Charles the Bald to worry about who was going to sow and harvest the crops.

4. Case Study 3: The Danelaw

When I first began to work on the Danish place-names in the Danelaw, it was generally thought that the distribution of place-names in *bý* in England marked areas of Danish colonisation of vacant land, but it has always been acknowledged that some of the settlements with names in *bý* there must have been established before the arrival of the Danes. Derby, for example, was already a thriving borough when it was first occupied by the Danes in the 9th century. It is to the Chronicle compiled by the Englishman Æthelweard in about 1000 that we owe a comment to the effect that the Danes came in 871 to the place which is called *Northuuorthige* but which is known in Danish as *Deoraby* and the identification of the English name of the place is confirmed by a reference to it as the burial place of St Ealhmund in a 9th-century list of saints' burial-places (Fellows Jensen 1978: 43-44). This Derby, as well as a lost Darby in Lincolnshire and West Derby in Lancashire, would all seem to have been given their Danish names because of the presence of a deer-park in their immediate vicinity. Similarly, the 47 settlements known as Kirby or Kirkby would all seem to have begun life as English settlements and to have been given this appellatival name by the Danes because they already possessed a church at the time when the Vikings arrived on the scene. These stone structures would have been bound to impress the Danes, who were not used to seeing such buildings in the landscape. They must have decided to refer to the settlements by the name *kirkju-bý* because they were 'settlements with a church'. We do not have concrete confirmation that there were pre-Conquest churches at all the settlements known as Kirby or Kirkby but some of them do actually contain fabric that can be dated to the pre-Norman period, e.g. Kirby Cane in Norfolk, Kirby Underdale in the East Riding of Yorkshire and Kirby Hill in the North Riding (Taylor & Taylor 1965: 354-357). Nor was it all the settlements with existing churches that were actually referred to as *kirkju-bý*. Pre-Norman fabric has also been recorded in the churches at settlements with other names in *bý*, for example Barnetby le Wold, Coleby, Lusby, Thurlby and Worlaby in Lincolnshire, Hornby and Whitby in the North Riding of Yorkshire (Taylor & Taylor 1965: 48, 165, 402, 615, 688, 319, 654), and in Derby (Taylor 1978: 1072). It is probably not without significance that the specifics of Barnetby and Worlaby are personal names of Old English origin, *Beornnōth* and *Wulfrīc* respectively.

In Yorkshire, there is stone sculpture which can be dated to the 10th century in several of the settlements with names in *bý*, not only in eight of the settlements with Kir(k)by names, Kirby Grindalythe, Kirby Hill, Kirby Knowle, Kirby Misperton, Kirby Sigston, Kirby Wiske, Kirkby in Cleveland and Kirkby Moorside (Bailey 1980: 45; Lang 1991: 150-158; Lang 2001: 129-139) but also in *bý*s whose names contain other specifics, for example Amotherby, Hawnby (Lang 1991: 124-125, 225-226) and Baldersby, Birkby, Danby Wiske, Easby, Haxby, Ingelby Arncliffe. Melsonby, Ormesby and Whitby (Lang 2001: 57-58, 63, 98-102, 124-127, 175-178, 188-189, 231-266). Even earlier sculpture is recorded at Whitby, where there are some plain crosses which might be of late 7th-century date, and Easby, where the scroll work reflects Carolingian influence (Bailey 1996: 51-55), while at Hunmanby, the fragments of a cross-head and cross-shaft that are now built into the north wall of the nave outside, have been dated to the 8th or the early 9th centuries (Lang 1991: 148-149).

All in all, there is little to suggest that the *bý*s as a class are new settlements established by the Danes on vacant land, even though their names are undoubtedly new. I am tempted to think that these names may have been given to them to mark a change in their status, perhaps to indicate that they were now to be taxed independently and not as a dependent unit of some large estate. I should like to compare them with the settlements with names in *bý* in Denmark that have been recently discussed by my colleague Bent Jørgensen. He has suggested that the giving of new names to old settlements in Denmark marked the development of a new category of denotata, namely 'settlements with associated rights over territory and preserves' (Jørgensen personal communication), a definition that would apply in broad outline to the Danelaw *býs*. Jørgensen also notes that the specifics of the names tend to be words for very simple and basic conditions, normally of a cultural, topographical, zoological or botanical nature (e.g. *dal* 'valley', *sal* 'hall', *ved* 'timber', *skov* 'forest', etc.), as in Dalby near Roskilde.

One thing would seem to be certain, however, and this is that the previous tenants of these settlements with new names in *bý* had not been exterminated by the Danes. Life as a new Danish tenant was probably not a dance on roses but only the least courageous of the tenants probably regularly feared being murdered by their labourers and the labourers in their turn would not have found a significant difference between paying their dues and services to these new Danish tenants rather than to the pre-existing great estates. The explanation for the lack of records of so many of the pre-Norse place-names in the Danelaw is probably to be sought in the destruction of monastic archives in the initial raids and the assumption of a fiscal significance by the place-name element *bý* as an indication of independent taxable status.

5. Conclusion

The complete absence of pre-Norse place-names from Shetland, their rarity of occurrence in Man and La Hague and the lack of information about the pre-Viking names of settlements with names in *bý* in the Danelaw all reflect an absence of written documentation for these names, possibly in the Northern Isles and Man because no such records had been kept, but in La Hague and the Danelaw certainly because of the pillage and destruction wrought by the invading Vikings. The survival of Scandinavian names in Man after the end of the period of Norse rule would seem to reflect the influence of English scribes, who found it easier to deal with Norse names than with Manx Gaelic ones, and the fact that the Manx language, although it survived in use until the early 20th century, would never seem to have been used for administrative purposes. The survival of Scandinavian names in La Hague and the Danelaw, in spite of the fact that French and English regained their status as the written and spoken languages of Normandy and the Danelaw respectively, would suggest that a form of Scandinavian administration must have survived long enough in both areas for the

Scandinavian place-names to have gained a firm foothold and for most of their French and English predecessors to have fallen into oblivion. The fact that the English names of more considerable settlements tended to survive in the Danelaw, while hardly any French names of this type are to be found in La Hague, supports the view that there was more destruction that can be attributed to the Vikings in Normandy than in the Danelaw. It is also possible that the Viking raids on the Northern Isles were even more destructive than those on Normandy. The complete absence of pre-Norse place-names from Orkney and Shetland is not necessarily, however, exclusively a result of destruction by the Vikings. It may in part reflect a swifter adaptation to economic exploitation and literate administration by the Scandinavians than by the Pictish or Celtic natives, perhaps because Christian institutions in the Northern Isles were less securely anchored and less powerful than those in England and France.

Literature

Adigard des Gautries, J., 1951: 'Les noms de lieux de la Manche attestés entre 911 et 1066', *Annales de Normandie* 1, 9-44.

Armstrong, A.M., Mawer, A., Stenton, F.M. & Dickins, B., 1950: *The Place-Names of Cumberland*, 1-3. English Place-Name Society 20-22. Cambridge.

Bailey, R.N., 1980: *Viking Age Sculpture in Northern England*. London.

Bailey, R.N., 1996: *England's Earliest Sculptors*. Publications of the Dictionary of Old English 5. Toronto.

Barnes, M., 1998: *The Norn Language of Orkney and Shetland*. Lerwick.

de Beaurepaire, F., 1986: *Les Noms de Communes et Ancienne Paroisses de La Manche*. Paris.

Dauzat, A., 1926: *Les Noms de Lieux*. Paris.

Dolley, M., 1969: 'New Light on the 1894 Douglas Hoard', *The Journal of the Manx Museum* 7, 121-124.

Dolley, M., 1983: 'Toponymic Surnames and the Pattern of Pre-1830 English Immigration into the Isle of Man', *Nomina* 7, 47-64.

Fellows Jensen, G., 1978: *Scandinavian Settlement Names in the East Midlands*. Navnestudier 16. Copenhagen.

Fellows-Jensen, G., 1983: 'Scandinavian Settlement in the Isle of Man and Northwest England: the Place-Name Evidence'. In: C. Fell *et al.* (eds), *The Viking Age in the Isle of Man*. London, 37-52.

Fellows-Jensen, G., 1984: 'Viking Settlement in the Northern and Western Isles – The Place-Name Evidence as seen from Denmark and the Danelaw'. In: A. Fenton & H. Pálsson (eds), *The Northern and Western Isles in the Viking World: Survival, Continuity and Change*. Edinburgh, 148-168.

Fellows-Jensen, G., 1985: *Scandinavian Settlement in the North-West*. Navnestudier 25. Copenhagen.

Fellows-Jensen, G., 1993: 'Tingwall, Dingwall and Thingwall'. In: *Twenty-Eight Papers presented to Hans Bekker-Nielsen on the occasion of his Sixtieth Birthday 28 April 1993*. Odense, 53-67.

Fellows-Jensen, G., 1995: *The Vikings and Their Victims: The Verdict of the Names*. The Dorothea Coke Memorial Lecture in Northern Studies delivered at University College London 21 February 1994. London. 2nd edition. 1998.

Fellows-Jensen, G., 1996: 'Tingwall: The Significance of the Name'. In: D.J. Waugh (ed.), *Shetland's Northern Links. Language & History*. Edinburgh, 16-29.

Fellows-Jensen, G., 2001: 'The Mystery of the *bý*-names in Man', *Nomina* 34, 33-46.

Fellows-Jensen, G., 2003: 'Thingland and Fingland: The Danish Tongue in Contact with French, English and Gaelic'. In: H. Galberg Jacobsen *et al.* (eds), *Take Danish – for Instance. Linguistic Studies in Honour of Hans Basbøll*. Odense, 75-82.

Fraser, I.A., 1974: 'The Place-Names of Lewis – The Norse Evidence', *Northern Studies* 4, 11-21.

Gammeltoft, P., 2001: *The Place-Name Element* bólstaðr *in the North Atlantic Area*. Navnestudier 38. Copenhagen.

Gelling, M., 1991: 'The Place-Names of the Isle of Man'. In: P.S. Ureland & G. Broderick (eds), *Language Contact in the British Isles*. Tübingen, 141-155.

Girard, F., 1972: *Les noms de lieux de canton Beaumont-Hague (Manche)*. Saint-Lô.

Jackson, K., 1955: 'The Pictish Language'. In: F.T. Wainwright (ed.), *The Problem of the Picts*. Edinburgh, 129-166.

Jørgensen, B., 1994: *Stednavneordbog*. 2. udg. Copenhagen.

Lang, J., 1991: *York and Eastern Yorkshire*. Corpus of Anglo-Saxon Stone Sculpure 3. Oxford.

Lang, J., 2001: *Northern Yorkshire*. Corpus of Anglo-Saxon Stone Sculpture 6. Oxford.

Lepelley, R., 2002: 'L'héritage maritime viking dans les noms de lieux des côtes du Nord-Cotentin'. In: É. Ridel (ed.), *L'héritage maritime des Vikings en Europe de l'Ouest*. Caen, 483-500.

Marstrander, C.J.S., 1932: 'Det norske landnåm på Man', *Norsk Tidsskrift for Sprogvidenskap* 6, 40-386.

Megaw, B., 1978: 'Norseman and Native in the Kingdom of the Isles. A Reassessment of the Manx Evidence'. In: P. Davey (ed.), *Man and Environment in the Isle of Man*. British Archaeological Reports British Series 54ii, 265-314.

Morris, C.D., 1985: 'Viking Orkney: A Survey'. In: C. Renfrew (ed.), *The Prehistory of Orkney*. Edinburgh, 210-242.

Musset, L., 1955: 'Les destins de la propriété monastiques durant les invasions normandes (IXe-XIe s.). L'example de Jumièges'. In: *Jumièges: congrès scientifique du xii centenaire*. Rouen, 49-55.

117

Musset, L., 1979: 'Participation de Vikings venus des Pays Celtes à la Colonisation Scandinave de la Normandie'. In: *Cahiers du Centre de la Recherche sur les Peuples du Nord et du Nord-Ouest*. Caen, 107-117.

Page, R.I., 1983: 'The Manx Rune-Stones'. In: C. Fell *et al*. (eds), *The Viking Age in the Isle of Man*. London, 133-146.

PNIM = Broderick, G., *Placenames of the Isle of Man* 1-6. Tübingen, 1994-2002.

Renaud, J. & Ridel, É., 2001: '*Le Tingland*: l'emplacement d'un *þing* en Normandie', *Nouvelle Revue d'Onomastique* 35-36, 303-306.

Ridel, É., 2002: 'La Hague, terre des Vikings'. In: B. Bioul *et al*. (eds), *Les Vikings en France, une synthèse inédite*. Dossiers d'Archeologie no 277. Dijon, 34-43.

Ritchie, A., 1993: *Viking Scotland*. London.

Sandnes, J. & Stemshaug, O., 1976: *Norsk stadnamnleksikon*. Oslo.

Smith, B., 2001: 'The Picts and the Martyrs or Did Vikings Kill the Native Population in Orkney and Shetland?', *Northern Studies* 36, 7-32.

Stevenson, R.B.K., 1955: 'Pictish Art'. In: F.T. Wainwright (ed.), *The Problem of the Picts*. Edinburgh, 97-128.

Stevenson, R.B.K., 1981: 'Christian Sculpture in Norse Shetland', *Fróðskaparrit* 28-29, 283-291.

Taylor, H.M. & Taylor, J., 1965: *Anglo-Saxon Architecture* 1-2. Cambridge.

Taylor, H.M., 1978: *Anglo-Saxon Architecture* 3. Cambridge.

Trench-Jellicoe, R., 2002: 'Manx Sculptured Monuments and the Early Viking Age'. In: P. Davey & D. Finlayson (eds), *Mannin Revisited. Twelve Essays on Manx Culture and Environment*. Edinburgh, 11-31.

Wallace-Hadrill, J.M., 1975: *The Vikings in Francia*. Reading.

Wilson, D.M., 1970: 'Manx Memorial Stones of the Viking Period', *Saga-Book* 18, 1-18.

Wilson, D.M., forthcoming a: 'The coming of Christianity'. In: P. Davey (ed.), *A New History of Man*, vol. 2.

Wilson, D.M., forthcoming b: 'The Viking Age'. In S. Duffy (ed.), *A New History of Man*, vol. 3.

Islands Great and Small: a Brief Survey of the Names of Islands and Skerries in Shetland

Peder Gammeltoft

1. Introduction

The archipelago of Shetland is situated in the North Atlantic, some 170 km north of Scotland and about 350 km west of Norway. Shetland is the first part of the British Isles one reaches when sailing from Norway, which, according to saga reports, could be done in a couple of days from Norway. Running in a general north-south direction for 130 km, Shetland is relatively easily spotted when sailing westward from Western Norway. Shetland is thus a prime candidate for having been one of the first of the North Atlantic islands to have received a Scandinavian influx.

Shetland consists of numerous islands, islets and skerries, and so far I have recorded the names of close on 200 of them. The majority of these, between 130-140 names, are of Scandinavian origin, whereas 50-60 names are relatively late Scots constructions. An additional handful of names are of unknown age and origin. My interest in the island-names of the Northern Isles stems from the fact that Scandinavian research has shown that islands are likely to be among the first localities to be named (cf. e.g. Hald 1971: 74-75; Hovda 1971: 124-148). Therefore, they constitute an important group in so far as they might be able to yield invaluable information about the colonisation of the North Atlantic area and how it took place.

2. Types of island-name formation

As I mentioned briefly above, the island-names of the Northern Isles consist partly of Scandinavian-language coinages and partly of later Scots-language coinages. Owing to the differences in age and structure between Old Norse and Scots, it is mostly no great problem to sort out which name was coined in which source language. Once this is said, however, there are a fair number of instances in which it is impossible to ascertain the exact source language of an island-name coinage.

Both Old Norse and Scots have more ways than one in which to coin island-names. In the following I shall attempt a brief overview of the various ways of coining island-names, starting with Scandinavian coinages and moving on to the Scots constructions.

2.1. Scandinavian coinages

In Scandinavia the very oldest strata of island-names are generally acknowledged to be simplex or derived formations. Island-names of this type are generally thought to have been coined in the Common Scandinavian period (CSc), possibly earlier. A large number of Scandinavian island-names are thus original uncompounded or derived constructions. Of uncompounded names may be mentioned e.g. the Norwegian island of Frøya in Sogn og Fjordane fylke (< CSc **Fraujÿ* 'The foremost one' cf. *NG* XII.376), whereas names like Aspona in Akershus fylke (< ON **Aspund* 'The aspen-grown one', an *-und*-derivative of ON *ösp* f., 'aspen'. cf. *NSL* 1997: 77), Gjerdinga in Nord-Trøndelag fylke (< **Gerðing* 'The fencing one', an *-ing*-derivative of ON *gerði* m., 'a fence', cf. *NSL* 1997: 173); and Losna in Sogn og Fjordane fylke (< **Losna* 'The detached one', probably an *-n(a)*-derivative of ON *laus* adj., 'loose, not fixed', cf. *NSL* 1997: 295) are but a few examples of derived island-names.

As far as I can see, no island-names of Scandinavian origin in Shetland, nor in the Northern Isles as a whole, appear to be of the derived type. Similarly, uncompounded island-names of Scandinavian origin are also exceedingly rare there. In Shetland, there are only a couple of known possible uncompounded island-names, such as Uyea in Unst, which originates from *eyju*, dative sg. of ON ey f., 'an island' (*Eyiu, Eyio* 1360 *DN* III, no. 310), and Clett, Sandsting, which may either be from ON *klettr*, 'cliff, rock, crag' or Shetl. and Norn *klett*, sb. 'detached rock, esp. on the sea-shore'. A name-type closely related to uncompounded place-name constructions is the group of names of the so-called comparative type. Although the two are structurally similar, uncompounded place-name formations and comparative place-name formations differ considerably semantically. Whereas an uncompounded place-name describes the locality typologically, a comparative place-name describes the locality according to what it resembles in shape, size or colour. Comparative island-names of Scandinavian origin are also rare in Shetland. Examples are Noss in Bressay (< ON *nös* f., 'a nose, nostril' (1490 Nws *DN* VIII, no. 426)), Giltarump in Sandsting (< ON **gyltarumpa* f., 'a gilt's backside') and The Cleiver in Northmaven (< ON *klauf* f., 'a hoof' or possibly ON *klofi* m., 'a cleft'). To the group of comparative island-names should probably also be added names like The Skult and The Nev. An ON origin is, however, not entirely certain as the origin could be either ON *skoltr* m., 'skull, forehead', or Shetl. *skolt, skult* 'a skull, knoll, bare top' and ON *nef* f., 'a nosebone, nose' or Shetl. *nev* 'a beak, point', respectively. The definite article does suggest a Shetl. Scots origin, but owing to the survival of the appellatives *skolt* and *nev* in the local dialect, this feature could well be a late addition to an original ON name. Compare for instance the above-mentioned The Cleiver, which seems to have attained a definite article because of its likeness to the English appellative *cleaver*, is ultimately an ON plural comparative or uncompounded place-name - although The Cleiver could alternatively be a Scots comparative name.

Instead, the most frequently occurring island-names of Scand-inavian origin in Shetland are compounded island-names. This type makes up almost the entire island-name material. Typologically, compounded island-names appear to have originated in the Common Scandinavian period, and had become the standard type of island-name formation by the start of the Viking Age (cf. *NK* V.37; Hald 1971: 72). The construction consists of a generic element compounded with a specifying element, normally in the word-order *specific + generic*. This type of construction quickly became popular and has become the standard way of coining island-names, even to the extent that a number of the originally uncompounded and derived island-names in the course of time have been supplied with an epexegetic or descriptive element in order to resemble a 'proper' island-name. An example of this is the Norwegian island of Mosterøy in Rogaland fylke, which is first mentioned as *Moster* (2/6 1558 (*DN* VI.8 18)) but which shortly after had the epexegetic element Norw. *øy* 'island' affixed to the name (cf. the discussion of the principle in Hald 1971: 71-84). The generic element indicates the type of locality, here typically ON *ey* f., 'an island', ON *holmr* m., 'an islet' or ON *sker* n., 'a skerry, rocky island, reef', etc., whereas the specific describes in which way the locality differs from other localities of the same kind (cf. Jakobsen 1936: 61, 97, 121-124; *NSL* 1997: 47-49). For instance, the name of Linga, Whalsay, is compounded of ON *lyng* n., 'heather' and ON *ey* f., 'an island'. (*Liwngøy, Linga* 1485 (*REO* p. 72)). Here, the generic element describes the type of locality whereas the specific states that the occurrence of heather was seen to be the foremost feature of the locality at the time of naming.

As I have already mentioned, the normal word order for compounded Scandinavian place-names is specific + generic structure. In Common Scandinavian, however, word order was not yet fixed to the present structure and could in a number of situations equally well be of a reversed generic + specific structure, especially if the specifying element was an adjective or adverb (Sandnes 2003: 294-300). The importance of this reversed structure diminished steadily from the Viking Age and onwards, and there are only a few traces of this word order in place-names today. This is mainly owing to the fact that the original reversed word order in place-names has often been revised to the increasingly normal *specific + generic* structure, as in Helgøya, Hedmark fylke, Norway, which is first recorded as *j øynni heigho* and *j øynne heigho* (10/2 1353 (*DN* II.31) and 15/11 1409 (*DN* I.624)). Belonging generally to the older layers of place-names, island-names have a relatively high frequency of names with reversed word order. In Shetland, there are no known early examples of island-names of Scandinavian origin of this type, but a few examples are recorded in Orkney, most notably Eynhallow, which is written as *Eigin helga* in c. 1350 (*DI* III, p. 50n.), as are *i Papey ina littlu* (c. 1300 *Orkn*, p. 77 (Orkn325I)) and *til Papeyiar hinnar meiri* (1300-1350 *Orkn*, p. 79 (Orkn325III)), the earliest recorded forms of Papa Stronsay and Papa Westray (cf. Callisendorff 1964: 110). It is perhaps also worth noting in this respect that Iona is called *Eyin helga* in Magnus Barefoot's saga (*FMS* VII.427).

2.2. Scots coinages

Being of Germanic origin just like Old Norse, the genuinely Scots coinages may, superficially, be somewhat hard to distinguish from coinages of Scandinavian origin. Not only are the Scots constructions in some cases structurally similar to the Scandinavian coinages, the transfer and subsequent adaptations of place-names and place-name elements of Scandinavian origin into the local Scots dialect also help to muddy the picture (cf. Berit Sandnes' article pp. 192-200, below). Nonetheless, it is possible to establish the principles lying behind Scots island-name formations.

Compounded island-names are by far the most common constructions in Insular Scots, too. A fair number of these are of the normal specific + generic structure, which make them difficult to distinguish from genuine ON island-names, as place-name elements like *holm*, *skerry* and *stack* have been borrowed from ON and have become popular place-name elements in Insular Scots. The easiest way of knowing that we are dealing with a Scots construction is if the specific element contains another place-name, as this construction is virtually unknown from the island-names of Scandinavian origin. Examples of this are e.g. Burwick Holm, Tingwall, and Gloup Holm, Yell, which are named from the nearby areas of Burwick and Gloup, respectively. Most of the island-names of Scots origin, however, make use of of-periphrasis. Names of this type abound in Shetland – from Northmaven alone, islets like Isle of Gunnister, Isle of Westerhouse and Holms of Burravoe are but a few examples. This type of construction is not found in ON and is, therefore, a certain sign of a non-Scandinavian origin. Again the specific is normally another place-name, often a settlement name.

3. Why is the study of island-names important?

I mentioned above that islands are likely to be among the first localities to be named. Island-names are, therefore, important in a wider cultural historical context, as they may constitute a gateway into the mind of the early Scandinavian settlers in the area. However, only a few names in the Northern Isles have been studied in any great detail, most notably those that may convey information about the former inhabitants of Shetland and Orkney and their relationship to the incoming Scandinavians. Especially the *Papey*-names, possibly signalling early monastic activities, and the possible pre-Norse names of Unst, Yell and Fetlar have been discussed by a number of scholars (cf. e.g. MacDonald 1977: 107-111; Fellows-Jensen 1996: 116-117; Gammeltoft 2004: 31-49). Much has already been written about these names and I shall not elaborate any further on them in this paper. Instead, I shall present a brief outline of what else the island-name material of Scandinavian origin in Shetland may yield of relevant linguistic and cultural historical information.

Between six and eleven island-names have, or may have, a personal name as the specific. Owing to the relatively late recording of most place-names in Shetland, the origin of many of the names of islands is somewhat uncertain. The seven most certain instances of island-names with personal name specifics are: Atla Holm (< ON pers.n. *Atli* m.,), Balta (< poss. ON pers.n. *Balti* m.,), Egilsay (< ON pers.n. *Egill* m.,), Hildasay (< ON pers.n. *Hildir* m.,), Samphrey (< ON pers.n. **Sandfríðr* f.,), Trondra (< ON pers.n. *Þróndr* m.,) and Vementry (< ON pers.n. *Vémundr* m.,). Most of these are well known ON personal names, apart from the only alleged feminine name, **Sandfríðr*, which is otherwise completely unattested (cf. Lind 1905-1915, col. 869). That we are most probably dealing with a personal name, however, is evident from the earliest forms of the name from 1512, *i Sandffriarøø* and *Vm Sanffrijdar ey*, which clearly show the ON feminine genitive singular *-ar* form, which indicates that the specific is a personal name. Furthermore, *Sand-* cannot be said to refer to any special feature of the island, as sand is largely absent from the island. The occurrence of a personal name as the specific in an island-name probably signals original ownership or it may possibly reflect a particular event involving the named person and the island in question.

Stating a topographical relationship of a locality by means of its position in relation to another locality is a commonly used naming motif. For instance, in my study of the settlement-names in ON *bólstaðr* m., some 44% of the compound formations in the Scottish Isles belonged to this naming category (Gammeltoft 2001: 245). It is, therefore, somewhat surprising that only seven of the island-names of Shetland (i.e. less than 6% of the entire material) belong within this category. Of these, the specifics in the names Foreholm, Inn Holm, Nizta and possibly South Holm, state the relative relationship to another locality, being fore (i.e. in front of), inner, lowest and south of another and presumably more important locality. The remaining examples, such as Taing Skerry in South Nesting, named after the local feature of Taing, and Bruray in the Skerries (< *brúrar*, gen.sg. of ON *brú* f., 'a bridge'), which takes its name from the unnamed natural bridge which links this island with Housay, state their situation in relation to another, named or unnamed, topographical feature.

In the region of half of the island-names of Scandinavian origin, however, have been named with reference to their shape, size or colour (35 names in total), or in terms of which animals, plants or objects the islands contained at the time of naming (37-43 names in total). Of these, some 25 island-names feature an animal designation as their specific. I have previously argued that this naming motif relates to what the islands were generally used for. Island-names such as Lamba in Northmaven (*Lambay* 1599 (*SheDoc* no. 281)), Gult Holm in Nesting and Oxna in Tingwall (*Oxna Ile* 1587 (*SheDoc* no. 99)), contain the elements ON *lamb* n., 'a lamb', ON *göltr* m., 'a hog' and ON *øxn* m. pl., 'oxen', respectively. These specifics would thus signify that the islands were used for rearing the above-mentioned animals. It has, however, been brought to my attention that Norwegian island-names containing words for pigs, dogs, oxen, etc., are often thought to signal dangerous water or passage with submerged reefs and strong currents, etc. Norwegian island-names such as Galten, Oksen and Svinøy are used of islands and skerries in whose vicinity sea-passage is dangerous or difficult (*NSL* 1997: 164, 342, 440, 462). Needless to say, such a possibility must be taken into account when dealing with the island-names of the Northern Isles. I am, nonetheless, still inclined to favour a utilisation interpretation, as most of the Norwegian island-names signalling danger are uncompounded formations like Galten and Oksen, whereas all of the Northern Isles examples are compound formations. In comparison, Svinøy is normally interpreted as either signalling danger or signifying that the island was used for grazing pigs during summer (*NSL* 1997: 440). That the reference is typically to what the island is being used for is shown very eloquently with the example of the island of Horse Isle in Dunrossness. Horse Isle is first recorded as *Hundholmi* in the *Orkneyinga Saga* (c.1600-50 Orkn702), later as *Swineholm* (Stewart 1987: 17) and now as *Horse Isle*. The oldest known name for the island is a compound of ON *hundr* m., 'a dog' and ON *holmr* m., 'an islet', whereas the later form of *Swineholm* derives from ON *svín* n., 'a pig' or Eng. *swine*, sb. and ON *holmr* m. or Shetl. *holm*, sb. The modern name, Horse Isle, is a compound of Eng. *horse* and Eng. *isle*. It is hardly conceivable that these name changes reflect aspects of danger. Instead they seemingly relate to changes in the utilisation of the island. In some instances, however, if the islands bearing names of this type are very small or consist solely of bare rocks, then the aspect of signalling danger should be preferred.

4. Rounding off

It is my hope that this brief survey has shown that the island-name material of Shetland is of relatively great morphological and semantic complexity. Although the Shetland material covers in the region of 200 island-names, the majority of these relate to everyday life, such as how they are located in comparison with other localities, who lived on them, what they could be used for and what dangers and difficulties they and their surroundings offered. One aspect of naming which I have only just touched upon relates to the many islands whose specific refers to the appearance of the island. Here, the shape, size or colour of an island was of prime importance, perhaps as a means of identification for sailors and fishermen. The prime intention behind the naming of islands in Shetland appears to be linked to aspects of everyday life. When most of the islands of the Northern Isles were named, the system and culture was Norse in character. Later Scots has also made its imprint on the island-name material, albeit to a much smaller degree. The centuries-long language contact between Norn and Scots in Shetland has ensured that a large part of Shetland island-name material of Old Norse origin still survives today.

Islands Great and Small: a Survey of Names of Islands in Shetland

Literature

Calissendorff, K., 1964: 'Helgø', *Namn och Bygd* 52, 105-151.

DI = Diplomatarium Islandicum: Íslenzktfornbréfasafn, sem hefir inni að halda bréf og gjörnínga, dóma og máldaga, og aðrar skrár, er snerta Ísland eða íslenzka menn 1-16. Gefið út af hinu íslenzka bókmenntafélagi. Copenhagen, 1857-1872.

DN = Diplomatarium Norvegicum. Christiania/Oslo, 1847-.

Fellows-Jensen, G., 1996: 'Language Contact in Iceland: the Evidence of Names'. In: P.S. Ureland & I. Clarkson (eds), *Language Contact Across the North Atlantic. Proceedings of the Working Groups held at University College, Galway (Ireland), August 29 - September 3, 1992 and the University of Göteborg (Sweden), August 16-21, 1993*. Tübingen, 115-124.

FMS = Fornmanna sögur. Eptir gömlum handritum útgefnar að tilhlutun hins norræna fornfræða félags 1-12. Copenhagen, 1825-1837.

Gammeltoft, P., 2001: *The Place-Name Element* bólstaðr *in the North Atlantic Area*. Navnestudier 38. Copenhagen.

Gammeltoft, P., 2004: 'Among *Dímons* and *Papeys*: What Kind of Contact do the Names Really Point to?', *Northern Studies* 38, 31-49.

Hald, K., 1971: 'De danske ønavne', *Namn och Bygd* 59, 71-84.

Hovda, P., 1971: 'Til norske elvenamn', *Namn och Bygd* 59, 124-148.

Jakobsen, J., [1936] 1993: *The Place-Names of Shetland*. Kirkwall.

Lind, E.H., 1905-1915: *Norsk-isländska dopnamn ock fingerade namn från medeltiden*. Uppsala/Leipzig. Supplementband 1931. Oslo/Uppsala/Copenhagen.

MacDonald, A., 1977: 'Old Norse "Papar" Names in N. and W. Scotland: Summary'. In: L. Lang (ed.), *Studies in Celtic Survival*. British Archaeological Reports 37, 107-111.

MacDonald, A., 2002: 'The *Papar* and Some Problems. A Brief Review'. In: B.E. Crawford (ed.), *The* Papar *in the North Atlantic*. St Andrews, 13-30.

NG = Norske Gaardnavne 1-19. Kristiania/Oslo, 1897-1936.

NK = Nordisk Kultur: Samlingsværk 1-30. Red. af J. Brøndum-Nielsen, O. v. Friesen, S. Erixon & M. Olsen. Stockholm/Olso/Copenhagen, 1931-1956.

NSL = Norsk stadnamnleksikon. J. Sandnes og O. Stemshaug (eds). 4. utg. Oslo, 1997.

Orkn = Nordal, S. (ed.), 1913-1916: *Orkneyinga saga*. Reykjavík.

REO = Records of the Earldom of Orkney, 1299-1614. Edited with introduction and notes by J. Storer Clouston. Edinburgh, 1914.

Sandnes, B., 2003: *Fra Starafjall til Starling Hill. Dannelse og utvikling av norrøne stedsnavn på Orknøyene*. Dr.art.-avhandling, Norges teknisk-naturvitenskapelige universitet. Trondheim.

SheDoc = Ballantyne, J.H. & Smith, B., (eds), 1994: *Shetland Documents, 1580-1611*. Lerwick.

SheDoc2 = Ballantyne, J.H. & Smith, B., (eds), 1999: *Shetland Documents, 1195-1579*. Lerwick.

Stewart, J., 1987: *Shetland Place-Names*. Lerwick.

The Origin of the Ayrshire *Bý* Names

Alison Grant

1. Something of a mystery

The Ayrshire *bý* names present something of a mystery, as they seem to indicate Scandinavian settlement in an area for which there is little other evidence of Scandinavian presence. The six names are located chiefly in the Ardrossan area, near to the coast of the Firth of Clyde (see Figure 1, below). Geoffrey Barrow (1998: 70-72) has advised caution in ascribing a Scandinavian origin to place-names in *bý* in the Central Lowlands of Scotland, particularly in instances where there are no topographical or ancillary settlement names. He argues that geographically isolated *bý* names are more likely to reflect the borrowing of Scandinavian place-name elements into the local dialects of the English and Gaelic languages. Similarly, Fellows-Jensen (1989-1990: 54-55) notes that it is difficult to date many of the *bý* names in the Central Lowlands. Whilst they may represent Scandinavian settlement in the 9th and 10th centuries, she admits that, in cases where there are parallel formations in England, it is also possible that the names were commemorative transfers brought from the Danelaw in the 12th century.

In this context, it is noteworthy that David I was raised at the court of the English king Henry I, and that he brought Anglo-Norman supporters with him when he acceded to the Scottish throne in 1124. During the 12th and 13th centuries, David and his successors transplanted Anglo-Norman and Flemish retainers from their English to their Scottish estates (see, for example Lynch 1991: 53, 58). Since five of the six Ayrshire *bý* names have English doublets, this might indicate that the Ayrshire names were transferred from England as part of the Anglo-Norman settlements in Southern Scotland. Alternatively, these parallel forms might suggest that the names were coined analogously in the post-Scandinavian period by either Gaelic or Scots speakers using the element *bý* as a loan-word, in a manner similar to that which Barrow has proposed for names in Fife, Angus and Berwickshire.

One of the main difficulties in identifying the origins of the Ayrshire *bý* names is the lack of early historical forms. There are no records of any of the names prior to the 13th century, and in most cases, the records start in the 15th century, which is rather late to be of use (see the Appendix for a list of these historical forms). However, this does not necessarily indicate that the *bý* names are late coinages, or commemorative transfers. Fellows-Jensen (1989-1990: 52) has pointed out that the Anglo-Norman settlements of the 12th and 13th centuries are characterised by *-tūn* names with a Norman or Flemish personal name as their specific. She notes that none of the *bý* names in the Central Lowlands of Scotland contain such Continental personal names, and in fact, most appear to contain Scandinavian specific elements. Fellows-Jensen (*ibid*: 54-55) argues from this that these names in *bý* may represent an earlier phase of purely Scandinavian immigration from the Danelaw.

As the specific elements of the Ayrshire *bý* names may also be Scandinavian in origin, the focus of this article will be to examine the possibility that these names represent genuine Scandinavian settlement on the west coast of Scotland. This influx could potentially have comprised of the same predominantly-Danish immigrants from the Scandinavian colonies in the Danelaw who settled in Fife and the Lothians. Alternatively, given the proximity of the Ayrshire *bý*-name sites to the Southern Hebrides, it is possible that these names may instead have a connection with the Gaelic-Scandinavian settlements in the Western Isles and parts of the North-West of England.

It is well established that the Southern Hebrides and adjoining mainland were less densely settled by Scandinavian immigrants than were the Northern Hebrides (see, for example, Crawford 1987: 97), but the presence of *bólstaðr* names on Coll, Tiree, Mull, Islay and Jura indicates that the Scandinavians did settle there. Additionally, Jennings (2004: 109-119) notes that there are two *ból-* names on the Kintyre peninsula, as well as the *bý* name Smerby. There is also good archaeological evidence of Scandinavian presence. Graham-Campbell and Batey (1998: 88-89) note that a Viking period silver hoard was found on the island of Inch Kenneth off Mull in the 19th century. Further south, they point out that 'Colonsay, Oronsay and Islay are relatively rich in pagan Norse burials, with a total of eleven reasonably well-documented examples and a further ten or more possible graves on record'. Closer to Ayrshire, there is evidence of two Viking burials on Arran at Lamlash Bay, which is across the Firth of Clyde from Ardrossan (Graham-Campbell and Batey 1998: 95-96).

It is true that there is little onomastic evidence of Scandinavian settlement on the western mainland of Scotland, in the region where the *bý* names are located. There are, however, three hogback sites, at Luss on Loch Lomond, at Dalserf on the upper Clyde and a major site at Govan (Ritchie 1993: 96). Graham-Campbell and Batey (1998: 100) note that at least one of the Govan hogbacks is very closely matched to those found in Northern England, which might suggest a connection with Scandinavian colonies in the south as well as those in the north. There is also another *bý* name, Busby, in Renfrewshire, south of the Clyde. Additionally, there was a Viking period silver hoard found near Port Glasgow at the end of the 17th century. Also relevant is the archaeological evidence of a seasonal beach-market at Stevenson Sands, near Ardrossan, 'where eighth/ninth century objects have been found, as well as an Arabic silver dirham of early tenth-century date' (Graham-Campbell and Batey 1998: 98-102).

2. Sorbie

The wider Hebridean context is particularly important when considering the Ayrshire *bý* name Sorbie. The name is explained by Nicolaisen (2001: 132) as ON *saur-býr* 'mud village' or 'swamp village'. As the name would therefore be entirely Scandinavian in construction, it seems there is little possibility that the name was a late coinage by either Gaelic or English speakers using *bý* as a loan-word. There are several reflexes of this name in the west of Scotland. Soroba is near Oban, and there is another Soroba at Craignish. There is a Soroby on Tiree and Soriby on the Isle of Mull, and there may also have been two Saurbie names in the Trotternish region of Skye, both recorded in a 1733 Rental as *Swerby* (Gordon: 1965). This name type is also commonly found further south, in areas of Gaelic-Scandinavian influence, including Galloway, Dumfriesshire, the Isle of Man, the North-West of England, and Yorkshire. It would appear that the Ayrshire 'Sorbie' name may be connected to this overall Gaelic-Scandinavian continuum.

The fact that there are so many *saur-býr* names might alternatively suggest that at least some of the names were transferred to western Scotland at some point in the post-Scandinavian era, as has been suggested for some of the Central Lowlands *bý* names. In this context, Taylor has recently demonstrated that the name Sorbie in Fife was a late 18th century transplant, created when the Harrays from Sorbie in Galloway acquired the land where Sorbie in Fife is situated (see Fellows-Jensen 2000: 141). Given this, the possibility of a similar transfer in the case of the Ayrshire Sorbie should not be ruled out entirely.

The large number of these names in Scotland, England and also Iceland might also be seen to indicate that it was a common name-type applied to any farm with poor soil or adverse conditions (Nicolaisen 2001: 132). It should also be noted that in the case of the Icelandic instances, Guðmundsson has postulated that there may be a connection between **saur-*

bær names and sacred heathen sites (see Fellows-Jensen 1984: 156). In the case of the British instances, Nicolaisen (2001: 132) has also suggested that *saur* in these names might 'sometimes refer to mud-flats covered by water at high tide and dry at low tide'. The Ayrshire instance of Sorbie is a mile or two inland from the coastal mud-flats, so that explanation would not be applicable here, but *saur* in the sense of marshy land liable to flooding does appear to be appropriate to this Sorbie site. Similar English or Scots names in the area include Bushy Bog, Bogside Flats, Bogend, Boghead and Meikle Myre. Sorbie itself is on a hillside above which a series of reservoirs have been formed in the modern period, fed by a number of burns. This tiny settlement is just beside what is now the Mill Glen Reservoir, and there is a burn running right across the land at Sorbie itself. It would therefore appear plausible that the name was given by Scandinavian-speakers to describe a farm with marshy conditions. Thus, despite the existence of numerous English parallels of the name, there is no reason to suppose that the name was transferred to Ayrshire either by Anglo-Norman settlers, or at a later period.

3. Crosbie

The Crosbie names also have a number of doublets. These names appear to contain ON *krossa-býr* 'cross farm' or 'farm with crosses' (Nicolaisen 2001: 132, 147). There are no parallels in the Western Isles, which might suggest an alternative connection with the secondary Scandinavian settlements along the coast of Southern Scotland and the North-West of England. Instances of these names occur in Galloway and Berwick as Corsbie, and the Ayrshire names are also sometimes recorded in this metathesized form. There are two Crosby names on the Isle of Man, and in Cumberland there are three instances, two directly across the Solway Firth from Galloway and one by the River Eden close to the Dumfriesshire border. There are two further Crosby names in Westmorland and one in Lancashire.

As there are so many doublets in areas of Scandinavian settlement, it seems unlikely that the names might have been coined independently by Gaelic or English speakers using *bý* as a loan-word. However, because of the more southerly parallels, the possibility does exist that the names are transfers from England during the Anglo-Norman period. There are no recorded forms of either name until the 13th century, when Crosbie near West Kilbride is recorded *a.* 1214 as *Crosby*, in 1230 as *Crosseby* and in 1367 as *Corsbi* (Johnston 1934: 146). This is perhaps the only one of the Ayrshire names to have such early historical attestations, and as such it is difficult to establish the precise linguistic and chronological background of these names.

In the case of the more northerly of the two instances of Crosbie in Ayrshire, it is significant that this was apparently an ecclesiastical site. This might suggest that the name may have been coined as a *kross-býr* name by Scandinavian-speaking immigrants from the North-West of England by analogy with the Crosby names in that region, rather than being an essentially random commemorative transfer introduced by Anglo-Norman immigrants from their estates in the Danelaw. The surrounding area provides evidence of both Christianity and Celtic ecclesiastical monuments. Crosbie is situated just outside West Kilbride, which contains *cill*, the Gaelic word for a chapel or church, and the name of St Brigid. Graham-Campbell and Batey (1998: 43) note that across the firth, on the tiny island of Inchmarnock (just west of Bute), a small fragment of a cross-slab of Scandinavian origin was found, marked with 'a ringed cross carved in the same manner as those in the Manx monuments'. They also record that the memorial inscription on the stone 'includes the Celtic loan-word *kross*, as is the standard usage on Man, in place of the expected Norse word *steinn*'.

Further south, the potential inversion-compound name Crossraguel indicates the presence of a cross, and there are also six *kirk*-compounds in southern Ayrshire: Kirkbride, Kirkconstantine, Kirkcudbright, Kirkdominae, Kirkmichael and Kirkoswald. It may be significant that the *kirk*-compound name type seems to have had its origins in Gaelic-Scandinavian contact. Thus, it would appear quite plausible that Crosbie was coined by Scandinavian immigrants to describe a settlement with a cross, rather than representing a later Anglo-Norman transfer.

The second Ayrshire Crosbie name survives on the modern Ordnance Survey map as Crosbie House, and is marked as a historical monument. As it is only a few miles from Crosbie at West Kilbride, it is possible that this second Crosbie name was transferred from the site at West Kilbride, which has given its name to the Crosbie Reservoir and the Crosbie Hills in that vicinity. The more southerly Crosbie is situated just to the north of Prestwick, OE *prēost wīc* 'priest's dwelling' or OE *prēosta wīc* 'priests' dwelling' (Nicolaisen 2001: 103), and is close to Monkton, which also suggests an Anglian ecclesiastical context. This might imply that the name was also coined by Scandinavian-speakers to refer to a settlement with one or more crosses, rather than being a transfer from Crosbie near West Kilbride or being an Anglo-Norman transfer of an estate name in the Danelaw.

4. Busbie

Another pair of names is the Busbie names. The modern Ordnance Survey map reveals that at the more northerly site there is a farm called Meikle Busbie adjacent to Busbie Muir, and at the southern site there is a hamlet called Busbiehill and two nearby farms called Busbie Mains and Busbie Head. As mentioned above, there is another Busby name in nearby Renfrewshire, and there is a further instance in Perthshire. Fellows-Jensen (1989-1990: 51) argues that the specific is likely to be Scandinavian *buski* 'shrubbery'. As these names are once again entirely Scandinavian in construction, there is little likelihood that ON *bý* was used as a loan-word to form place-names by either Gaelic or English speakers. However, as these names have a doublet in northern Yorkshire, it is possible that the name was transferred to Ayrshire by Anglo-Norman immigrants. Yet it may be significant that the Yorkshire instance of Busby is situated in a region which is a focal point for hogback monuments, some of which are similar to those found in Scotland. Thus it may be possible that the Ayrshire names reflect an earlier influx of Scandinavians from this part of the Danelaw (Fellows-Jensen 1995: 184).

As it seems unlikely that the four or five Scottish *Busbie/Busby* names could all be commemorative transfers of a single Yorkshire name, it is possible that the names were actually coined *ad hoc* by Scandinavian-speaking immigrants to the Ayrshire coast in reference to farmsteads at bushy sites. In the vicinity of the northern Busbie the names Bushglen and Broomhill would appear to suggest a terrain of bushes and shrubs, as would the Rowanside Hills amongst which Meikle Busbie and Busbie Muir are situated. Around the southern Busbie there is another Broomhill, together with a Rowan Hill and a Wood Hill, and there is a village named Thorntoun adjacent to Busbiehill. All of this would support the theory that the names were coined by Scandinavian-speakers in response to the terrain in the region, rather than representing later transfers in the post-Scandinavian period.

As the Busbie names discussed above appear to contain ON *buski* 'shrubs, bushes', then this may have a bearing on the interpretation of the Galloway name Bysbie. Oram (1995: 137) argues that this name contains ON *biskup* or the OE cognate *biscop* 'Bishop's Farm', based on the 1305 form *Biskeby* and the proximity of Whithorn, where a bishopric was established in 1128. Yet the numerous Busby formations seem to lend weight to Fellows-Jensen's alternative theory (1989-1990: 43) that Bysbie may originally have been a *buski* name which was later altered due to the establishment of the Whithorn bishopric.

5. Magbie

The final Ayrshire *bý* name is Magbie. This is a problematic name, because the specific is unclear. Fellows-Jensen (1989-1990: 51) notes that 'the specific of *Magby* AYR cannot be identified with certainty on the basis of recorded forms but it may be the Scandinavian common noun *maki* "customer, partner, mate".' Johnston (1934: 247) had earlier suggested 'Dwelling of *Mæg*'. This is the only one of the Ayrshire group without a parallel in either England or Scotland, and as such cannot be attributed to Anglo-Norman immigrants from the Danelaw. Yet, as the form of the name is similar to Mabie in Galloway, one possibility might be that the two names contain the same etymology. In this context it is noteworthy that the Sorbie, Crosbie and potentially the Busbie names are all paralleled in Galloway, which might suggest a link between the settlement of the two areas. However, Fellows-Jensen (1991: 84) gives the etymology of Mabie as 'Scandinavian *mey(ja)* or *mær* "maiden, kinswoman" or the related OE *mæge*. There is no obvious explanation as to how any of these specific elements might have led to the development of a velar plosive sound which is currently present in Magbie in Ayrshire (see the Appendix for a list of historical forms). As such, it seems unlikely that the two names could be doublets.

What is striking about the Magbie forms is that they all contain English 'hill', and Magbiehill is the form given on the modern Ordnance Survey map. As the current Magbiehill is a farm or small hamlet, rather than a topographical feature, it is possible that 'hill' is a later addition to what was originally a habitative *bý* name. The consistent *mak* forms in the historical records might also suggest a surname in Gaelic 'mac' functioning as a specific element, with English 'hill' as the generic. Interestingly, there is a very similar name, Macbie Hill, near Dolphinton in Lanarkshire, which Johnston (1934: 246) records as being bought and named in 1712 by a man named Montgomery 'after MacBeth or Macbie Hill, Ayrsh[ire]'. Due to the notoriously unreliable nature of Johnston's dictionary, it is uncertain whether his information is accurate. Yet the lack of historical forms without the element 'hill' attached might suggest that this name actually contains the Scottish surname MacBeth or a variant form such as MacBeith, McBay or McBey, all of which are from the Gaelic name *Mac Beatha* (Hanks and Hodges 1988: 355).

I was, however, unable to find any historical forms of the name prior to the 15th century, by which time the original form could have undergone considerable alteration. If Magbie were a Scandinavian name in *bý*, to which 'hill' was later suffixed, it is likely that by the 15th century its meaning would have become semantically opaque. As such, Magbie could have been mistaken for a surname, which would have influenced how the name was recorded orthographically. It may be significant that there is a Hill of Beith approximately five miles from Magbiehill which may also have influenced the interpretation of the latter name. Given these difficulties, it seems impossible to determine whether or not this name originally contained Old Norse *bý*.

Even if Magbie were excluded from the list of Ayrshire *bý* names, it should be remembered that the Sorbie and Crosbie names have parallels in Galloway and in North-West England and the Busbie names have a potential parallel in Galloway and several certain parallels in Southern Scotland. For such similar nomenclature to emerge, it is likely that these areas were all settled by the same linguistic group. As the Ayrshire names contain no English or Continental elements, there is no evidence of coinage either by a non-Scandinavian speech community utilising *bý* as a loan-word, or of post-Conquest transfer of names from the Danelaw. Rather, the essentially Scandinavian make-up of these Ayrshire names suggests that they are connected to genuine Scandinavian settlement around the coast of Western Britain. It seems likely, therefore, that the various parallel formations were coined by Gaelic-Scandinavian emigrants from the Scottish Isles, who settled in North-West England, before settling along the coast of South-West Scotland.

As is the case with the *bý* names in the Central Lowlands, there are no other Scandinavian habitative or topographical place-names in Ayrshire, which contrasts with the settlements in Cumberland and South-West Scotland. This might suggest that the names are more likely to have been transplanted from the Danelaw by Anglo-Norman immigrants. There is, however, an alternative explanation for this lack of ancillary settlement evidence. It is possible that Scandinavian settlement was extremely limited, with little or no opportunity for secondary expansion or utilisation of natural resources beyond the original *bý* sites. It is perhaps significant that none of the *bý* names has a personal name as a specific element, as Oram (1995: 131) has argued of the Scandinavian settlements in South-West Scotland that:

> the scarcity of personal-name forms associated with any of the various generics indicates that the immigration was not sufficiently intensive for these initial settlements to be speedily broken down into smaller farms.

Additionally, Jennings (2004: 109-119) has argued that a lack of ancillary names in areas of Scandinavian settlement might indicate that a linguistic shift occurred within one or two generations, so that the Scandinavians 'had become naturalised before any significant secondary settlement took place'. Given this, it is possible that the settlement in Ayrshire was a later detachment from the Scandinavian colonies in either Galloway or coastal Cumberland, comprising of Scandinavians who may even have been invited to settle amongst the established native population (see Oram *ibid*: 131) rather than representing settlement directly from the Scottish Isles.

Yet, in the case of the coastal Ayrshire *bý* names, their proximity to the southern end of the Hebridean settlements should also be taken into consideration (see Figure 1, below). The Ayrshire settlements are directly across the firth from the island of Arran, and an alternative explanation for the lack of names indicating that the area was being exploited by the incoming Scandinavians is that there were better resources available on Arran. Both Nicolaisen and Fraser have commented on the lack of Scandinavian habitative names on the island, and Nicolaisen (1992: 8) suggests that, 'Not one Norse name indicates that its giver ever stayed on during winter or had any permanent dwelling in the island'. Similarly, Fraser (2000: 53) records that the small number of Scandinavian names on Arran are purely topographical, whose content suggests that '[i]f they had a serious interest in the island, it was in terms of its natural resources – timber, fish and game'. Examples include Glenashdale (ON *ask-dalr* 'ash-tree valley'), Chalmadale ('Hjalmund's valley'), Ormidale ('Orm's valley'), and Brodick and Sannox (*breið-vík* 'broad bay' and *sand-vík* 'sandy bay' respectively). Of these two bays, Fraser (*ibid*: 53) notes:

> it is significant that these are east facing, with good beaches, where ships and boats could be drawn up, and with good anchorages. Moreover, a supply of good arable land, grazing and timber would have been available during the Norse period.

The Ardrossan area of Ayrshire, where the *bý* names are located, is directly opposite these two bays, and in fact the present day ferry to Arran runs from Ardrossan to Brodick.

In the case of names such as Ashdale, where ON *-dalr* is coupled with a tree-name, Crawford (1995: 24-28) has suggested that nomenclature of this type reflects Scandinavian exploitation of timber resources, particularly in areas where Scandinavian place-names are otherwise scarce. Nicolaisen

(1992: 8) also suggests that the Scandinavian place-names on Arran are indicative of 'seasonal interlopers depleting the rivers and grazing their heifers and their yearlings on shielings on the best grassland easily accessible from the shore'. He argues that these interlopers were 'water-riding Norsemen who ultimately came from Norway via the Northern Isles and the Hebrides'. Yet it seems plausible that some of these Scandinavians came from settlements slightly closer to hand, namely across the firth at Ardrossan.

It should be noted that the Scandinavians in Ayrshire probably did not constitute the only Scandinavian presence on Arran, and some of the Scandinavian place-names may already have been coined by settlers who had made a more direct immigration from Norway. Scholars such as Waugh (2000) and more recently Kruse (2004) and Jennings (2004) have argued that topographical names with generics such as -dalr and -nes are often indicative of permanent habitation. Jennings (2004: 109-119) notes that Scandinavians often gave topographical names to the earliest settlements in any given area. Kruse (2004: 97-107) suggests that a name of this type 'will have a dual designata; it will refer both to the topographical feature and the settlement itself, and the latter will probably be the most important'. He argues that the survival of these names indicates that they were permanent Scandinavian settlements because '[t]here was no reason for locals to accept new, foreign names from visitors for a topography that they already had names for in their own language'. It would therefore appear that some of the Scandinavian names on the island, such as the small group of names in -dalr, may represent an earlier phase of Scandinavian settlement on the island, into which the Ayrshire colonists insinuated themselves in order to exploit Arran's natural resources. A secondary influx of this type might have augmented the Scandinavian toponymy on Arran, and aided in the preservation of existing Scandinavian names on a predominantly Gaelic-speaking island.

In conclusion, it would appear that, despite being outside the regions of recognised Scandinavian settlement, the Ayrshire bý names show some clear affinities with the Scandinavian nomenclature of Gaelic-Scandinavian colonies around the western seaboard, particularly in the case of Galloway. Given this, there is no reason to suppose that the names might reflect the borrowing of bý into a non-Scandinavian language. Similarly, as the names themselves seem to fit the topography of northern Ayrshire, there is no need to ascribe them to a later stratum of Anglo-Norman immigration from the Danelaw into this region. The lack of other Scandinavian names in the vicinity does not preclude a genuine Scandinavian presence in this area, as settlement under restrictive circumstances may have impeded any opportunity for ancillary development. Alternatively, there may be a connection with the topographical names on nearby Arran, representing a seasonal exploitation of island resources from the mainland.

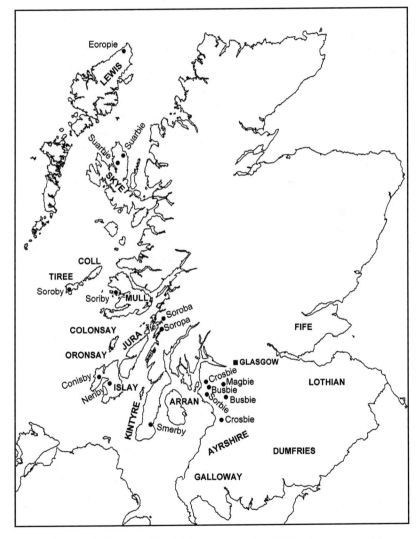

Figure 1. The Ayrshire bý names seen in a Hebridean context.

Appendix: Historical Forms of the Ayrshire *Bý* Names

Busbie, West Kilbride < ON *buski* 'shubbery'.

Busby	(1527)
Busby	(1539)
Busbie-Lytill	(1582)
Busbie	(1583)
Busbie	(1607, 1611)
Busbie Meikill et Littill	(1612)
Busbeyis	(1623)
Busbie	(1625, 1628)
Busbies	(1628, 1636)
Busbie	(1667)

Busbie, Kilmaurs < ON *buski* 'shubbery'.

Busby	(1467-68)
Busbeyis	(1599)
Busbeyis	(1611)
Busbyes	(1613, 1614)
Busbie(s)	(1614)
Busbie	(1620-33)
Busbiehead	(1620-33)
Busbie-Fergushill	(1621, 1628, 1636, 1667)
Busbieheid	(1625)
Busbeyis	(1635)
Busbie(s)	(1636)
Busbies	(1663)
Busbiehead	(1663, 1667)

Crosbie, West Kilbride < ON *kross* 'cross'.

Crosby	(a.1214)
Crosseby	(1230)
Corsbi	(1367)
Corsbe	(1549-50)
Corsbie	(1626, 1634)
Corsbie	(1637)

Crosbie, Prestwick < ON *kross* 'cross'.

Corsby	(1464)
Corsbie, Corsby	(1548)
Corsbie	(1587)
Corsby	(1590)
Corsbie	(1591-2)
Corsbie	(1603)
Corsbie	(1634)
Carsbie	(1642)

Magby, Stewarton < ON *maki* 'customer, partner, mate', pers. n. *Mæg*, or surname *MacBe(i)th*.

Makbehill	(1451)
M'behyll	(1451)
Makbihill	(1476)
Makbehill	(1507)
Makbehill	(1537)
Makbehill	(1587)

Sorbie, Ardrossan < ON *saur* 'mud or swamp'.

Sorbie	(1612)
Sorbie-craigs	(1612)

Sources

All historical forms are taken from *The Register of the Great Seal of Scotland*, except for the earliest forms of Crosbie near West Kilbride, which are taken from Johnston's dictionary.

Literature

Barrow, G.W.S., 1998: 'The Uses of Place-Names and Scottish History: Pointers and Pitfalls'. In: S. Taylor (ed.), *The Uses of Place-Names*. Edinburgh, 54-74.

Crawford, B.E., 1987: *Scandinavian Scotland*. Scotland in the Early Middle Ages 2. Leicester.

Crawford, B.E., 1995: *Earl and Mormaer: Norse-Pictish Relationships in Northern Scotland*. Rosemarkie.

Fellows-Jensen, G., 1984: 'Viking Settlement in the Northern and Western Isles – The Place-Name Evidence as Seen from Denmark and the Danelaw'. In: A. Fenton & H. Pálsson (eds), *The Northern and Western Isles in the Viking World: Survival, Continuity and Change*. Edinburgh, 148-168.

Fellows-Jensen, G., 1989-1990: 'Scandinavians in Southern Scotland?', *Nomina* 13, 41-60.

Fellows-Jensen, G., 1991: 'Scandinavians in Dumfriesshire and Galloway: The Place-Name Evidence'. In: R.D. Oram & G.P. Stell (eds), *Galloway: Land and Lordship*. Edinburgh, 77-95.

Fellows-Jensen, G., 2000: 'Vikings in the British Isles: The Place-Name Evidence', *Acta Archaeologica* 71, 135-146.

Fraser, I.A., 2000: *The Place-Names of Arran*. Glasgow.

Gordon, B., 1965: 'Some Norse Place-Names in Trotternish, Isle of Skye', *Scottish Gaelic Studies* 10, 82-112.

Graham-Campbell, J. & Batey, C., 1998: *Vikings in Scotland: An Archaeological Survey*. Edinburgh.

Hanks, P. & Hodges, F., 1988: *A Dictionary of Surnames*. Oxford.

Jennings, A., 2004: 'Norse Place-Names of Kintyre'. In: J. Adams & K. Holman (eds), *Scandinavia and Europe 800-1350: Contact, Conflict and Coexistence*. Turnhout, 109-119.

Johnston, J.B., 1934: *Place-Names of Scotland*, 3rd edition. London.

Kruse, A., 2004: 'Norse Topographical Settlement Names on the Western Littoral of Scotland'. In: J. Adams & K. Holman (eds), *Scandinavia and Europe 800-1350: Contact, Conflict and Coexistence*. Turnhout, 97-107.

Lynch, M., 1991: *Scotland: A New History*. London.

Nicolaisen, W.F.H., 1960: 'Norse Place-Names in South-West Scotland', *Scottish Studies* 4, 49-70.

Nicolaisen, W.F.H., 1992: 'Arran Place-Names: A Fresh Look', *Northern Studies* 28, 1-13.

Nicolaisen, W.F.H., 2001: *Scottish Place-Names: Their Study and Significance*, new edition. Edinburgh.

Oram, R., 1995: 'Scandinavian Settlement in South-West Scotland with a Special Study of Bysbie'. In: B.E. Crawford (ed.), *Scandinavian Settlement in Northern Britain*. London/New York, 127-140.

Ritchie, A., 1993: *Viking Scotland*. London.

Thomson, J.M., Stevenson, J.H., Dickson, W.K. & Paul, J.B., 1882-1912: *The Register of the Great Seal of Scotland*. Edinburgh.

Waugh, D., 2000: 'A Scatter of Norse Names in Strathnaver', In: J.R. Baldwin (ed.), *The Province of Strathnaver*. Golspie, Strathnaver, 13-23.

Explorers, Raiders and Settlers. The Norse Impact upon Hebridean Place-Names

Arne Kruse

This article is a discussion about how the Norse during the Viking period related to the native peoples in the west of Scotland and how this relationship impinged on the Norse naming of their new land. It will assert that the earliest Norse contact phase resulted in the creation of certain island names through actual communication with the local population. However, it is likely that this contact situation did not last very long, and it was rapidly followed by blanket Norse naming, which paid no regard to the previous naming tradition. The discussion will then develop the proposition that the Norse met two different ethnic groups in the islands and that this pre-Norse ethnic divide might help to explain some place-name patterns on the west coast of Scotland.

1. Some island names

There is a general consensus concerning the intensity of the Norseness of the place-names of Shetland and Orkney. It is agreed that the Norse almost totally re-named the islands. The only name which reflects a pre-Norse onomasticon for certain is Orkney, recorded as *Orchades* by Diodurus Siculus in the first century BC, and echoed by Pliny, who calls the islands *Orcades*. The name is reflected in Old Irish as *Insi Orc*. It is also more or less agreed that the three northernmost islands on Shetland, Unst, Yell and Fetlar, may be based upon pre-Norse names. For the large northern Hebridean island Skye, we have both the Latin *Sketis nesos*, Ptolemy, 2nd century AD, and the Old Irish *Sci* and *Sceth*, and it is obvious that the Old Norse *Skíð* is a phonological adaptation of this (and actually, thanks to a shared Indo-European origin, both the Old Irish and the Old Norse name carry the semantic content 'split', originally most likely to refer to the long inlets in the western part of the island).

141

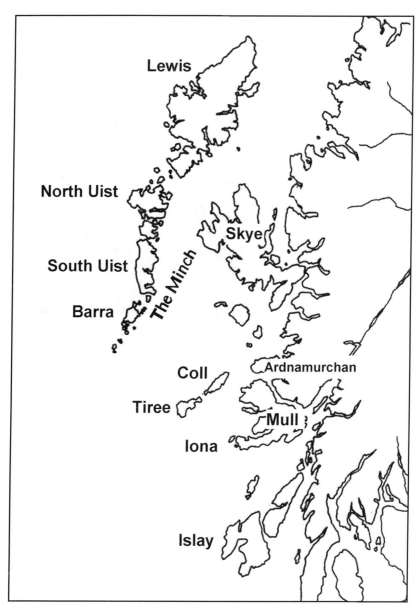

Figure 1. A map of the west coast of Scotland, with locations mentioned in the text.

Although there are no recorded pre-Norse names of the largest islands in the Outer Hebrides, Lewis and Uist, their Old Norse names *Ljóðhús* and *Ívist* are also likely candidates for having been transformed into Norse from a pre-Norse language. For island names their semantic content is highly suspicious, respectively meaning 'house of people' and 'in-dwelling'. Together with Unst, Yell and Fetlar, these islands stand out from the rest, not only for their northern location within their respective groups of islands, but also because their names are typologically different from other Norse island names. They are unusual because they are all among the very few island names in the Norse colonies without the generic *-ey*, and semantically they are atypical because they do not have a content which instantly relates the island to a location, shape or ownership in the form of a personal name. In fact, their meanings are obscure – which is somewhat unusual, as island names in the Norse colonies are largely fairly transparent. The island names in question strongly hint at native originals which have been squeezed into Norse phonology and 'meanings' that may be easy to memorise although they do not really refer to anything characteristic about the location. The names stand out as the likely products of an initial meeting of peoples, probably coined at a very early contact phase by explorers or maybe early raiders from the north, eager to determine the northernmost and therefore the first important points of reference they arrived at by establishing the names of the largest islands from the local population.

From other parts of the world there are many examples of other types of expeditions registering names in a similar way. We can think of Spanish explorers in Latin America and French and British trappers and map-makers in North America, all of them registered the Native American names of tribal areas and important natural features. This is how names like Andes, Iowa and Mississippi have made it onto modern maps. Old Norse names from elsewhere have a similar origin. During expeditionary raids the Vikings for example picked up the French river-names Seine and Loire and adapted them to Scandinavian pronunciation in the forms *Signa* and *Leira*. Likewise, the Mediterranean island-names Sicily and Cyprus were referred to as *Sikiley* and *Kípr*. (This is at least how the names turn up in Snorri Sturluson's 13th century *Heimskringla*.)

Although there is no certain historical, linguistic or archaeological evidence for pre-Viking trade between Scotland and Norway, it does not eliminate the possibility that it happened, and naming important features from native originals would naturally have taken place within such a setting. The other possibility is organised expeditions at an early stage in the Viking period, and, without entering this discussion, it is evident that scholars are increasingly abandoning the idea of small, spontaneous raiding bands of Vikings in favour of the idea that the Viking advance was a set of highly organised ventures (Stylegar 2004: 5-30).

2. Settlement names and nature names on the Western Isles

Contrary to the names of the large islands, the other Norse names in the islands are typologically and semantically remarkably ordinary, and although it is impossible to be entirely certain that there do not exist other names coined in the early Norse period as translations or phonological adaptations from a previous language – it is clear that they are well within the frame of what one would expect to find in a Norse colony. There is in principle no difference between nature names and settlement names in the Western Isles and similar names on the Faroe Islands or Iceland, where there was no population prior to the arrival of the Norse.

As stated, there is no dispute about the completeness of the Norse onomasticon in Shetland and Orkney (apart from, of course, the later Scots names). The situation in the Hebrides is not quite so straightforward, but when it comes to the Western Isles most scholars do accept that there was more or less a clean break with the arrival of the Norse – again with the exception of the names of some of the islands. George Henderson (1910: 185) was the first important scholar to postulate that there must have been a clear-cut linguistic break. Nearly all place-name scholars after Henderson have confirmed this amazing discontinuity with what must have existed in the Western Isles before the arrival of the Norse. (I refer to scholarly work by A. MacBain (1922: 70), W.J. Watson (1926: 38-39), I. Fraser (1974: 18-19; 1984: 40), and A.-B. Stahl (1999: 365). G. Fellows-Jensen (1984: 151) seems to be in two minds but suggests that a Gaelic-speaking presence is likely to have survived since it was finally able to absorb the Norse element in the population.

There is an important counter-claim to the dominant view. A detailed study of the names of central western Lewis was carried out by Richard Cox (1987) and his conclusion is that a substantial amount of the place-names of Lewis appear to be of a pre-Norse date (Cox 1991). As a result, he strongly supports the idea that the Gaelic language spoken on the island before the arrival of the Norse survived throughout the Norse period. This work is important because it is one of the very few in-depth studies of place-names in the Western Isles and also because his conclusions contradict all other studies on the onomastics in the area. It is appropriate therefore to scrutinise his work in some detail.

Before Cox, Magne Oftedal (1962: 48-49) showed that place-names can contain the evidence to pinpoint where the settlers came from in Norway. He points to the names [tãũNəraj], containing ON *hafn*, and [tamànəvaɣ] containing ON *hamn* (both 'harbour') on opposite sides of Lewis. The difference reflects a dialectal difference in Norway, where the consonant group *fn* was assimilated to *mn* in the northern part of Western Norway but not in the southern part. Although the assimilated *mn* is younger than *fn*, Oftedal does not claim this to be as evidence for any early or late 'freezing' of the names into Gaelic. Oftedal also discussed how Norse names could be shown to have been borrowed into Gaelic at different times, illustrated by two names on opposite sides of Benbecula, the name [sdãiN´əvaL] which Oftedal (1962: 48) says is 'evidently from early O.N. *Staina-fjall* "mountain of the stones"', and [elaN´ˈʃd´eiʃaj] 'from O.N. *Steins-øy* "island of the stone"'. He continues:

> The first name must have been adopted in its older form, as witness the initial cluster of 'broad' consonants. The second name must have entered Gaelic after the raising of the diphthong from *ai* to *æi* or *ei*, which took place in the Viking ages (at different times in the various dialects), because the initial consonant cluster is 'slender'. If I stress the importance of the consonants here it is because they are much more reliable evidence than the vowels, which are much more exposed to changes. In cases like this it is possible to establish a relative chronology.

Surely, Oftedal is right about the relative chronology concerning these two names based on the surviving consonants in the names. However, he makes an unnecessary shortcut when he states that the first name is 'evidently from early O.N.' because of the diphthong *ai*. He states that the raising to *æi* or *ei* happened during the Viking age at different times in the various dialects but fails to mention that this raising never happened and remains *ai* in many west Norwegian dialects, such as in Hardanger, Voss and Sogn (Beito 1973: 278-306).

Both the assimilation of *fn* and the raising of *ai* reflect dialectal differences actually still evident in Norway and her former colonies. As such, the variations could have been transferred at any time from Norway or they could represent dialectal differences in the Norse spoken locally in the Hebrides.

Richard Cox (1991: 485) repeats Oftedal's point about diphthongs:
There are several forms which clearly belong to the earliest
strata of loan-words, and which can be ascribed to the 8th
century, e.g. *aoidh* 'ford, isthmus' ON **aið* later *eið*; *Rostainn*
with ON **stainn* later *steinn* 'rock, stone'; the personal-names
Uisdean ON **Aystein*, acc. later *Øysteinn*, and *Amhlaigh* ON
*Āleif acc. later *Ólaf*.

Cox obviously believes these are examples of early Scandinavian diphthongs
which have been 'frozen' and preserved in Gaelic phonology before they
developed into the 'classic' ON diphthongs *ei/æi* and *ey/øy*. His discovery of
these forms is interesting, however, rather than being evidence for the
survival of Gaelic through the Norse period, they may indicate where in
Norway the settlers came from, or possibly variations in Hebridean Norn.

Cox (op.cit.) further uses a group of names of the type *Steinn Langa*,
with noun+qualifier structure, normally associated with Gaelic word-order,
as evidence for the survival of Proto-Scandinavian in the Gaelic
nomenclature of Lewis. Such an assumption is problematic because this
morphosyntactic structure is typically found in so-called noa-names (to avoid
naming-taboo, especially used by fishermen) in Scandinavia as well as all
over the Norse expansion area, including Iceland which was settled after the
transition from Proto-Scandinavian to Common Scandinavian is normally
considered to have happened. The structure is also found in other types of
names in the Norse colonies, e.g. in Orkney. According to Berit Sandnes
(2003: 294-307), the survival of noun+qualifier names in Orkney indicates
the conservative nature of Orkney Norn, as the structure seems to have been
productive much longer there than in Norway, where this particular word
order in names is hardly seen after 1400. We know next to nothing about
Hebridean Norn, but it would not be surprising if the Hebridean variation of
Norn could be shown to be linguistically conservative in a similar way. The
point to be made here is that the survival of this structure in other parts of the
Norse colonies makes it difficult to use noun+qualifier word order as
evidence for 'frozen' Proto-Scandinavian in Lewis.

Cox's advocacy of a pre-Norse Gaelic presence in Lewis may suffer
from a major flaw; he has not been able to provide evidence for any Gaelic
place-names incorporated in Norse names. There does not seem to be any
names such as **Benmor+vatn* or **Tarbert+vík*. This is what one might
expect to find when colonisers settle amongst people they communicate with;
that the Norse would have adopted parts of the native nomenclature, at least

for the most important natural features and settlements, and integrated them into their own onomasticon. This does not seem to have happened on Lewis, nor on Barra, where a similarly detailed study has been carried out (Stahl 1999).

This situation is significant, as it links the nomenclature of the Western Isles to that of the Northern Isles. In both places we know there were settlements when the Norse arrived but there is no evidence in the onomasticon that the inhabitants of these settlements ever existed. No names, apart from the few aforesaid major island names, provide evidence of anything pre-Norse. Although perhaps not the only possible scenario behind an onomastic change of this magnitude, the most obvious one is ethnic discontinuity; it happens when one population is replaced by another.

In contrast to this situation, the many hybrid Norse-Gaelic names in the west of Scotland – where Norse place-names have been adorned with Gaelic tautological additions, of the type Loch Langavat and Ben Tangaval – were obviously created at a later stage when Gaelic had replaced Norse to such a degree that the Norse names were no longer meaningful. This process, along with the survival of the thousands of other Norse names transferred into the medium of Gaelic, constitute clear evidence that when Gaelic eventually replaced Norse in the west of Scotland it was a replacement of language, not of people.

When it comes to the local place-names in the Inner Hebrides and the west coast littoral – the names of settlements, headlands, skerries, glens, hills and burns – we are still waiting for equally thorough investigations as those done on Lewis (Cox 1987, 2002) and Barra (Stahl 1999), and nothing definite can be said about this topic before such in-depth studies are carried out. However, research done on the settlement patterns of Wester Ross (Fraser 1995) and of Coll and Tiree (Johnston 1995) strongly suggests a similar blanket Norse settlement familiar from the Western Isles, while Jennings (2004) puts forward a more clustered Gaelic/Norse settlement distribution in Kintyre, further south.

Although the west coast littoral and the Inner Isles today show a percentage of Norse settlement and nature names that is lower than that found in the Outer Isles, it does not necessarily indicate the degree of intensity of the initial Norse settlement. It could equally well be an indication of how early Gaelic replaced Norse as the dominant language in the various regions in the west. Again, in-depth studies might in the future reveal secrets about the intricacies of the relationship between place-names and language shift on the local level (an example of such a study from Orkney is Sandnes 2003).

3. Picts and Gaels on the west coast of Scotland

It is of course reflected in today's place-names that Norse was succeeded by Gaelic in the Western Isles, and at an earlier stage than Scots took over on the Northern Isles. Otherwise, the Norse nomenclature of the Western Isles is very similar to that of Orkney and Shetland, both typologically and in terms of completeness. One tempting explanation for this similarity is that the Norse might have met the same people in these groups of islands and that the Norse therefore interacted (or not) with the natives in the same way in all these islands. The following will be a discussion on this subject and on how a possible Pictish/Gaelic divide along the Minch[1] could explain a few cultural divides and linguistic isoglosses that are still evident today.

Leslie Alcock (1971) coined the term 'Peripheral Picts' to describe the pre-Norse inhabitants of the Western Isles, to indicate both the distinctiveness in their use of pottery and lack of imported wares, as well as a link with the Pictish Mainland. The distribution of pottery production is particularly distinctive, showing the Western Isles and Skye as long-standing producers of pottery, in sharp contrast to the surrounding areas (Lane 1983). There is support for the Western Isles and Skye being culturally different from the rest of the Hebrides in a knife inscribed with Pictish ogham discovered on Vallay, North Uist, and five Pictish Class I symbol stones from Skye as well as two from the Western Isles. (See further discussion in Fisher 2001: 11-12.)

The distribution pattern of the brochs is similar to that of the Pictish stones. Apart from one broch registered on Islay and two on the northernmost tip of Mull, all brochs are found north of the southern Minch, telling us that there might have been a cultural divide here well in advance of the historical Picts. Many broch sites were inhabited through the Pictish period up to 800 AD – at the time of the arrival of the Vikings – when there is a sudden abandonment (Armit 1996: 202; Sharples and Parker Pearson 1999: 48; Gilmour and Harding 2000).

Archaeology appears to point strongly to a Pictish-linked material culture north of the Minch and in this context it is slightly worrying that there are onomasticians who seem to take pre-Norse Gaelic for granted and not even consider the possibility that the language in the Western Isles and Skye around the arrival of the Vikings could have been anything other than Gaelic.

Admittedly, the linguistic situation in the west of Scotland in the late 8th century is hard to make out. One can be sure that Gaelic was spoken in the kingdom of Dál Riata, by then stretching from the Mull of Kintyre to Ardnamurchan, including Tiree and Coll. The language spoken north of this

Arne Kruse

area, in Skye and the Outer Hebrides, is not certain but it is as likely to have been a variation of the old P-Celtic spoken by all other pre-Gaelic Celtic tribes of Scotland as Gaelic. It could well be that Gaelic was starting to gain ground in the Outer Hebrides and Skye as a prestigious language or maybe a language attached to trade or to Christian activity directed from Iona. In Adamnan's *Life of Columba* (Book I, chapter 33) we hear that Columba, while on Skye, baptized *primarius Geonae cohortis* 'leader of the *Geona* band'. It is not clear what people this tribe is meant to belong to but what is interesting, however, is that Columba at this occasion needed an interpreter.

Even if the Gaelic language had started to make advances northwards, it is difficult to believe that by the time of the arrival of the Vikings P-Celtic was wiped out on Skye and the Western Isles, down to the level of a complete change in the onomasticon. For such a dramatic shift to have happened one must envisage an ethnic change; in practice it implies that Gaels from Dál Riata would have replaced the native Picts. Such a development is problematic because the Outer Isles and Skye are never mentioned as part of the Scots' sphere of interest. Iona is the provider of information on matters concerning Dál Riata and it is striking how the sources from Iona are completely silent about the stretch of islands on the horizon to the west. During the 7th and 8th centuries the kingdom of Dál Riata was oriented south and westwards in such a way that there seems to have been a significant cultural divide in the southern part of the Minch.

There is a series of entries in the *Annals of Ulster* which reinforce the impression that Skye was in the Pictish political sphere:

U668.3 nauigatio filiorum Gartnaidh ad Hiberniam cum plebe Sceth
[The voyage of the sons of Gartnait to Ireland with the people of Skye.]
U670.4 Uenit genus Gartnaith de Hibernia
[The sept of Gartnait came back from Ireland.]
U688.2 Occisio Canonn filii Gartnaidh
[The slaying of Cano son of Gartnait.]

Garnait is a name with definite Pictish associations (Binchy 1963: xviii). It occurs several times in the Pictish King Lists. Indeed this Garnait may have been a king of the Picts. The Pictish king Bruide son of Maelchon, who died in 586, was succeeded by Gartnait son of Domelach (Bannerman 1974: 92-94), who, it has been suggested, was the son of Aedán mac Gabráin, king of

149

Explorers, Raiders and Settlers

Dál Ríata, Domelach being his Pictish mother (op.cit.: 93-94). However, there are chronological difficulties. The historical content of these annals is obscure; were the sons of Garnait driven from Skye, and if so, by whom? Why did they return? Who slew Cano, the eponymous hero of the 9th century Irish tale *Scéla Cano Meic Gartnáin* (Binchy 1963)? This saga describes conflict between Aedán mac Gabráin and Cano, which although chronologically impossible might reflect conflict between Dál Ríata and Skye in the second half of the 7th century.[2]

Although they are far from contemporary to this period and therefore must be used with care, the Norse written sources appear to support a divide along the Minch. In Hermann Pálsson and Paul Edward's English translation of the *Orkneyinga saga* (ch. 41, p. 86) the name *Skottlandsfjörðr* is rendered 'the Minch'. From the context in the saga this makes sense, and this name is likely to imply that, seen from the Western Isles, the Norse located the Gaelic-speaking *Scots* to the south-east of the Minch, just as, from Orkney, the name *Péttlandsfjörðr* (*Orkneyinga saga*, chs 25-29) refers to the *Picts* across the firth on the northern Mainland of Scotland. *Skottlandsfirðir*, in plural, is used in *Magnus saga berrfætt* (chs 8, 11) to describe where Magnus' men rowed in order to claim the islands of the Hebrides to the Norwegian crown. The generic here probably refers both to 'sealochs' and to 'sounds', the latter as in *Skottlandsfjörðr* and *Péttlandsfjörðr* – a meaning of *fjörðr* also found in Norwegian names. The specific in this case refers to the location of these sealochs and sounds, which is 'the land of the *Scots*'. *Skottlandsfirðir* is more an appellative than a place-name, and similar appellatives are still used in Norwegian in e.g. *vestlandsfjordane* or *finnmarksfjordane*, respectively 'the firths of Vestlandet' and 'the firths of Finnmark'. However, the usage in the sagas of both the name *Skottlandsfjörðr* and the appellative s*kottlandsfirðir* indicate that 'the land of the Scots' is to the south-east of the Western Isles.

A group of names with an intriguing distribution pattern is that with the element *pap*, found in Iceland, the Faroes, and the Northern and Western Isles and Skye. It is more or less agreed that this group of names dates back to the earliest period of Viking activity and that the Old Norse term *papi* m., is a likely borrowing from Old Irish (cf. a review article by Peder Gammeltoft (2004: 31-49)). However, seen purely from the distribution pattern, which, I have argued, is not likely to include any Gaelic-speaking area, there is reason to believe that the term could just as well be a Norse borrowing from Pictish.

There is no need here to speculate any further about the distribution pattern of the *Pap*-names. The importance in this context is that it implies that

150

the southern Minch constitutes a southern limit of some sort of Norse interaction or experience with people they related to.

It is remarkable that in the Northern and Western Isles more than 30 place-names refer to what must surely have been only a relatively small number of *Papar*, while the Norse do not refer to *Picts* in more than one early name, *Péttland*, found in secondary names as Pentland Skerries and Pentland Firth, indirectly referring to 'the land of the *Picts*' as the northern and eastern parts of the Mainland of Scotland at the time of the Norse colonisation (op.cit.). Considering names in England like Walsingham, Normanby and Denby – denoting farms of Welsh, Norwegian and Danish settlers within predominantly English, Danish and Norwegian settlements respectively – one would have expected the Norse settlers in the Northern and Western Isles to refer to their Pictish neighbours in settlement names. The fact that **Petbœr*, **Petaskaill* or **Petabus* are non-existent names tells us either that Pictish settlements were so frequent in the Norse colonies that naming them would not have constituted specific enough denotations to function well as place-names, or that Picts for some reason or other did not establish themselves on independent settlement units within the Norse-dominated community. One further explanation, which is going to be explored in the following, would simply be that there were no longer any Picts there.

4. What happened to the natives?

If the Western Isles were ethnically/linguistically Pictish at the beginning of the Viking Age, we would expect to find a Pictish or P-Celtic stratum in the Norse names, but such a stratum has not been identified. There appears to be a total absence of names containing P-Celtic elements like *aber*, *pren* or *pert*. This absence means there is no obvious linguistic link between the Iron Age and the modern populations of the Western Isles. This is significant and difficult to explain if a native population, in some form or other, survived the Norse impact.

The newest archaeological discoveries from the Western Isles relating to the native/Norse interface have not come up with convincing evidence for the survival of a pre-Norse culture. On the contrary, the new work done on buildings, pottery, graves and environmental studies appears to indicate that there must have been a fundamental change around 800AD, so fundamental that the most satisfying explanation is an ethnic replacement (cf. Jennings and Kruse 2005, forthcoming).

Brian Smith (2001) suggests that the native Pictish population in the Northern Isles was killed by the Norse. If we also allow for the possibility that they were taken away as slaves or that they fled to the Mainland as a result of repeated attacks and raids by the Norse, it is possible that the scenario Smith suggests in the Northern Isles could be extended to the Western Isles. We should not forget that these are all islands with no hinterland to escape to. The population is exposed and would have been vulnerable to raids by pirates after goods, food supplies and slaves. It is easy to envisage the intense insecurity suffered by the locals in such a situation, especially if it stretched over several years, and it is likely that the raiding period did involve years of disruption for the local population before the Norse became involved in a phase of settlement (Crawford 1987: 40).

One could argue that it does not make economical sense to deprive an area of future slaves in such a way, but it could be that several years of raids would have left the islands so empty that when the Norse started to settle, they would have had to import slaves from elsewhere. In other words, the Norse settlers to the Northern and Western Isles may have been accompanied by Gaels, presumably as slaves and wives, imported from Ireland and maybe the Inner Hebrides. This is what we see in the other Norse colonies, and the presence of imported slaves could have been just as high in the Norse areas of Scotland as say, in Iceland, where, today, the mitochondrial DNA shows that more than half of the Icelandic female ancestresses must have been of Celtic origin (Helgason *et al.* 2001).

Figure 2. Slave-taking on the west coast of Scotland? 9th or possibly early 10th century illustration on a stone from a chapel site at Inchmarnock, Bute. Copyright Headland Archaeology, Edinburgh.

The presence of Gaels at an early date in the Western Isles may be corroborated by the onomastic record. In his most recent publication, Richard Cox (2002) who until recently has advocated pre-Norse linguistic survival, appears to have revised his position. He now concludes that there are no certain pre-Norse names in the area of the Carloway Registry of Lewis, but that there are Gaelic names dateable to the period prior to the Scottish annexation of the Hebrides in 1266, and indeed, there is evidence of 'a continuous Gaelic-speaking presence during the Norse period' (op.cit.: 118). Though it is regrettable that he doesn't discuss the matter any further, this statement is intrinsically reasonable, because it confirms what the archaeological data strongly suggest, namely that there was a clean break with the past, and that there may have been a Gaelic presence from quite early on in the Norse period. For example, when analysing the pottery from the Western Isles Alan Lane (1983: 379) finds the changes in both style and technique around 800 AD to be so sudden and fundamental that he pronounces the new pottery must have been made by new potters. He further suggests that the new potters are likely to have come from Co. Antrim in Ireland where there are close parallels in time and style to the pottery found from c.800 in the Western Isles (see further discussion in Jennings and Kruse 2005, forthcoming).

5. The other Hebridean island names

As with the island groups further north, most names of islands in the Inner Hebrides are Norse coinages: Jura, Gigha, Colonsay, Staffa, etc. Similarly, island names are found which are known to be of pre-Norse origin. Mull has developed from *Malaios*, recorded by Ptolemy in the 2nd century AD, and Islay was recorded as *Ili* in 568 AD. However, the island names in the Inner Hebrides are in one way different in that many of the modern names seem to have developed from a pre-Norse Gaelic tradition and not via Norse. The Norse name for Mull, *Mýl*, doesn't seem to be what the modern Gaelic name *Muile* is based on. Iona, in Norse *Eyin helga*, carried parallel names in Gaelic and Norse, but only the former has survived. Tiree has the modern Gaelic forms *Tireadh* and *Tir-idhe* that does not seem to have developed from Norse *Tyrvist* (although the Norse name is reflected in the expression *Tiristeach* 'Tiree man') (Watson 1926: ch.III).

This difference in the genealogy of the island names on the west coast may be another reflection of the Pictish/Gaelic division. The user-group for macronyms like island names will typically include administrative institutions like the church, and it will include neighbours on the other islands and the adjacent mainland, who will need to refer to the islands. The reason why the island names north of the Minch are passed down through a Norse tradition can be explained by the collapse of the Pictish neighbourhood to the islands. Although there is a lot of uncertainty around the amalgamation of the Scottish and the Pictish kingdoms in the 9th century, the event eventually resulted in the demise of the Pictish language as well as the Pictish church and other institutions. Such institutions are the likely prerequisites for keeping alive a macronym tradition, and if they did disappear it could have seriously undermined, for example, a pre-Norse name tradition supported by the organisation of the Pictish church in the north-west of Scotland. In addition, the Norse impact in the form of settlement on the adjacent mainland to the Western Isles and Skye is likely to have been so comprehensive that it eliminated a pre-Norse neighbourhood user-group for the island names. There is good reason to believe that the thin coastal strip of land available for settlement on the west mainland of Scotland, which leans on the 'Spine of Britain', the long and broad mountain chain that separates west from east, was at one time essentially Norse (Kruse 2004).

Further south, Norse may also for a time have been overwhelmingly dominant. However, Gaelic would have continued to be spoken in an unbroken tradition perhaps on the Inner Hebrides but certainly in Ireland and on the Scottish Mainland. This continuity would have kept alive the pre-Norse names of some of the main islands of the Inner Hebrides. When Norse eventually died out in the Western Isles and Skye, what took over was not the old pre-Norse native language of the area, but rather a new language, Gaelic, first spoken in this area by people who had been there only as long as the Norse had and who owed their presence there to the Norse.

Literature

Adomnán of Iona: *Life of St Columba*. Transl. by Richard Sharpe. London 1995.

Alcock, L., 1971: *Arthur's Britain: History and Archaeology*. London.

Armit, I., 1996: *The archaeology of Skye and the Western Isles*. Edinburgh.

Bannerman, J., 1974: *Studies in the History of Dalriada*. Edinburgh/London.

Beito, O., 1973: *Norske målføretekster*, Skrifter frå Norsk målførearkiv XVIII. Oslo.

Binchy, D.A., 1963: *Scéla Cano Meic Gartnáin*. Dublin.

Cox, R.A.V., 1987: *Place-Names of the Carloway Registry, Isle of Lewis*. Unpublished Ph.D. thesis, University of Glasgow. Glasgow.

Cox, R.A.V., 1991: 'Norse-Gaelic Contact in the West of Lewis: The Place-Name Evidence.' In: P.S. Ureland & G. Broderick (eds), *Language Contact in the British Isles: Eighth International Symposium on Language Contact in Europe, Douglas, Isle of Man, 1988*. Tübingen, 479-493.

Cox, R.A.V., 2002: *The Gaelic Place-Names of Carloway, Isle of Lewis. Their Structure and Significance*. Dublin.

Crawford, B.E., 1987: *Scandinavian Scotland*. Scotland in the Early Middle Ages 2. Leicester.

Fellows-Jensen, G., 1984: 'Viking Settlement in the Northern and Western Isles – the Place-Name Evidence as seen from Denmark and the Danelaw.' In: A. Fenton & H. Pálsson (eds), *The Northern and Western Isles in the Viking World: Survival, Continuity and Change*. Edinburgh, 148-168.

Fisher, I., 2001: *Early Medieval Sculpture in the West Highlands and Island*. Edinburgh.

Fraser, I.A., 1974: 'The Place Names of Lewis – The Norse Evidence', *Northern Studies* 4, 11-21.

Fraser, I.A., 1984: 'Some Further Thoughts on Scandinavian Place-Names in Lewis', *Northern Studies* 21, 34-41.

Fraser, I.A, 1995: 'Norse Settlement on the North-West Seaboard'. In: B.E. Crawford (ed.), *Scandinavian Settlement in Northern Britain*. London/New York, 92-105.

Gammeltoft, P., 2004: 'Among *Dímons* and *Papeys*: What Kind of Contact do the Names Really Point to?', *Northern Studies* 38, 31-49.

Gilmour, S. & Harding, D., 2000: *The Iron Age Settlement at Beirgh, Riof, Isle of Lewis: Excavations 1985-95*. 1. *The Structures and Stratigraphy*. Edinburgh.

Helgason, A., Hickey, E., Goodacre, S., Bosnes, V., Stefansson, K., Ward, R. & Sykes B., 2001: 'mtDNA and the Islands of the North Atlantic: Estimation the Proportions of Norse and Gaelic Ancestry', *American Journal of Human Genetics*, 68(3), 723-737.

Henderson, G., 1910: *The Norse Influence on Celtic Scotland*. Glasgow.

Jennings, A., 2004: 'Norse Place-Names of Kintyre'. In: K. Holman & J. Adams (eds), Scandinavia and Europe 800-1350: Contact, Conflict, and Coexistence. Turnhout, 109-119.

Jennings, A. & Kruse, A., 2005 (forthcoming): 'An Ethnic Enigma – Norse, Pict and

Gael in the Western Isles'. In: A. Mortensen & S.V. Arge (eds), *Viking and Norse North Atlantic, Select Papers from the Proceedings of the Fourteenth Viking Congress, Tórshavn, 19-30 July 2001.* Tórshavn.

Johnston, A., 1995: 'Norse Settlement Patterns in Coll and Tiree'. In: B.E. Crawford (ed.), *Scandinavian Settlement in Northern Britain.* London/New York, 108-126.

Kruse, A., 2004: 'Norse Topographical Settlement Names on the Western Littoral of Scotland'. In: J. Adams & K. Holman (eds), *Scandinavia and Europe 800-1350: Contact, Conflict and Coexistence.* Turnhout, 97-107.

MacBain, A., 1922: *Place-Names of the Highlands and Islands of Scotland.* Stirling.

Oftedal, M., 1962: 'Norse Place-Names in Celtic Scotland', *Proceeding of the International Congress of Celtic Studies, Dublin 1959.* Dublin, 43-50.

Orkneyinga Saga. The History of the Earls of Orkney. Translated by H. Pálsson & P. Edwards. London, 1978.

Rivet, A.L.F. & Smith C., 1979: *The Place Names of Roman Britain.* London.

Sandnes, B., 2003: *Fra Starafjall til Starling Hill. Dannelse og utvikling av norrøne stedsnavn på Orknøyene.* Dr.art.-avhandling, Norges teknisk-naturvitenskapelige universitet. Trondheim.

Sharples, N.M. & Parker Pearson, M., 1999: 'Norse Settlement on the Outer Hebrides', *Norwegian Archaeological Review* 32, 41-62.

Smith, B., 2001: 'The Picts and the Martyrs or Did Vikings Kill the Native Population of Orkney and Shetland?', *Northern Studies* 36, 7-32.

Stahl, A-B., 1999: *Place-Names of Barra in the Outer Hebrides.* Unpublished Ph.D. thesis, University of Edinburgh. Edinburgh.

Stylegar, F.-A. 2004: '"Central places" in Viking Age Orkney', *Northern Studies* 38, 5-30.

Watson, W.J., 1926: *The History of the Celtic Place-Names of Scotland.* Edinburgh.

Notes

[1] In want of a more precise name, the name Minch here is meant to refer to what really is the southern part of the Minch, namely the wide stretch of water between Ardnamurchan, Coll and Tiree in the south-east and Barra and Uist in the north-west. Unconventionally, Skye will in this article be north of the Minch, as the name is used here. The point is to cluster the Western Isles and Skye into a geographical unit separated from the rest of the Hebrides by a large stretch of exposed sea. Because too little is known about the nomenclatures of Canna, Rum, Eigg and Muck, these islands are in this study unfortunately left in a limbo (although a cross from Eigg has 'strong Pictish connections' (Fisher 2001: 94)).

[2] I am grateful to Andrew Jennings who has pointed to these passages in the Irish sources.

Shetland *Mead* Names – Some Notes on their Structure and Character

Gunnel Melchers

1. Introduction

The word *mead* (*meed*, *meid*, *meith*, *methe*, *meath*, *mi(d)*, *me(d)*) (forms listed by the *Concise Scots Dictionary* and Jakobsen (1928-1932)), Norwegian *méd*, Swedish *me(d)* (western part of Sweden only) is etymologically complex, if not dubious. It may be related to Scandinavian *med(e)* 'the runner of a sleigh or toboggan', but is beyond doubt derived from ON *mið* n., 'a fishing-bank marked by landmarks'. It has also been associated with Latin *meta* 'a turning-point, a prominent, protruding place' (cf. ME *mithe* 'indicate'). On the other hand, Kruse (2000: 55), quoting Hovda 1961, relates it to Latin *medius*, interpreting it as 'that which is in the middle', i.e. the intersection of two bearings. According to the *English Dialect Dictionary* the word is not found in the traditional dialects of England (it is included but the provenance is given as Scotland only; cf. Widdowson 1972, however, quoted below). In his dictionary of the Scandinavian element in the Shetland dialect, Jakobsen states that the word may refer to a fishing-ground as well as a landmark taken in sight when finding a fishing-ground, when two or more marks, mostly prominent pieces of land, are brought in a certain relation to each other. This paper focuses on the latter, secondary (cf. Kruse 2000: 56) significance of the word. To complement the lexicological definitions it should be pointed out that meads are also employed for positioning at sea in general, i.e. not necessarily related to fishing.

The designations of meads and fishing-grounds are currently being collected on a massive scale within the framework of the Shetland Place Names Project, as reported by Eileen Brooke-Freeman in another contribution to this volume. These designations are viewed as having great biological as well as historical significance and are given a certain priority in the fieldwork ('a rescue operation'). The general purpose is in line with the overall aim of the project, i.e. the actual localisation of place-names in Shetland. With regard to the collection of mead names in particular, it is explicitly stated in the project's preliminary notes and instructions to fieldworkers that it includes an interest in the actual fishing activities and the locations of the fishing-grounds. An unpublished collection, entitled *Shetland*

Amenity Trust: Meeds Project, kindly placed at my disposal for the purpose of this paper, indicates that it is, in fact, the fishing-grounds that constitute the core or framework of the collection. In spite of the project's title, the meads are secondary, listed and described to a varying degree in connection with each fishing-ground. Incidentally, this is also the framework used by Jakobsen in his work on place-names (cf. Jakobsen 1936: 248f.), where he focuses on the names of fishing grounds and lexical items constituting elements in the designations of meads. The relationship between fishing-ground and mead can be further illustrated by expressions such as 'the southwest edge [of a fishing-ground] *was meided by* two houses at Underhoull' (quoted from the Amenity Trust project). According to the project report, the function of the meads could be 'cardinal', i.e. indicating the exact position of a fishing-ground or 'limiting' the area suitable for fishing. The herring meads, in particular, are characterized by 'a cardinally-based positioning system of considerable ingenuity' (quoted from the Amenity Trust project).

This paper, by contrast, is above all concerned with mead designations *per se*, in particular with linguistic aspects such as their formation, classification, and somewhat problematic onomastic status. The study is based on a limited set of data, partly collected in passing by myself during my dialectological fieldwork in various localities, partly supplied by the Shetland Archives and also taken from the unpublished collection described above. Comparisons are made with Swedish and Norwegian mead names as documented in studies by Falck-Kjällquist (1987, 1990), Hovda (1961), and Kruse (2000).

2. The collection and presentation of data

With regard to data collecting, the secrecy surrounding meads has been known to cause problems for ethnologists and linguists:

> In earlier days the meiths were kept secret from neighbouring fishermen, and if a strange boat approached, the local boat would move off or run down bare hooks to mislead the visitor. No boat would ask another for bait, nor would anyone give another a bearing (Fenton 1978: 589).

There is indeed a great deal of anecdotal evidence relating consciously misleading information to the degree of removal of objects and painting over colour-based 'markers'. This kind of complication in data collecting is, incidentally, well known to me from my work on textile terminology. Recipes for plant dyes are generally, even though they are now documented in scholarly articles as well as DIY books, still surrounded by myths and secrecies. The secrecy surrounding particular locations can also be compared to the way Scandinavians tend to 'monopolize' their mushroom or cloudberry finding-places. With reference to fishing, however, there may also be another dimension to secrecy, viz. fishermen's taboo language. Names of churches, which obviously provided easily distinguishable marks, were, for example, often transformed in mead designations (cf. Olsson 1996: 97).

Interestingly, Kruse (2000: 68), in discussing taboo as a reason for avoidance of certain vocabulary, e.g. denoting domestic animals, in so-called 'sea names', discards Jakobsen's theories with regard to the use of these names. Rather, he subscribes the difference between 'sea-names' and 'land-names' to ignorance of local geography on the part of the fishermen and to a kind of jargon.

Another and very different kind of problem in collecting and presenting data has to do with the actual pinpointing of these somewhat 'shifting' designations. In the Shetland Place Name Project, the problem has been solved in a laudable way, as outlined in the (unpublished) preliminary notes and introduction to the project:

> The grounds are described by the meids, each identified by its National Grid 6-figure reference. Where possible, each feature is identified with a point reference. In practice, different locations on a land feature might be used, and these will be qualified by prefixing a grid reference with the word *say*. This is particularly applicable to the use of Scords for meids, relying upon the intersection of two distant hills to create a notch on a skyline, and impossible to locate in terms of the National Grid. Similarly, off the west coast of Shetland, much use was made of the near-45° south slope of the North Hill of Quarff; here the point of intersection of the slope with the skyline of Burra Isle was the datum point for taking meids, so the actual location would vary with the height of the lower fore-land, as was equally the case when features of the Bressay coast came in sight with the same slope.

The following example (1) from the investigation of haddock line grounds, collected for the project in 2001, will demonstrate the character of the mead designations as well as the clarity of the description outlined in the quotation above. As mentioned earlier, it is the designation of the fishing-ground that is seen as the pivot. Square brackets here and in the subsequent exemplification of mead names from other sources enclose translations/explanations for the benefit of the readers of this paper. Proper names are often abbreviated in the translations. For reference, all examples of mead designations in this paper are numbered.

1. The Oot Rentils [elongated banks in the sea where boat-fishing is carried on] o' Vaila:

    Depths: 67-80 metres, max. nearly 90.

    This line shoot starts at GR273410, meided as the Point of Skeld (say 300405) with Uradale Scord (say 419381), and 'The Rump in a Lump' as in 5. above. Shoot all along the line of the first meid, as far as the Spindle in the middle of the Wester Mouth: "A very good place for haddocks; best at back end of the year up to mid-January".

Similarly, although not suggesting the same degree of exactitude, the ethnologist Alexander Fenton states that the positions of the ling seats (= inshore grounds) and other productive fishing spots were marked by lining up two meads (referred to as *hands* in parts of Shetland, e.g. Fair Isle) or bearings from opposite directions (Fenton 1978: 588). The following examples (from the island of Fetlar) are given:

2. Seat: Stranda Sands   Meads: W: da Haa [the Hall] door o' Hollo (at Hestaness).
   E: Hosta and da Tind in line.

3. Seat: Seah or Se-a   Meads: W: Taings [low, narrow tongues of land] of Helersness and Sheniberg in line.
   E: Heog Stack at Hoga.

4. Seat: Da Wrak   Meads: W: Tower of Brough (Kirn) at Foreland.
   E: Skerry o' Quoda i da Maamy Soond.

This kind of notation is also found in the Swedish *bö*-books, which are hand-written notebooks from the West Coast of Sweden, accounting for the *böar* ('seats') in a certain area and their *me(d)* ('meads'), as in the following example, quoted from the collections of the Institute for place name and dialect research, Gothenburg University:

5. Bö: Lyrbonden   Me: Skansen på utare vandholma udden.
                                         [the fortlet on the outer v-holm headland]
                                         Herrö vårtera på ortskär.
                                         [H-island wards on o-skerry]

Ideally, then, a listing of mead names should always include the name of the seat, which, unfortunately, is not always the case with the data collected in my dialectological fieldwork or excerpted from the Shetland Archives oral history material. This is not to say that my informants would not have been able to specify the position of a fishing-ground with a high degree of precision. During an interview, George Stout, Fair Isle, for example, indicated several meads on a detailed map of his native island and the surrounding sea by means of an intricate system of lines. A number of elaborately marked maps of this kind, some of which are quite old, can also be found at the Shetland Archives. Hand-written notebooks on meads can be very informative and contain detailed drawings of hills and other marks as viewed from the recommended angles.

The following examples will illustrate the somewhat 'looser' character of more naturally occurring data as found in transcribed oral history recordings and my own notes from conversations with dialect informants:

6. Dis man found dis place where da two small stones in da gio wis a mead.

7. Dats da Heog, dats dis hill up here, dey call da Heog. Now, and da mead in line with sharp stones sticking up in outer side of deck end in sight. Dis is da name, dis is da Horil, Frammar Fladdick an face o da Bush an inner nose of Liversee Gio, in line with Helior, of Liversee Gio. (Examples 6 and 7 both from SA 1971/221).

8. King Harald Street open (Captain Michael Gray, personal communication).

9. Glör ida Soond and the Punds [small tongues of land, Westing, Unst] taegedder [together] (George Jamieson, Unst, quoting from a family 'mead-book').

10. Clovie's old house asight and Willie Johnson's house over Scarf Stone (Florence Shearer, personal communication, quoting from a Cunningsburgh family mead-book).

In addition to demonstrating different types of data, the ten examples above display some of the most frequently employed types of marks as well as structures in designations. Before turning to a more detailed linguistic commentary on these, a brief summary will be given of relevant research carried out in this field.

3. Linguistic work on mead designations

It seems more than likely that systems of positioning at sea like the mead designations exemplified above exist or have existed in all fishing and sea-faring communities around the world. This is not to say that universal structural uniformity can be assumed. As shown by Falck-Kjällquist (1987), for example, there are typological differences in the way meads are indicated in the three areas she has investigated, viz. the west coast of Sweden, Vänern/Vättern (the two major lakes in central Sweden), and in the Baltic (the Turku archipelago). To some extent, these differences can be explained by the character of the coastscape, type of fishing, and time-depth. Thus structures such as 'the points together' (cf. example 9, above), which represent a 'modern' way of stating a position are but rarely used in the easternmost area. Similarly, it emerges from the Amenity Trust collections that the use of meads at the herring fishing differed markedly from what was customary in other types of fishing:

> meids were used not so much to find herring in the first instance, *but to inform others of the location.* The various meads ... revealed a cardinally-based positioning system of considerable ingenuity. There were *two distinct sets of meids*, the first for direction, and the second for distance from a known reference point. This is distinct from the meiding methods used to locate position in hook- or net-fishing where the nature of the seabed is uppermost in mind; in that context there are no sailing directions for reaching such meids,

although the processes are similar. Accordingly, these meids
have little biological significance, but are of interest through
their involvement with place-names.
(from: *Boy, where came yon herrin' fae?*, p.1, unpublished
material, Shetland Amenity Trust Meids project)

The use of some kind of mead system may be universal, but appears to be
remarkably under-researched, at least from a linguistic point of view.
Admittedly, in *The Place-Names of Shetland*, Jakobsen (1936: 248-254) has
a section called *Names of fishing-grounds and their landmarks* and he also
lists names under various entries in his monumental etymological dictionary.
His material is of course of enormous interest, but there are few examples of
complete mead designations and no discussion.

In England, John Widdowson, studying fishermen's language (mostly
terminology) in the East Yorkshire town of Filey (1960's), discusses in
passing some traditionally worded 'bearings', locally referred to simply as
'marks'. Interestingly, in a later article he includes the following example
among 'miscellaneous traditional sayings':

11. *Kirk* at High Brigg. ... A bearing or 'meet' taken between the church and
    a high point on Filey Brigg when the cobles are coming to land
    (Widdowson 1972: 69).

It is pointed out that this example, like many sayings and proverbs in his
collection, demonstrates a linguistic form no longer in use. Here the
interesting form is *kirk*, whose provenance is now restricted to the borders
and Scotland. In addition, the realization of *kirk* in the 'meet' is – curiously –
with an /l/ instead of an /r/.

Widdowson, who has done no further research on mead designations,
has suggested that research in this field might well have been carried out in
Newfoundland where he himself recorded 'lengthy lists of coastal features
memorised by fishermen who had no training in navigation' (personal
communication). Yet inquiries directed to various Canadian place name
scholars and dialectologists have yielded no results, nor have consultations
with language institutions elsewhere in the English-speaking world. I am, of
course, not claiming to have exhausted all possible sources.

The only geographical area where substantial empirical as well as
theoretical work seems to be at hand is, in fact, in the Nordic countries,
especially Norway and Sweden. Names of fishing-grounds and meads were

a life-long preoccupation with the renowned Swedish onomast Ingemar Olsson, who has already been referred to in this paper. His seminal work on Gotland has had great impact on the three following major contributors to research in the field, viz. Per Hovda, Arne Kruse, and Birgit Falck-Kjällquist.

Until recently, Hovda's monograph on Norwegian fishing meads (1961) remained the only full-length study on the topic. The focus of his work, which is above all a massive data collection, covering the Norwegian Atlantic coast as well as those parts of the West Coast of Sweden that used to belong to Norway, is etymological. There are, however, also descriptions of systems for positioning as well as a brief discussion of naming principles.

In his recent work *Mål og méd* Kruse (2000) gives an exhaustive, presentation of the traditional dialect and mead names of a clearly delimited area, viz. the island of Smøla in the Trondheim area. Some 400 names are presented in this volume, whose target group is local fishermen as well as anyone interested in language, ethnology and history. It is based mainly on interviews and private name collections, often including detailed drawings. Kruse's definition of *méd* (cf. e.g. Kruse 2000: 73) is actually 'fishing-ground', which he claims to be the usual significance of the word today. As we have seen, this is in line with the set-up of the Amenity Trust data presentation. Confusingly, however, Kruse (2000: 56) also writes, quoting Hovda, that the use of *méd* in the sense of *médline* ('bearing') is common all along the coast.

The thrust of Kruse's study thus constitutes a difference with the interests of the present paper, which tries to investigate expressions for the actual bearings, i.e. phrases rather than single lexical items. Yet 'full meads' are sometimes referred to in his study and are often exemplified in extensive quotes from mead books and interviews. The following observations have been noted as significant for the purpose of this paper and for comparison with data from Shetland:

a) As in Shetland dialect, the word for mead has a derived verb, also used reflexively. Two good marks constituting a mead can be said to 'mead themselves well'; *Finméda* ('fine meading') refers to the employment of three meads.

b) As in Shetland, names of land markers, especially hills and mountains, are often totally different when they are 'sea names', i.e. as viewed from the sea (cf. e.g. the point of Shaldi Kliv in Fair Isle which is known as Knockhammer when viewed from the sea, when it appears bulky).

Further variation in these names may occur according to the point from which a mead is taken.

c)   A special type of 'measure' used in the indications of meads in the sense of 'bearings' to express the width of a passage is *dørabreidd* ('door's width'), *seglbreidd* ('sail's width'), *benkebreidd* ('bench's width'), etc.

d)   As in Shetland, words no longer in active use in the dialect, are used in characterizing marks, e.g. *haud* ('highest point') and *sport* ('low land'). Hence the detailed listing which constitutes the bulk of Kruse's work is of the utmost interest for comparative studies.

At two place-name conferences in the last two decades, Birgit Falck-Kjällquist (1987: 1990) has reported from her ongoing studies of names from fishing-grounds and meads in three different Swedish-speaking regions, from each of which she has collected some 500 names. She has made valuable contributions to a more theoretical discussion of the character and status of these names and has also inspired further research at Gothenburg University.

Falck-Kjällquist is particularly concerned with 'natural landmarks' which she claims are synonymous with '*meiths*, as found in Scotland'. In contrast with some other scholars mentioned in this paper, she does not include the sense of 'fishing-ground' in the concept, which she sees as:

either 1) sights, silhouettes or shapes of certain geographical entities like oddly shaped hills, rocks, mountains or in fact any part of the coastline or "coastscape" that has an unusual or striking form, or 2) geographical entities that give rise to those sights, silhouettes and shapes. These entities can either be one single natural formation of some kind or a conglomerate of two or more, which from a certain angle look like one (Falck-Kjällquist 1990: 307).

Although Falck-Kjällquist expresses great interest in the linguistic expressions of bearings as indicated under 2) above, most of her data presentation is devoted to a description and classification of the toponyms constituting the elements of the natural landmarks, i.e. the referents. In particular, she considers names where a comparison is made, e.g. with a part of the human body, animals, or well-known articles in general use, such as boats or tools.

With regard to meads in the sense of 'bearings', her most important contribution is a very insightful analysis and clarifying graphic representation of cross-bearing systems (Falck-Kjällquist 1987: 152f.). She further emphasizes the different character of bearings employed in the 'inner archipelago' and further out at sea. There is hardly any discussion of the linguistic structure of the mead designations, but her paper appears to have generated a lively discussion on their onomastic status, judging by the included questions and comments.

4. Towards a typology

The collections of Shetland mead designations are characterized by remarkable lexical richness and creative language use. In the following brief classification, a selection of elements and figures featuring as markers, *Natural* (cf. 4.1.1.) as well as *Man-made* (4.1.2.) is first listed and described. The typology of meads is then extended to the actual bearings, which can be characterized as 'configurations', i.e. usually relationships between two or more components.

4.1. Elements featuring as markers

4.1.1. Natural

Elevations: *bank, cliff, height, hill, houll* ('height'), *knowe* ('hillock'), *stack, tind* ('spike, peak'), *toog* ('mound') *wart (ward)* ('mountain-top, originally with cairns').

Indentations: *burn, daal, gio (geo)* ('cleft in a rocky coast'), *scord* ('deep depression in the ridge of a hill'), *slackie* ('low-lying hollow'), *sneek* ('incision'), *voe*.

Individual, 'loose' entities: *ord* ('big boulder'), *stone*.

Types of land: *brake* ('slope'), *mire, moss*.

Promontories, points: *edge, point, pund, taing*.

Islands: *holm, isle, skerry*.

Shapes (metaphors): *e'e* ('eye'), *face, head, hog, horn, horseshoe, mouth* (of a gio), *rump, shoulder, stack, throat, toom* ('thumb'), *tuus (tusk)* ('a rock finger').

4.1.2. Man-made

broch, byre, cairn, church, guns, haa, hill-dyke, hotel, house, hut, lighthouse, lookout, manse, quarry, radar station, street, tower, ward (cf. Elevations in 4.1.1., above), wreck (especially from WWI and II).

The above should be viewed as a rough classification and the categories are clearly not mutually exclusive. In the actual mead indications, elements may be 'naked' as in the above list but are generally qualified by pre- or post-modifiers, as exemplified below:

sandy brakes, sandy face, tari ('sea-weed, kelp') *geo, the muckle knowe of Oxna, sharp (white, red, scarf* ('cormorant'), *three-cornered ...) stone, Sandwick church, Sumburgh Hotel, Clovie's old house, coastguard hut* (lookout), *King Harald Street, tower of Brough, da throat o' Lungie Geo.* It goes without saying that an established proper name may denote an element as well, e.g. *Vaila* (an island), *Quinerahevda* or *Whinner Hevda* (a dip on the land between Little Hevda and Muckle Hevda). An environmentally based difference between elements used in Shetland and the Nordic countries is the frequent reference to tall or otherwise remarkable trees in the latter region.

The metaphors listed above are a mixture of widely used, 'codified' place name elements such as *head* and *mouth*, and more 'creative' and localized denotations such as *horseshoe* and *tuus*. Similarly, analyzing her Swedish data, Falck-Kjällquist (1990: 309f.) found that a great number of the toponymical elements were names of comparison, simplex as well as compounds. Parts of the body, animals, and well-known articles in general use were the most common referents. The shape or silhouette of the entity constituting the landmark will vary when viewed from different positions; hence the same entity may be referred to by different names or metaphors in different mead designations. An interesting comment is found in the Amenity Trust report (Mainland North coast and North Isles seine net grounds, p.1), where the name Da Mires (applied to the low land between the Skerries hills when seen from a distance), is claimed to be a 'virtual' rather than a real place!

As in Scandinavia (cf. Kruse 2000), some of the vocabulary employed in denoting marks is no longer in active use in the local dialect, e.g. *scord, slackie, tuus, ward*. It is, in fact, generally assumed that many of the mead names are very old, but as seen from some of the *Man-made* (cf. 4.1.2.) elements, this is not always the case.

4.2. Configurations

A complete mead in the sense of 'bearing-line' (Swedish *enslinje*) can be expressed by a single toponym (with or without modifiers) of the metaphor type, i.e. when a shifting natural landmark is viewed from the 'right' position (Falck-Kjällquist 1990: 312). However, a mead is usually expressed by a configuration, i.e. the relationship between two marks, as illustrated in example 11, above. The most reliable indications for fishing-grounds are given as cross-bearings, often with references to cardinal points (cf. examples 4 and 10). The following brief account of configuration types focuses on the character and structure of single bearings. It is introduced by exemplifying the most common structures.

12. The Rump in a lump.
13. Da Hill o' da Rump shaain [showing] be Vaila.
14. Clovie's old house asight (cf. (10) above, giving the cross-bearing).
15. North Havera shut in (i.e. out of sight) at Sanda.
16. The Hoevdi blinded (out of sight).
17. Skerry doon.
18. King Harald Street open.
19. Soond a Fura Skerry open.
20. Keep open between Ramna Stacks and Mainland.
21. Water between Papa and Forwick Holm.
22. Roesound closed.
23. Da Punds taegedder.
24. Da knowe idda voe.
25. Da stack ida burn.
26. Da light (Eshaness) ida Horn (Papa).
27. Gordo Banks in the middle of the Houll Sound.
28. A three-cornered stone in the mouth of the Rum.
29. Taings of Helersness and Sheniberg in line.
30. A bit o' Vaila out at the Rump.
31. Hoog Stack at Hoga.
32. Da haa at Uyea bearing at the south point of Haaf Gruney.
33. White stone over the Greff Stack.
34. Feallie below Sandness Hill.
35. Baagie Stack on the Haa o' Øya.
36. The face of the Noup at the sneek on the low part of the Skerries at Burrafirth.
37. Kurkaby on the point of Spoo Ness.
38. Haa of Øya on point of the Skuda.
39. The old church of Sandness at highest point on the Holm of Melby.
40. Isle of Ueya through Stacks of Fethaland.
41. The holm of Papa showing through the cave of the ... of Lyra Skerry.
42. Sandy Brecks with North Hill of Quarff.
43. Skerries of Skea with Holms of Burravoe.

44. Mioness just clear of Griff Skerry.
45. The Filla coming out at Mioness.
46. When Hill of Haggista comes to Hamarsland Hill.
47. Head of Yisness an' Da Burrian.

Examples 12-47 give a fair representation of the names/designations found in the data. Since the data is taken from different 'genres' (private mead books, transcripts of recorded interviews, and carefully planned, scientifically based investigations such as the current Amenity Trust project) and collected over a period of more than a century, there is considerable variation in style and form, not least in spelling. No attempt has been made to 'modify' or 'normalize' the text, however. Examples 20 and 46 – the latter with a Shakespearean ring about it – are the only structures consisting of a clause rather than a noun phrase and make a 'conversational' impression; yet they were taken from a mead book and not from an interview. Obsolescent forms include the use of *benorth*, *bewest* etc., frequently found in old mead books. The use of *bearing* in example 32 may seem very modern but this example, too, is taken from an old mead book. Descriptive terms frequently found in the Amenity Trust material but not elsewhere include *gripping* and *touching* (e.g. a hill reaching the edge of a promontory).

Example 12 illustrates the use of one topographical entity functioning as a mead when viewed from a certain angle. It is described in the Amenity Trust material (West Side of Shetland, p.3) in the following way: '... a mile or so south of the Rump, with the bare south face of the Rump showing clean. This aspect of the rock was known as "The Rump in a lump"'. Examples 13-17 basically illustrate the same type, although their grammatical structures are different and two of the examples are related to a second landmark by a spatial preposition. With reference to the minimal, yet adequate structure of no. 17, Eunson (1961: 184), after stating that fishing hands, i.e. meads, must be easy of utterance to the local men and probably unintelligible to the stranger because of the speed of utterance, writes:

'Skerry doon' (down) is just one more interesting piece of navigational knowledge. This was the Skerry off the south end of the Isle just disappearing when at sea in a small boat and was reckoned about 6 miles. This distance guide was used a lot in the old days when boats were out bartering with passing ships.

Nos. 18 and 19 which have the same grammatical structure as the preceding example, exemplify a type of designation claimed to be more modern by Falck-Kjällquist (cf. above). This seems to be the case with the Shetland data as well. Examples 20-23 illustrate the same type of positioning, although the configurations are obviously different.

Although all the types presented so far are richly exemplified in the data, examples 24-46 represent the most common category of all, i.e. the relationship of one entity to another expressed through a spatial preposition or prepositional phrase. The exact significance of some of these spatial expressions should be well worth investigating in their own right by a dialectologist. The meaning of *with* (*wi'*), for example, as in 42 and 43, is interesting. In Jakobsen's dictionary, where it is only entered as the latter form, various meanings are assigned to this lexical item, which is, incidentally, even recorded in the Norn fragments. It may function as an adverb in the sense of 'along' and is used in several expressions for cardinal directions, such as *ut wi* 'south-easterly or southerly'. Even in present-day Shetland dialect *wi'* may stand for 'by' (in its spatial sense), which shows its Scandinavian connection (cf. ON *við*). Within the context of mead designations, it is particularly interesting to learn that a special sense of the word is 'in a certain angular position, in a line with' with particular reference to fishing-marks. Jakobsen refers to certain (abbreviated) names of fishing-grounds, where the preposition *wi'* is always placed after the noun it governs, e.g. *gjona wi'*, recorded from Unst, named after a cleft which was kept open during the rowing outwards. There are no recent records of names with post-positioned *wi'*.

Example 47, finally, which seems to illustrate yet another way of expressing a relationship with two entities and a different grammatical structure, is, essentially, similar to the previous category, in that *and* corresponds to a spatial preposition. To the outsider it makes the impression of a less precise indication.

5. Onomastic status

As mentioned earlier, the presentation of Falck-Kjällquist's seminal 1987 paper was followed by a lively discussion, a transcript of which was added to the published article. Interestingly, although the paper is basically concerned with description and categorization, the discussion is almost exclusively devoted to a topic not addressed in the paper, viz. the onomastic status of the mead designations. These are more often than not referred to as 'names', not only in Scandinavian name studies and the title of this paper but also in mead books and informal interviews. It is true that 'mead names' may also refer to 'fishing-grounds', in which sense their status of place-names proper is beyond doubt. This is of course also the case with many of the toponymical elements of which the meads are built up. When *mead* refers to 'bearing', there are several question marks, however.

A special problem has to do with the fact that we are not dealing with fixed points or areas, but with lines and shifting configurations. A comparison with street or road names, which obviously also denote lines, albeit more tangible ones, tells us that a term such as 'the Oxford Road', which symptomatically has kept the definite article, is not – or was not for a considerable time – viewed as a place name to the same degree as Oxford Street. Like many mead names, 'the Oxford Road' has simply been used as an integrated phrase in everyday language, and we can assume that a mead such as 'the points together' originates in expressions such as 'take the boat out as far as a point where you can see that the points are together'. The abbreviated forms briefly discussed above in connection with 'Skerry doon' have then gone down as codified phrases and been taken down in mead books. In this context it is also worth mentioning that Widdowson (cf. above) discusses his examples of meads in an article on traditional proverbs and sayings. Codification indicates name status; in addition, it tells us that the denotations were shared, which is a characteristic of proper names. According to one definition of what constitutes a place name, a prerequisite is that it should be known by at least two people, i.e. not necessarily beyond a family. This was probably often the case with mead names as well as names of small, cultivated strips of land, runrigs. Considering the shifting character of meads, it is true that they are perhaps better characterized as images rather than actual places. Still, their constituents are concrete landmarks. For comparison, consider the well-known configuration from Swedish Lapland known as Lapporten ('the Lapp Doorway'), which looks strikingly like a doorway only when viewed from a sizeable distance. Nevertheless, it definitely qualifies as a place name and is generally regarded as such.

An interesting criterion for place-name status is whether the actual users of a denotation consider it to be a name. This was discussed at some length in connection with Falck-Kjällquist's paper, and there was a certain consensus as to the great importance of this aspect. It was, for example, suggested that a possible way of testing name status would be to investigate the acceptability of constructions such as 'Let us go to "points together"'. It would be interesting to follow up this recommendation with reference to the rich data from Shetland. The interesting transcripts of spoken data found in the Shetland Archives are worth looking at from this aspect as well. The context is all-important for an understanding of the significance and status of these intriguing names.

Literature

Eunson, J., 1961: 'The Fair Isle Fishing-Marks', *Scottish Studies* 5, 181-198.

Falck-Kjällquist, B., 1987: 'Struktur och namnsemantiskt innehåll som mönsterbildande faktorer i namn på fiskeplatser i tre svenskspråkiga områden'. In: G. Hallberg, S. Isaksson & B. Pamp (eds), *Nionde nordiska namnforskarkongressen*. Skrifter utgivna genom dialekt- och ortnamnsarkivet i Lund 4. Lund, 151-162.

Falck-Kjällquist, B., 1990: 'On Toponyms of Local Coastal Navigation Systems'. In: E.M. Närhi (ed.), *Proceedings of the XVIIth International Congress of Onomastic Sciences*. I. Helsinki, 307-313.

Fenton, A., 1978: *The Northern Isles: Orkney and Shetland*. Edinburgh.

Hovda, P., 1961: *Norske fiskeméd. Landsoversyn og to gamle médbøker*. Oslo/Bergen.

Jakobsen, J., 1928-1932: *An Etymological Dictionary of the Norn Language in Shetland*, 1-2. London/Copenhagen.

Jakobsen, J., 1936: *The Place-Names of Shetland*. London/Copenhagen.

Kruse, A., 2000: *Mål og méd*. Trondheim.

Olsson, I., 1996: *Gotländska ortnamn*. Visby.

Robinson, M. (ed.), 1985: *The Concise Scots Dictionary*. Aberdeen.

Shetland Amenity Trust: *Meeds Project*. Unpublished documents.

Stewart, J., 1987: *Shetland Place-Names*. Lerwick.

Widdowson, J.D., 1972: 'Proverbs and Sayings from Filey'. In: M.F. Wakelin (ed.), *Patterns in the Folk Speech of the British Isles*. London, 50-72.

What is Norse, what is Scots in Orkney Place-Names?

Berit Sandnes

1. Introduction

Since 1994 I have studied the place-names from four parishes in Orkney. When working with this place-name material, it becomes clear that earlier scholars have focused almost exclusively on the Norse stratum. There is of course also a Scots stratum in Orkney place-names, and in this paper I will try to establish criteria to distinguish between Norse and Scots formations, a distinction which is obviously also relevant for the dating of names. Norse is here used somewhat vaguely of both Old Norse and the local dialect Norn that developed from Old Norse, whereas Scots is used about English-based dialect.

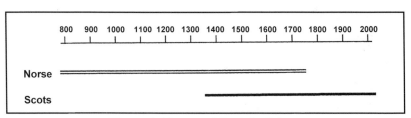

Figure 1. Norse and Scots in Orkney

Norse name formations are possible throughout the Old Norse and Norn-speaking period. Old Norse was introduced by Scandinavian settlers c. 800. An exact date for the death of Norn cannot be established, but we are fairly safe in assuming that it died out in the latter half of the 18th century (cf. Barnes 1998: 26).

Scots was introduced in Orkney by Lowland settlers from the 14th century, and Scots coinages are possible from the first Scottish settlement until today.

2. Norse place-name elements

As we see, there was over 400 years of language contact in Orkney, and during this period a large number of appellatives and place-names of Norse origin were borrowed into local Scots. Marwick records some 3,000 words of Norse origin in *Orkney Norn*. Once words or place-names have been borrowed, they become part and parcel of the local Scots dialect, and the loans may be used in every context, including new place-name formations. The place-name *Lerwick* and the bird's name *shalder* 'oyster-catcher' are two examples of such imported elements that are integrated parts of Shetland Scots today. And Orcadians may still know the meaning of words/place-name elements of Norse origin such as *crue* (< *krú* 'small enclosure'), *oyce* (< *óss* 'mouth of a burn') and *taing* (< *tangi* 'point'), to mention just a few.

When studying place-names in Orkney, we should thus be careful not to assume a Norse origin on the basis of isolated Norse elements. The names may still be purely Scots formations. We have to distinguish between the linguistic origin of the individual place-name elements and the origin of the place-names as a whole (cf. Cox 1989: 2f).

To exemplify this, I will briefly consider some of the farm-name elements treated by Marwick. In *Orkney Farm-names* (1952: 227ff.) he presents a chronology of nine farm-name elements, which are supposed to represent the oldest layer of farm-names:

> *bær* 'farm' (primary)
> *bólstaðr* 'farm', *garðr* 'farm', *land* 'land' (secondary)
> *bú* 'estate', *skáli* 'building, hall', *staðir* 'places'
> (presenting chronological problems)
> *setr* 'seat, dwelling place', *kví* 'enclosure' (younger)

Figure 2. Marwick's chronology of farm-name elements

A closer scrutiny makes it clear that several of these elements are by no means limited to the Norse period. First of all *land* is common to Norse and Scots, and could be used in name formation from 800 until today. In addition *garðr/garth* 'farm' (possibly also used of enclosure, ON *gerði*) and *kví/quoy* 'enclosure' have been borrowed into the local dialect. According to Thomson (1995:48), the two elements have been productive in place-name formation until the 19th century. In many cases the Scots origin of these late *quoy*- and *garth*-names will be obvious from the fact that the other elements are Scots: e.g. Heathery Quoy, Quoy Sinclair.

Whereas the *land*, *quoy* and *garth*-names may be either Scots or Norse formations, the *Bu of* ... names stand out as being exclusively Scots in origin. This can be seen from the form; *bu*-names are invariably formed with the Scots ... *of* ... periphrasis. In this case the Scots settlers in Orkney borrowed the Norse appellative *bú* neutr. meaning 'estate' and applied it to land they acquired in Orkney, as an alternative to *Mains of* ... or *Manor of* ... used in other parts of Scotland. The estate in question would either be originally large and central farms or new large units, created by amalgamation of several old farms. Consequently, *Bu of* ... often refers to large farms, and in many cases old farms. As a class, however, *Bu of* ... names are Scots, always post-dating 1300. *Bu of* ... names are first recorded in rentals of 1492, and in most cases *Bu of* ... is an addition to an original name: e.g. *Kjarrekststaupum* (Orkneyinga saga) > Bu of Cairston, i *Orfioru*, *Aurfuru* (Orkneyinga saga) > Bu of Orphir.

My main point in this context is to show that some of the place-name elements in Marwick's chronology are not limited to the early Norse period. For further discussion (and criticism) of Marwick's chronology, I refer to Thomson 1995.

In some cases Jakobsen and Marwick's keen interest in the Norse heritage makes them suggest a Norse origin for elements where a Scots origin is equally plausible or even more plausible (cf. Smith 1995: 27). One example is the element *Wind-* in Orkney place-names. Marwick suggests the interpretation *vin* fem. genitive sg. *vinjar*, genitive pl. *vinja* 'grassland, clearing'. As a generic in Norwegian names, *vin* is regarded as pre-Viking Age. In the Northern Isles, the element never occurs as a generic. In some Shetland names, such as *Winja depla* and *Winjawels* (Jakobsen 1901: 164ff.), the case morphology points to a Norse origin: the *j*-insertion corresponds to the conjugation of feminine *jō*-stems. Orkney names like *Windywas* (or *-walls*) and *Windbreck* show no traces of case morphology, however. Both names are rather common, but apart from the small unit of *Wyndbreck* in Orphir, recorded in the 1492 Rental (Thomson 1996), none is recorded before the 17th century. Most of the localities are peripheral, not likely to be named particularly early, and it seems unlikely that they should contain an element virtually extinct when Orkney was settled. For this reason, Scots *wind* or the synonymous Old Norse *vindr* 'wind' should be preferred. Whereas *Windywalls* is purely Scots, probably of a draughty house, the generic in *Windbreck* is of Norse origin, *brekka* 'slope'. This element was borrowed into Scots, however, and could be used in a Scots formation. *Windbreck* in Rendall, in the area I have studied, lies on a ridge fairly close to the sea and can certainly be windswept.

3. Language of formation – criteria
We may conclude from the discussion so far that elements of Norse origin do not allow us to conclude that names are Norse formations. Are there other criteria to help us determine the language of formation? I will suggest three criteria.

3.1. The language of the generic is of primary importance.

The names *Boat Meadow* and *Boats Hellia* share the same specifying element, which may be Scots *boat* or the synonymous Old Norse *bátr* 'boat'. Calling a flat rock on the coast *hella* requires competence in Norse language. This means that *Boats Hellia* should be regarded as a Norse formation. On the other hand *Boat Meadow* is a Scots formation, because the word 'meadow' only exists in Scots. This is the case even if the first element is Norse. In Nistaben Meadow, Nistaben is an original Norse *Neztabœrinn* 'the lowermost farm'. The formation is still Scots, but here the generic is specified by an existing farm-name.

Problems arise for the name Boat Geo. The origin of the generic is Norse *gjá* n. 'cleft, ravine', but this has been borrowed into the dialect in the form *geo*. This is the common term used of steep narrow inlets in the dialect, and is also frequent as a place-name element. The formation language of this name must thus remain uncertain.

3.2. All elements of the name should be taken into account.

If the generic of the name does not reveal the formation language, the specific may help us. A few geo-names may serve as examples. The specifics tell us that Knocking Stane Geo and Peat Geo are Scots formations, whereas Ramna Geo contains the Norse bird's name *hrafn* masc. 'raven'. And while there is no linguistic way of telling whether an uncompounded *Garth* is a Scots formation with a borrowed appellative, the specific of Evrigar is Norse *øfri* 'upper', and this is an indication of a Norse formation. In the case of Garth, early records will of course increase the probability of it being of Norse origin.

3.3. Morphology

Morphology is probably the best indication of source language. Place-names containing reflexes of Norse morphology must have been coined while the Norse grammatical system was still in function.

A large number of Orkney place-names have the endings *-en, -an, -on*, which reflect the Norse suffixed definite article: Lyron < *leirin* fem. def. 'the clay(ey place)', Breckan < *brekkan* fem. def. 'the slope', *Tooin* fem. 'the hillock'. These can be regarded as certain Norse formations.

The gen. pl. morpheme in Old Norse is *-a*. We can thus distinguish between a Scots formation Lambsqouy 'lambs' enclosure' and the synonymous Norse formation Lamaquoy < *lambakví*, with the medial -*a*-reflecting the ON genitive morpheme.

The morphological criterion should also be used with care. Again, Marwick often prefers a Norse origin where a Scots origin is more plausible. Most importantly, he considers the frequent -*y*/-*ie*-ending to be reflections of Norse masc. nom. -*i*. But in the name material I have studied, many -*ie*-endings cannot be rooted in an original -*i*-ending, e.g. Skibby Geo < *Skipagjá* 'inlet of the ships', Ernie Tooin < *arna(r)þúfan* 'hillock of the eagle(s)' Wadi < *vað* neutr. 'ford' and Quinni, some form of *kví* fem. 'enclosure'. For the latter two, there are no forms at all in the paradigm ending in -*i*.

The endings in these names should rather be interpreted as the very productive Scots *ie*-suffix. All Norse names that are borrowed into Scots are adapted to the Scots language system to a greater or lesser degree. As a group, morphological endings are probably more liable to adaptation than place-name elements, the reason being that place-name elements in some cases correspond to appellatives that are still comprehensible, whereas the meaning of morphological endings is normally lost in a language shift. The incomprehensible endings are likely to be dropped or substituted by Scots suffixes, and consequently we should be very careful about trying to reconstruct the original morphological form of Norse names.

On the basis of the criteria above, the following table can be made:

Norse formation	- Certain if the name contains reflexes of Norse articles or case morphology: *Ernie Tooin*
	- Likely if the generic is of Norse origin, and supported if there are additional Norse elements: *Fisk Hellya*
Scots formation	- Likely if all elements are Scots, including local borrowings from Norse
	- Certain when a Scots generic is specified with an existing place-name of Norse origin: *Breckan Park*
	- Certain for *of*-constructions: *Bu of Hoy*.
Uncertain	- If all elements are known in both Norse and the local Scots dialect: *Boat Geo, Midhouse*.

Figure 3. Indications of formation language.

4. Word order

Thus far I have demonstrated that some assumed Norse formations are more likely to be of Scots origin. In this final section I will provide one example of the opposite, namely the so-called "inverted compound names". By choosing the term "postpositive specifics" one avoids the notion of names having changed from a "normal word order".

In the Orkney material I have studied, there are c. 20 examples of names with postpositive specifics. In most cases the generic is *kví/quoy* 'enclosure'. Some of the examples are found in the earliest records, e.g. *Kuikobba* 1329 (*DN* II 170, 1329), and *Queenamuckle* in the first Orkney rentals (1492, Thomson 1996). The latter name reflects some case form of Norse *kvín mikla*, literally 'the enclosure big'. The specific of *Kuikobba* seems to be genitive of a man's nickname *Kobbi*.

This order of elements has parallels in Northern England, e.g. *Briggethorfinn*, literally 'bridge Thorfinn's' for which Ekwall (1969: 35/1977: xxiii) assumes Celtic interference. In Orkney such an interpretation is problematic, as there has been no direct contact between Norse and Celtic in this part of the British Isles. For this reason we should look for an alternative explanation. And the pattern is actually well documented in early Scandinavian sources. In Danish runic inscriptions, more than half of the attributes in noun phrases are postpositive, according to Skautrup (1944: 142). Postposition is also common in the oldest Norwegian records (Lundeby 1965), but disappears after 1300. In place-names it survives for a little longer. Forms such as *i Œynni yttri* 'in the island outer' and *i æynni helgho* 'in the island holy' are found in the mid-14th century. The latter is a parallel to Orkney Eynhallow.

When postpositive attributes fall out of use, the place-names gradually adjust to the current word order. This is best demonstrated for Denmark. In her thesis Weise (1969) demonstrates that postpositive adjectives are rather common in place-names in Eastern Denmark in pre-1400 sources (107 instances in her material), but over the centuries up to 1700, c. half of these adjust to the normal word order. In Norway the development has gone even further; I know of only two Norwegian inverted compound names, the island names Holmengrå < *holmr hinn grái*, literally 'the islet grey' and Landegode < *land hitt góða* 'the land good' (*NSL*: 219, 282.).

It is interesting to observe that a pattern obsolete in the mother country has survived in the former colony. I should also add that the pattern is also common in the Faeroe Islands, as discussed by Matras (1963: 141ff.). In both archipelagoes gradually less direct contact may be the reason why the archaic form survives.

There is one more interesting aspect about postpositive specifics in Orkney names, namely that they seem to have been sufficiently frequent to function as a pattern for later Scots formations. Late examples such as *Quoyhenry*, first recorded in 1733 and *Quoy Sinclair* first recorded in 1841 are probably examples of late Scots formations with the loanword *quoy*. Additional examples are Ha'white, Brae Vingus and Cup Stephen. Since Gaelic has never been spoken in Orkney, an originally Norse pattern is more likely than a Celtic one also in the late Scots formations.

5. Summary

Place-names are arguably the area in which Orkney's Scandinavian-speaking past is most visible today. In the material of my study, about 75% of the names contain Norse elements. I have tried to demonstrate that on linguistic grounds and for the purpose of dating names, we should distinguish between actual names that have been borrowed into Scots and names that have been coined with borrowed appellatives. Certain Norse formations can be dated to the period before 1700-1750. I have also demonstrated that morphology is the most reliable indication of Norse formation. Names containing remains of Norse articles or case morphology must have been coined when the grammatical system was still intact.

Scots formations include names coined with Norse loanwords. Obviously these can be coined until the present date, and they always post-date 1300. In my material, I should add, Scots formations are actually extremely rare before 1600. This ties in with the literary references to Norn still being the common language for the majority of the population well into the 17th century.

What is Norse, what is Scots in Orkney Place-Names?

Literature

Barnes, M., 1998: *The Norn Language of Orkney and Shetland*. Lerwick.

Cox, R.A.V., 1989: 'Questioning the Value and Validity of the Term 'Hybrid' in Hebridean Place-Name Study', *Nomina* 12, 1-9.

DN = Diplomatarium Norvegicum. Christiania/Oslo, 1847-.

Ekwall, E., [1924] 1969: 'The Celtic Element'. In: A. Mawer & F.M. Stenton (eds), *Introduction to the Survey of English Place-Names*, part I. EPNS 1. Cambridge, 15-35.

Ekwall, E., [1936] 1977: *The Concise Oxford Dictionary of English Place-Names*. Oxford.

EPNS = English Place-Name Society county surveys.

Jakobsen, J., 1901: *Shetlandsøernes stednavne*. København.

Lundeby, E., 1965: *Overbestemt substantiv i norsk og de andre nordiske språk*. Oslo/Bergen/Tromsø.

Marwick, H., 1952: *Orkney Farm-Names*. Kirkwall.

Matras, C., 1963: 'Fjallið mikla, Áin í Dal, Millum Fjarða and Urd Mans'. In: A. Brown & P. Foote (eds), *Early English and Norse Studies*. Presented to Hugh Smith. London, 141-149.

NSL = Norsk stadnamnleksikon. J. Sandnes & O. Stemshaug (eds). 4. utg. Oslo 1997.

Skautrup, P., 1944: *Det danske sprogs historie* 1. København.

Smith, B., 1995: 'Scandinavian Place-Names in Shetland With a Study of the District of Whiteness'. In: B.E. Crawford (ed.), *Scandinavian Settlement in Northern Britain*. London/New York, 26-41.

Thomson, W.P.L., 1995: 'Orkney Farm-Names; a Re-assessment of their Chronology'. In: B.E. Crawford (ed.), *Scandinavian Settlement in Northern Britain*. London/New York, 42-63.

Thomson, W.P.L., 1996: *Lord Henry Sinclair's 1492 Rental of Orkney*. Kirkwall.

Weise, L., 1969: *Efterstillet adjektiv i danske stednavne*. København.

Onomastic Evidence for Faroese and Shetlanders in Norway?

Tom Schmidt

1. Introduction

On 15th March 1530 Mogens Gyldenstjerne, the commander of the castle in Oslo, wrote to his cousin, Eske Bille, at Bergen Castle. He asked for three or four men from Shetland or the Faroes, as he was desperately in need of labourers:

> er myn kierlig bøenn tiill eder athi wilde flye meg iij eller iiij arbeydz karle aff thee Heettlensche eller Færøer, jeg haffuer stoer trangh paa arbeydzfolch for thenne pestilentz som heer haffuer gaatth
>
> [It is my dear prayer to you that you would give me three or four working men from the Shetlandic [islands] or Faroes. I have great need of labourers because of the pestilence which has been going on here] (*DN* X 633)

This clearly indicates that men from Shetland and the Faroes were sought after, and naturally much easier to find in the western part of Norway than elsewhere. It is interesting to note that this letter was written 60 years after the king of Denmark had mortgaged Shetland to the Scottish crown.

A fair number of anthroponymics – first names as well as bynames – found in 16th century records indicate that some Shetlanders and Faroese seem to have settled more or less permanently in Norway. Cultural and economic contact across the North Sea must have been as important in previous centuries. In earlier sources evidence of this is much more scarce and it is often very difficult to prove, particularly as personal names were then to a greater extent identical on both sides of the North Sea. One has to rely on the rather few bynames which derive from designations of nationality, and on other, much more circumstantial evidence. Toponymics may contain useful information, though there are many difficulties in their interpretation and dating.

Below I first present some instances of personal names and bynames from medieval documents, and also names from early 16th century lists of tax payers and pay-rolls which indicate the presence in Norway of men (and a few women) from Shetland and the Faroes. I then go on to discuss some place-names which may be taken as indications of immigration. First of all, however, I shall look briefly at what can be said about the names of these islands, and of their inhabitants.

2. The Old Norse Names of the Islands and their Inhabitants

The Old Norse (ON) name of the Faroe Islands was *Færeyjar*, the inhabitants were called *færeyingar* m. pl. and the corresponding adjective was *færeyskr*. The generic element of *Færeyjar* is the plural of *ey* f., 'island', and the specific is a rare form of an old word for 'sheep', ON *fær* n., developed by *R*-umlaut from *fár*, which has developed into East Scandinavian *får*. The normal ON word for 'sheep' is *sauðr* m., and the word *fær* is according to Fritzner (I: 527) – apart from one instance in the Snorre-Edda – only found in the compound *færsauðr* (a 'sheep-sheep' as opposed to *geitsauðr*, 'goat-sheep'). Fritzner also claims that the word is found as the specific element in a field name *Færskinn*; this name may, however, preferably be interpreted differently.[1]

Apart from the name of the islands, Norwegian *Færøyene*, the corresponding adjective *færøyisk* and the noun *færøying* (even *færing*) the word *fær* has left no trace in modern Scandinavian, and it seems strange to me that the numerous Norwegian *Færøya* (and the like) are indiscriminately interpreted as 'sheep island', which – if the names were to be taken literally – would give these names a conciderable age. I shall return to this below.

The ON name of the Shetland Islands was *Hjaltland*. The development into *Shetland* is unproblematic, as evidenced by several instances of initial *hj-* being changed into *sh-* in Shetland (cf. Jakobsen 1932: pp. liv, 760-772, e.g. *sjel* p. 765, from ON *hjallr* m.). The same or a similar pronunciation is found in several Norwegian dialects, especially along the south-western coast.

The etymology of *Hjaltland* is, however, obscure. It is not even certain whether it is really a Norse name. It may be a Scandinavianisation of an older, indigenous name, though Jakobsen (1932: lxxxix) calls it 'the proper and original name for the main island'. I have only seen one Norwegian interpretation of the name, according to which the first element may contain the stem or the plural genitive of ON *hjaltr* m. (Vågslid 1959: 1031). This seems to be an older and a much more widely used designation for the inhabitants of the islands than the other form we find: *hjaltlendingr*. *Hjaltr* is even used in the weak form *hjalti* m. Vågslid's interpretation can be supported by several parallels: cf. *Norwegian*: *Skottland*, *Tyskland* (Germany), *Finland*, *Estland* (Estonia), etc., and a number of names of districts in which the first element corresponds to the word for a people or a tribe, e.g.: *Hordaland*, *Rogaland*, *Hadeland* and *Grenland*.

The reason why the Shetlanders were named in this way – again according to this theory – is that they carried a sword with a particularly elaborate *hjalt* n., English *hilt*. Originally the ON word *hjalt* was used of the hilt-guard, the part which protects the hand when holding the hilt (while the plural *hjölt* was used of the hilt as a whole). A good parallel is the derivation of Saxon from *sax* (a short sword), as given by the *OED*.

Vågslid was probably inspired by Jakob Jakobsen who – more down to earth, and influenced by Oluf Rygh – regarded *hjalt* as designating some topographical feature:

> the great piece of land called 'the Westside', jutting out in a westerly direction from the chief isle, 'the Mainland' (Shetland proper), while the southern part of Mainland is long and narrow, and may well be compared with a sword-blade ... (Jakobsen 1936: 127f.)

One may suspect that Jakobsen's interpretation was based on the shape of the island as seen from maps, and that he forgot that the name-giving Vikings hardly had the opportunity of a bird's eye view of the islands.

Whatever the origin of *Hjaltland*, *hjaltr* (pl. *hjaltar*) was an ON word for a Shetlander (and it may even have been used of the people whom they found living in these islands when they arrived, i.e. the Picts). *Hjaltlendingr* is a later formation, and so is the weak derivation *hjalti* from *hjaltr*. Younger Norwegian forms were *hjelt* and *hjelte*, and the plural form of both was *hjeltar*. This, or a word of the same root and similar appearance, seems to constitute the first element of some Norwegian place-names. Is it then possible that these names are the results of some association with Shetlanders? At first glance this looks like a good interpretation. It does seem, however, that other alternatives are possible, or even just as likely, but we had better turn to the data. I shall start off with a survey of the bynames and the personal names.

3. Bynames and Personal Names

3.1. Færeyjar – Færøyene – The Faroes

The ON adjective *færøyskr* has been found as a byname only a few times:

'FiNr fær-eyski' (*Sverris Saga* p. 158; ca. 1250), 'sira Þronder færœyski' (*DN* II: 71; Bergen 1306), 'um Erik Færœyska' (*DN* IV: 70; Bergen? 1307) and 'Eirikkir Færøyske' (*DN* XII: 35 Bergen? 1308-09; copy 1427).

In the 16th century the adjective appears mostly as *ferisk*, *færisk* – even written *ferest*, and it is often found in lists of imported goods such as sheep-skin, tallow and woollen cloth:

> Feriske (Fereske, Færeske) farskind
> Feriisk (Færiske, Feriske) taligh (talij, thelig)
> Ferisk (Ferest, Feresth) vadmal (vanmal)
> (*NRJ* I *passim*).

In more or less the same forms the adjective is used as a personal byname (or at least as a word designating persons). As shown in Figure 1 (see next page) most instances are from the west coast of Norway, but some are found as far north as Finnmark, a fact that was noted by Knut Liestøl as early as in 1941.

I have been unable to find ON *føreyingr* m. in the records I have examined, and Fritzner (I: 527) only gives *Olafs Saga* as his source for it. After the mid-19th century it is only recorded in modern Norwegian as *færing* and *færø(y)ing*. As these have become the common words for the inhabitants of the Faroes, it seems, however, reasonable to think they have also been used in earlier periods. Magnus Olsen (1931: 37) has interpreted the name of a ship coming to Lynn i 1306 as *Føreyingr*, but the corrupted form in which the name appears in this English (Latin) source makes this slightly doubtful. Even the skipper's byname is difficult to interpret.[2]

NAME	YEAR	LOCATION
Anne Fereske (Feriske)	1521	Bergen
Erik Ferrisk	1520-21	Skarsvåg, Finnmark
Erick Feriske	1521	Melfjorden, Nordland
Guren Færisk		
pa Horbergh	1520-21	Rissa, Trøndelag
Henrik Ffærrsk	1520-21	Silda, Finnmark
Joenn Feriske;		
Jonn Feriske	1521	Bergen
Niels Feriske	1521	Andenes, Nordland
Niels Ferisk	1519	Strandvik, Hordaland
Oluff Feriske	1520-21	Bergen
Oluff Ferisk	1521	Bergen

Oluff Feriske	1522-23	Bergen
Olaff dreng Feriiske	1520	Bergen
Olaff Feriske Portener	1522	Bergen
Syord Ferrisk hostrv	1520-21	Skarsvåg, Finnmark
Torsten oc Niels Feresk	1520-21	'som halshugne bleffwe' (Bergen?)
Østenn Feriske	1521	Andenes, Nordland

Figure 1. Færøysk *as a byname c. 1520. Sources: NRJ I-III passim.*

I had been hoping to find traces of the word *færøying* (*færing*) in Norwegian place-names, but so far I have had little luck. I should mention though, that Gillian Fellows-Jensen (1997: 20-22) has suggested that this word may be found as the specific of Ferrensby in the West Riding of Yorkshire.

3.2. Hjaltland – Shetland

According to the dictionaries *hjaltlendingr* is the ON word for an inhabitant of Shetland, but it does not seem to have been widely used. Again *Olafs Saga* is the only source mentioned by Fritzner (I 829), and I have been unable to find traces of the word prior to the modern Scandinavian period. In Norway the oldest form seems to be from 1901.

ON *Hjaltlenzkr* is found as an adjective (*hjaltneskr*, *hjatlenzkr* and *hjetlenzkr* have also been recorded) and **Hjaltlenzki* might be thought a fitting byname (cf. *Saxlenzki*, *Upplenzki*: Lind 1921: 304, 393). The bynames actually recorded are, however, *Hjaltr* and *Hjalti*, identical with the designations of nationality (Lind 1921: 145). *Hjalti* was also, according to Lind, a fairly common man's name in medieval Iceland, as shown by a number of entries in the twelfth century Icelandic *Landnámabók* and the sagas, but also in early documents (Lind 1915: 537ff.). There is nothing peculiar about this personal name, as shown by several parallels, such as *Danr*, *Finnr* (*Finni*), *Gautr* (*Gauti*) and others, which presumably originated as bynames designating a person as a Dane, a Finn or a Gaut (person from the Swedish province of Götaland). However, in the case of the *Hjalt*(*i*) personal names, another etymology has been suggested, according to which they may have been coined directly from *hjaltr*.

In Norway the personal name *Hjalti* has been thought to have gone out of fashion at an early stage; the bynames *Hjaltr* and *Hjalti* were, however, fairly common. They are found 13 or 14 times in Norwegian sources between 1285 and 1404, borne by at least eight men (Table 2, next page). All but one

185

of these (*Jon hiælltte*) represent the form *Hjaltr*. Note the German first name Konrad in 1309.

After the mid-15th century Danish gradually replaced Norse as a written language, and the name of the islands mostly appears in the form *Hetland* in documents (cf. 'Heettlensche' in Mogens Gyldenstjerne's letter, cited above). In early 16th century accounts, however, the name is still generally found as *Hieltland*, though once as *Hietland*, and I have found only two instances of the adjective 'Shetlandic' written without the *l* (*en Hietlandsk drengh*; *Hietlantz*). When prefixed, the adjective has the forms *hjelte* or *helte*, the former being by far the most frequent: *Hielte skiff*, *Hielthekwffthe* (sweater) and in numerous entries for 'vadmel' (woollen cloth), *hieltewadmel*, but even *Helthe wandmell* and *Helterotsze* (fish); cf. *NRJ* I-II.

Pall Hiæltir	*DN* XII: 7; Bergen 1285; copied 1427
Pall Hialtir	*DN* XI: 8; Bergen 1287; copied 1427
Kuanrade hiællt	*DN* I: 109; Bergen 1309
Siguardr hialttr	*NgL* III: 122; Bergen 1316; copy ca. 1350
Harallde hiallt	*DN* I: 132; No. 149; Voss 1317
Jon hiælltte	*DN* I: 181; Gausdal 1333; No. 223
Hakon hiælltr	*DN* V: 95; No. 112; Nidaros 1336
Hakon hialltr	*DN* II: 205; No. 246; Nidaros 1342
Hakon hiallter	*DN* VI: 321; No. 274; Nidaros, ca. 1370
Jone Hialt	*DN* IV: 478; No. 648; Oslo 1395
Hakon hiælter	*DN* VI: 392; No 356; Nidaros 1400
[Siurda hialtt	*DN* I: 427; No 492; Viðareiði, The Faroes 1404]

Figure 2. Hjaltr *(*Hjalti*) as a byname 1309-1427.*

The inhabitants are called *hjelter* or even *helter* in the plural, and *helt* in the singular. As a byname this noun is found in several variants, but with two exceptions always representing the form with *hj*. In Figure 3 they are listed according to the persons' first names. I have made no systematic attempts at discovering which entries refer to the same person, so the number of persons is definitely less than the 54 entries for the period between 1516 and 1523:

NAME	YEAR	OCCUPAT.	LOCATION
Anders Hielth	1520-21	Farmer	Kvernes, Nordmøre
Ditmus (Diennis?) Hielt	1522	Servant	Bergen
Ener Hielth	1520-21	Fisherman?	Grip, Nordmøre
Erland Hielt	1522-23	Fisherman	Finnmark
Hans Hielt	1520	Skipper?	
Hans Helt styremandenn	1522	Skipper	Bergen
Hans Hielt	1521	Fisherman	Andenes, Nordland
Helge Hielt	1522-23	Fisherman	Finnmark
Jnger Hielt	1521	Poor woman	Bergen
Joen Hieltt	1516-17	Servant	Bergen
Jon Hieltt arbedtzkarll	1518	Servant	Bergen
Jon Hielt smededrengh	1518	Servant	Bergen
Joen Hielt Tommisszen	1519	Servant	Bergen
Jon Hielt	1519-20		Bergen
Ion Hielt	1520	Skipper	
Jon Hielt	1520-21		Bergen
Ionn Hielt	1521	Fisherman	Andenes, Nordland
Jonn Hieltt paa Ask	1522	Farmer	Eikanger, Hordaland
Ionn Hielt	1522	Servant	Bergen
Karine Hielt	1521	Poor woman	Bergen
Clawess (Claws) Hielt	1518	Skipper	Bergen
Claues Hielt	1521	Skipper	Bergen
Claues Hielt	1521	Skipper	Bergen
Lasse Hielt	1519-20	Servant	
Lasse Hielt	1520-21	Servant	Bergen
Lasse Hieltt	1521-23	Servant	Bergen
Magge Hielt	1521	Poor woman	Bergen
Marine Hielt	1521	Poor woman	Bergen
Mogens Hielt	1521	Sailor?	Bergen
Mogens Helt	1522	Sailor?	Bergen
Mogens Hielt	1521	Fisherman	Lofoten, Nordland
Mogens Hielt	1522	Servant	Bergen
Magens Hielth	1520-21	Fisherman?	Edøy, Nordmøre
Nielss Hieltt	1516-17	Servant	Bergen
Niels Hielt bryggere	1518	Brewer	Bergen
Niels Tommessen Hielt	1518	Servant	Bergen
Nils Hielt	1519	Fisherman?	Troms
Niels Hielt	1519	Servant	Bergen

Niels Hielt	1521	Fisherman?	Hillesøy, Troms
Niels Hielt	1522	Servant	Bergen
Olaf Hielt	1522	Servant	Bergen
Oluff Hielt	1522-23	Servant	Bergen
Olaff Hielt bryggere drengen	1522	Brewer's boy	Bergen
Oluff Hielth	1520-21	Fisherman?	Stappen, Finnmark
Olaff Hielt	1522	Fisherman?	Stappen, Finnmark
Olaff Hielt [pa Skede]	1519	Farmer	Kvinnherad, Hordaland
Per Hielt	1522	Fisherman	Hillesøy, Troms
Powel Hielt	1521	Fisherman	Finnøy, Rogaland
Siwor Hieltt	1516-17	Servant	Bergen
Siurdt Hjelt	1521	Fisherman	Andenes, Nordland
Siwrd Hielt	1521	Fisherman	Andenes, Nordland
Siwrd Hielt	1521	Fisherman	Lofoten, Nordland
Stenffenn Hielt	1521	Servant	Bergen
Torbiorn Hielt [pa Skede]	1519	Farmer	Kvinnherad, Hordaland

Figure 3. Hjelt *as a byname c. 1520. Sources: NRJ I, III, V passim.*

There were certainly a number of Shetlanders in the country who were not known by such bynames, but given the limited information in the sources it is impossible to decide the nationality of each individual. In some cases a non-Scandinavian personal name such as *William, Robert, James* or *Archibald* may be taken as an indication of the name-bearer's nationality, in this case probably Scottish (and the number of persons with the bynames *Skotte* or *Skottekone* is nearly as high as that for *Hjelt*). However, it seems that the Shetlanders of this period still to a great extent bore Norse or adapted foreign names (cf. the list presented in Ballantyne and Smith 1999: 183-194). More or less by chance I stumbled upon the mention of four men and a woman who, judging from the context, must have been Shetlanders, several from Fetlar: 'Jenss Ericksen oc Siwor Toraldsen i Fedelaar', 'Adam Enerssen ... i Fedelaar', and 'the Hielther ... Moghens Olszen oc Maryon Oluffs dotther'. These islanders were buying a ship from a Norwegian in 1519 (*NRJ* I: 340f.). I should like to emphasise that from their Christian names and patronymics alone, these people would be very difficult to distinguish from native Norwegians, though *Adam* and *Maryon* do point to foreign naming traditions. But it should be realised that by 1519 a large number of foreign names had been adopted by native Norwegians, so the name material is not a reliable source in this connection.

Most of the Shetlanders I have identified are mentioned in connection with Bergen – as servants or labourers at the castle, or as skippers and sailors. But some are found as taxpayers among ordinary fishermen or even as farmers. These must be regarded as bona fide immigrants and not just guest workers. It seems the Shetlanders – like the Faroese – were not regarded as foreigners to the same extent as Germans and Scots – or Danes for that matter – and in contrast with these other nationals they were more accepted and allowed more extensive travel and opportunities for settlement within the country.

The number of Shetlanders greatly exceeds that of the Faroese, which can be explained both by the larger population of Shetland and by the much shorter distance from Norway. Even so, there is little doubt that for centuries both the Faroese and the Shetlanders had depended on contact with Bergen for most of their trade, and also on Norwegian coastal settlements for their supply of timber. Would it not then be reasonable to assume that some of these islanders left traces in Norwegian place-names, first and foremost along the western shores?

4. Toponymics

A number of Norwegian place-names seem to bear evidence of contact across the North Sea from the Faroes and from Shetland, and possibly also of immigration from the islands to the mainland. Among such names are Færøya, Færevik, Færingsholman – Hjelten, Hjelthavna, Hjeltnes. In the standard work on Norwegian names, *Norske Gaardnavne*, these names – when included – are without exception interpreted as having nothing to do with the Faroes or Shetland, and in most cases probably rightly so.

4.1. The Faroes – The Faroese

There is no room for any thorough discussion of the names starting with *Fær*, but I shall present those mentioned in Oluf Rygh's *Norske Gaardnavne* (*NG*; 'Norwegian Farm-Names'); cf. Figure 4 (see next page). The names are identified by location, volume and page in *NG*, and the final column gives the oldest written forms and the suggested interpretations.

No reference to either Faroese people or the Faroes is found in the comments, though for two names ON *fær* n. is suggested as a possible interpretation, and for the last name in my list, Færøyna, this is done without any reservation.

Many other names might have been included in this discussion, but as

these are the only ones treated in the volumes of *NG*, they are also the only
ones for which older written forms are available. *Norsk stadnamnleksikon*
(*NSL*; 'Dictionary of Norwegian Place-Names') has just two entries for
names in *Fær*: *Færder*, which is clearly irrelevant in this connection, and
Færøya. This latter name is described as 'frequent' and the specific is
explained as 'believed to be' ON *fær* n., 'sheep'. The name Færvik (a farm
next to a bay off the island of Tromøya by Arendal) is then said to be of
'probably' the same origin, and finally a semantic interpretation is added: 'As
is the case with *Sauøya* the island name of *Færøya* tells us that people have
let their sheep graze on these islands' (*NSL*: 162).

Initially it seemed likely that names in *Fær* + a word for 'bay' (*vik* and
våg) might indicate places where ships coming from the Faroes used to dock,
but after having compared the situation of the places with such names (and
there are many more than those listed in *NG*), I have found this interpretation
less likely. I shall mention a few instances:

NAME	LOCATION	NG	COMMENTS
Færstad	Nannestad, Akershus	2: 394	*i Færekstadum* 1316; **Færekr*?; intrusive *k*?
Ferstad	Strinda, Sør-Trøndelag	XIV: 347	*af Færixstadom* c. 1430; < **Færisstaðir*? – ???
Færden	Norderhov, Buskerud	V: 48	*A Ferðini* 1338; < **Førðvin*, 'ford' m.
Færder	Tjøme, Vestfold	VI: 256	*Ferderøe* 1723; < **Fjarðar-eyjar*?
Færsnes	Vegårshei, Aust-Agder	VIII: 4	< **Ferisnes* < **Førisnes* < *fyri* n., 'copse of pine'?
Færås	Sveio, Hordaland	XI: 106	*Furaass* 1610; < **feri* n. = *fyri* n., 'copse of pine'?
Færåsen	Vigmostad, Vest-Agder	IX: 152	*Feraas* 1668; < *ferd* f., 'journey, travel'?
Færen	Meråker, N-Trøndelag	XV: 4	< [lake] *Feren*; [river] *Fera* < **for* f., 'pine'.
Færevik	Skånevik, Hordaland	XI: 50	*Ferreuig* 1567; < *ferd* f., 'shoal (of fish)'. Now: Feravika.

Færevåg	Tysnes, Hordaland	XI: 164	*Fergeuag* c. 1520; < *ferd* f.? Now: Færavågen.
Færestad	Lærdal, Sogn	XII: 65	*Færestad, Feriæstad* ca. 1520; **ferjustaðr*?
Færestrand	Selje, Nordfjord	XII: 403	*Ferrestrandt* 1563; ???
Være	Voss, Hordaland	XI: 553	*a Færini* c. 1360; *får* n., 'sheep'? *far* n., 'path'?
Ferset	Vega, Nordland	VI: 33	*af Færesætre* c. 1430; < *fær* n.??? but cf. Foråsskardet, nearby
Færvik	Tromøy, Aust-Agder	VIII: 98	*Feruig* 1593; < *fær* n., 'sheep' or gen. pl. *færa*?
Færøyna	Solund, Sogn	II: 222	*Færøy* 1427; *fær* n., 'sheep'

Figure 4. Names beginning with Fær *listed in Oluf Rygh: Norske Gaardnavne.*

Færevik (in Skånevik, Hordaland) is not found in ON sources, the oldest form being *Ferreuig* in 1567. Magnus Olsen (*NG* XI: 50) emphasizes that this name cannot be old enough to contain the element *fær*, and he suggests the word *ferd* n., in the sense of 'shoal (of fish)'. I am not ready to accept his view on the age of the name, but on the other hand I cannot see that there is any reason for connecting it with the Faroes. The name refers to two separate farms by separate bays, but these are situated far from the coast proper and are not at all noteworthy or particularly suitable for landing ocean-going vessels.

Færevåg (in Tysnes, Hordaland) is first mentioned in the 1520's. There is an identical name in Bømlo (also in Hordaland), though with no older forms. Both names refer to well sheltered bays, certainly suitable for landing, but they are both unlikely places to do so if you come in from the open sea. In both cases there are plenty of better harbours further west.

Færvik (Tromøya, Aust-Agder) is treated by Amund B. Larsen in *NG* VIII, published five years before Olsen's volume on Hordaland, and his suggested interpretation is *fær* as, he says, is so often found in *Færøy(a)*. The farm of Færvik is fairly substantial, but its earliest written form is only from 1593. The bay which has given name to the farm, lies off the southern part of the island of Tromøya, going in from the open sea of Skagerrak. In this case I would not rule out a connection with the Faroes, but I fully recognize that such an idea can be little more than guesswork.

One name which is not included in *NG*, *Færingsholman* (Frøya, Sør-Trøndelag), may be thought to contain the word *færing* = *færøying*, 'person from the Faroes', but another possibility is perhaps more likely. *Færing* m., is a commonly used word for a certain type of boat with four oars. It is known along the entire coast and the oldest record of the word I have found is from the 17th century, though it is probably older, cf. modern Icelandic *færæringur* m., and the ON adjective *ferærðr*, 'supplied with four oars'.

Apart from *Færvik* on the south coast, the only name which without reservation is interpreted in *NG* as containing ON *fær* n., 'sheep', is *Færøya*. This name occurs in several places, and in slightly different variants: *Færøy*, *Færøya*, *Færøyna* and *Færøyni*, which I have registered in 17 different places along the coast, from Vest-Agder in the south-west to Troms in the north.

Only one of these names is mentioned in *NG*, Færøyna, the name of an island as well as a farm in the parish of Solund north of the mouth of the Sogne fjord. Three medieval forms are mentioned in *NG* XII: 222: *Fæøy* (1291, in a copy from 1427), *Færøy* in 1427 and 1463 (in a later copy) and *Færøn* from c. 1490. 16th century forms are *Førenn* and *Ferøenn*, and the name is found as *Ferrøenn*, *Ferøe*, and *Ferøen* in the 17th century.

The interpretation of the specific given in *NG* is ON *fær* n., 'sheep', and the editor of Vol. XII supports this by referring to a number of names of islands with other words for animals as their first elements.

As this island is the only one by this name which houses a farm, it is also the only name with really old recorded forms. This does not mean, however, that the other *Færøy*-names cannot be equally old – or older for that matter. What seems to be characteristic of the places called *Færøya* is the often rather exposed position towards the open sea. I have compared them to places called *Sauøya*, which can only mean 'sheep-island', and found that these much more frequent names have a somewhat different distribution; they are found over a larger part of the country, frequent even in the south-east and further to the north, though not least in the same areas as the *Færøy*-names, the west-coast. The islands bearing the name of *Sauøya* are, however, generally smaller than the ones called *Færøya*, and they have on the whole a much more sheltered position, screened by other islands, and they are also often found fairly close to old settlements (though there are of course exceptions to this). However, the most characteristic feature is that there are often other islands in the vicinity with names like *Lamøya*, *Lamholmen*, *Geitøya*, *Nautøya*, *Feøya*, all of them indicating that the islands in question have been used for the grazing of domestic animals.

Finally it is worth noting that there is no instance of *Fær* being the specific in names ending in *holm(en)*, while variants of *Sau+holm(en)* are found all along the coast from the Oslo fjord to the Russian border (73 entries in the Central Place-Name Register; SSR). Until I have proof of the contrary, I will reject the old interpretation of Færøya and maintain that these names ultimately reflect an association with the islands in the Atlantic.

4.2. Shetland – The Shetlanders

When looking for possible traces of Shetlanders in place-names in Norway, it seems reasonable to begin by looking at the farm-names which may be connected with the bynames *Hjaltr* or *Hjalti*. The number is not overwhelming. In *NG* I have found only the names listed in Figure 5 (see next page), and most of these may at best be labelled dubious or obscure.

Lind (1915: 538) suggests that the man's name *Hjalti* is part of the third name on this list, *Hjeltar*, but this seems at best impossible to prove, as the thirteen names in Norway ending in *arfr* are all regarded as obscure by other scholars. However there is nothing in the topography around the farm of this name to suggest a derivation from *hjalt*, 'hilt', which has been proposed for some of the names and seemingly substantiated in the case of *Hjeltnes*. Only the last two names on the list may safely be regarded as containing either the byname *Hjaltr/Hjalti* (rather than the personal name), or the designation of nationality. In both cases it is a question of a part of a divided farm; in the first case the two now substantial farms of *Skråstad* (< *Skrástaðir*), and the second in all probability indicating one third of the large farm **Sand*, since the 16th century known as *Hjellsand*, *Sørsand* and *Nordsand*.

NAME,	LOCATION	*NG*	COMMENTS
Hjelten	Brunlanes, Vestfold	VI: 315	*a Hioltini* c.1400; from *hjalt* n., 'hilt'.
Hjeltjelt	Nes, Hedmark	III: 59	*Hielckieldt* 1593; dubious: from *hjalt* n., 'hilt', or *hjalti*, m., *hjaltr* m., 'Shetlander'?
Hjeltar,	Skjåk, Oppland	IV.1: 38	*Hialttarfwæ* 1333; from *hjalt* n., 'hilt'?
Hjelten,	Hamre, Hordaland	XI: 342	cf. Hjeltnes.
Hjeltnes,	Ulvik, Hordaland	XI: 447	*Hialtnes* c. 1330; cf. Hjelten; a skerry outside the headland looks like a *hjalt* n., 'hilt'.

Jetland, Kyrkjebø, Sogn	XII: 179 *Hettland* 1567, *Jettland* 1603; obscure. *Hjaltland*, *hjalt* n., 'hilt', or *hesli* n., 'grove of hazel trees'?
Hjetlund, Sør-Fron, Oppland	IV.1: 127 *Hiætlundæ* (gen.) 1361; from *hjalti* m., *hjaltr* m., 'Shetlander'.
*Hjalta-Skrástaðir, Vang, Hedmark	III: 89 *Hiæltaskrastader* 1395; from *hjaltr* m., 'Shetlander'.
Hjellsand, Øksnes, Nordland	XVI: 386 *Hieltesand, Hielsand* 1614; from *hjalti* m., *hjaltr* m., 'Shetlander' (rather than *hjallr* m., 'shelf').

Figure 5. Possible Hjalt-*names according to Oluf Rygh's Norske Gaardnavne.*

Hjalta-Skrástaðir may well take its name from a man called Jón Hjaltr, who is mentioned in the same source as the place-name (*DN* IV: 479; Oslo 1395):

at þet sama Skrastader. sem Paal helt ok sat aa. eitir Hiælta
Skrastader ok at Rannogh Pals dotter med sinom husbonda
Jone Hialt þet aatte
[that this same Skrastader, which Páll held and sat in, bears the
name Hjalta-Skrastaðir, and that Rannveig Páll's daugh-ter,
with her husband Jón Hjalt, owned it]

It is worth noting that this place-name is found in the inland county of Hedmark, which shows that the Shetlanders were not confined to the west (cf. Figure 5).

Rygh overlooked another name, from the neighbouring county of Oppland, but it is nonetheless of interest. In a letter from the valley of Gausdal, in 1333, a man called *Hagbarðr í Hjaltabergi* appears. His grandfather *Jón Hjalti* is also mentioned, as owner of a part of a farm called Einstad (*DN* I: 181; *Hjaltaberg* 1333):

Þæir helldo handom saman Þorstæin Þœfuer ok Hagbardr j
Hiælltæbærghe vndir þui skillyrdi at Hagbardr væitti þui vidr

gangu at han hafdi þa fyrsta penigh ok sidusta ok alla adra þa
er þær j millim er af Þorstæini Þœfue firir alla þa jord er Jon
hiælltte fadur fader hans atte j Æinastadum ...
[Þorsteinn Þœfr and Hagbarðr í Hjaltabergi shook hands on the
agreement that Hagbarðr admitted that he had [received] the
first penny and the last, and all others between, for all that land
which Jón Hjalti, his father's father, owned in Einastaðir]

One may safely conclude that *Hjaltaberg refers to a part of the present farm
of Berge, very close to Einstad.

Finally I will mention Hjälteby in the parish of Valla in the island of
Tjörn, in present-day western Sweden, first recorded as j Hjaltabø c. 1400. It
has been suggested that the specific element contains either hjalta, the
designation of nationality hjaltr in the genitive plural, or the genitive singular
of the byname Hjalti.

One argument in favour of the former interpretation is the presence of
some other names which also indicate nationality: the now lost
*Íslendingabœr, part of the village of Bö in the neighbouring parish of
Stenkyrka, and Guddeby, also in this part of Båhuslen, which contains either
the genitive plural of gautr m., 'man from Götaland', or the genitive singular
of a personal name Gauti. As regards Hjälteby, the personal name cannot
completely be ruled out, but either way the name must ultimately refer to a
person or persons from Shetland. The same interpretation is also one of many
suggested for the name Hjältön, of an island in the not so distant parish of
Bokenäs.

Hjeltefjorden	Øygarden, Hordaland
Hjelteflua (skerry)	Øygarden, Hordaland
Hjelteskjeret	(skerry) Øygarden, Hordaland
Hjeltaneset	Askøy, Hordaland
Hjeltaskjeret, Hjelte?	(skerry) Askøy, Hordaland
Hjeltholmen	Austrheim, Hordaland
Hjeltneset	Austrheim, Hordaland
Hjelterinden	(ridge) Bergen, Hordaland
Hjeltevardneset	Fedje, Hordaland
Hjeltholmen	Fjell, Hordaland
Hjeltskjerneset	Lindås, Hordaland
Hjelthavna	(harbour) Os, Hordaland
Hjeltaflua	(skerry) Tysnes, Hordaland

Hjeltholmen	Gulen, Sogn og Fjordane
Hjeltøyna	(island) Gulen, Sogn og Fjordane
Hjeltneset	Bremanger, Sogn og Fjordane
Hjeltholmen	Herøy, Nordland
Hjeltfjellet	(mountain) Hattfjelldal, Nordland

Figure 6. More possible Hjalt-*names*

In addition to these few possible or probable instances of names referring to Shetlanders, I will finally present a list of names extracted from the on-line official place-name register SSR (see Figure 6, above). The names are mainly from coastal areas and may all be interpreted as containing some reference to Shetlanders (though some are clearly secondary formations coined in relation to names of major topographical features bearing a *Hjelte*-name). Furthermore, one cannot exclude the possibility that some contain a topographical appellative **hjalt*. A study of the local topography will, I feel sure, exclude the appellative in many cases, and we will be left with the choice between a personal byname or the designation of nationality.

I have had no opportunity to go and look at all these places with names in *Hjelt*, but judging from maps the two last names – both from Northern Norway – can probably be ruled out, as *Hjeltfjellet* is well inland, and *Hjeltholmen* definitely has a hilt-like shape. But for the other 16 names I maintain there is good reason to consider a Shetland connection. *Hjeltefjorden* is the name of the main sailing route into Bergen from the north, and is generally explained as having been named after the Shetlanders (cf. *NSL*: 216). The distribution of these 16 names – along the west coast centering on Bergen – is on the whole a strong indication of their having the same origin, and in my view these names of topographical features also strongly support a reinterpretation of other *Hjelt*-names in Southern Norway, especially on the west coast, where contact with Shetland and Shetlanders has always been close.

5. Conclusion

Initially, I briefly discussed the Old Norse names of The Faroes and of Shetland, and the corresponding designations of their inhabitants. The main aim, however, has been to discuss the extent to which it is possible to find onomastic evidence of Faroese and Shetlanders in Norway. Thus in section three, I have presented some personal names and bynames in medieval and early modern Norwegian sources which strongly indicate that the name bearers originated in, or had some other close connection to, these islands. There is all reason to believe that even Norwegian toponymics contain elements that show such a connection, though this is far more difficult to prove. In section four, a number of such place-names is discussed in some detail, focusing in particular on names with the specific elements *fær-* and *Hjelt-*. Though other interpretations are in some cases possible, I argue that there can be little doubt that a fair number of the place-names in question ultimately reflect the strong cultural bonds across the North Sea.

Literature

Ballantyne, J.H. & Smith, B. (eds), 1999: *Shetland Documents 1195-1579*. Lerwick.

DN = *Diplomatarium Norvegicum*. I-. Christiania/Oslo, 1847-.

Fellows-Jensen, G., 1997: 'Ferrensby: Vitnisburður um, at føroyingur hevur hildið til í Yorkshire í víkingøld', *Málting. Tíðarit um føroyskt mál og málvísindi* 21, 20-22.

Fritzner = J. Fritzner, 1883-1896: *Ordbog over det gamle norske Sprog*. 2. udg. Kristiania.

Jakobsen, J., 1928-1932: *An Etymological Dictionary of the Norn Language in Shetland* 1-2. London/Copenhagen.

Jakobsen, J., 1936: *The Place-Names of Shetland*. London/Copenhagen.

Liestøl, K., 1941: 'Det norrøne folkeviseumrådet', *Nordiskt Tidskrift*, published by Letterstedtska Föreningen, 1936, 271-283. [Reprinted in *Saga og folkeminne*. Oslo, 1941, 141-155.]

Lind, E.H., 1905-1915: *Norsk-isländska dopnamn ock fingerade namn från medeltiden*. Uppsala/Leipzig.

Lind, E.H., 1921: *Norsk-isländska personbinamn från medeltiden*. Uppsala.

NG = *Norske Gaardnavne* 1-19. Kristiania/Oslo, 1897-1936. (http://www.dokpro.uio.no/rygh_ng/rygh_form.html.)

NgL = *Norges gamle Love indtil 1387* 1-5. Edited by R. Keyser et al. Christiania, 1847-1895.

NRJ = *Norske Regnskaber og Jordebøger fra det 16de Aarhundrede* 1-5. Edited by H.J. Huitfeldt-Kaas et al., Christiania/Oslo, 1885-1983.

NSL = *Norsk stadnamnleksikon*. J. Sandnes & O. Stemshaug (eds). 4. utg. Oslo, 1997.

OED = *Oxford English Dictionary*: http://dictionary.oed.com.

Olsen, M., 1931: 'Gammelnorske skibsnavn', *Maal og minne* 1931, 33-43.

SSR = *Sentralt stedsnavnregister*: (http://ngis2.statkart.no/norgesglasset/default.html.)

Vågslid, E., 1959: 'Shetland', *Norsk allkunnebok*, vol. 9, 1031.

Notes

[1] 'færskinn, n. Faareskind; forekommer som Navn paa teigr' (Fritzner I: 527). In the source (DN VIII: 314; Bogge, Eresfjord, Møre og Romsdal, 1428) the word is written *Ferskin*, which may preferably be interpreted as 'four skins', cf. a name like *Niskinn* ('nine skins') and compounds such as *ferbyrðingr* m., *ferdagaðr* adj., *ferfalda* v., *ferfaldr* adj., *ferfætingr* m., etc. (Fritzner I: 404f.).

[2] Cf. *DN* XIX: 513: '...De Ermundo Skeype de eadem et eorum sociis. pro M/xx dur. pisc. valoris. L li. pro MMM. bord. valoris ix li. pro Cent et Lx boll. olei. valoris. xviij li. et pro. ix. CCC. croplinge. valoris iiij li. xiij s. intrando in **ffarroynke** xx s. v d.'

The Significance of Names: Scandinavian Personal Names in the Northern and Western Isles

David Sellar

The significance of place-names is well known and well explored; the significance of personal names rather less so, certainly in Scotland. In keeping with the theme of this conference, linking name studies in Britain and Ireland with those in Scandinavia, this paper explores the significance to be attached to the use of Scandinavian personal names in the Northern and Western Isles, with particular reference to the ruling dynasties of Orkney, and the Isle of Man and the Hebrides from the 10th to the 13th centuries. It also draws attention to the later history of some personal names of Scandinavian origin in the Hebrides, their adoption into Gaelic, and subsequent transmogrification into English. The paper has benefited from pioneering studies by Hermann Pálsson (1981), Gillian Fellows-Jensen (1995) and Brian Ó Cuív (1988). Ó Cuív's article on 'Personal Names as an Indicator of Relations between Native Irish and Settlers in the Viking Period', in particular, demonstrates how personal name research can contribute to more general historical debate.

Figure 1 shows the dynasty of the Jarls of Orkney from the tenth to the early thirteenth centuries, and Figure 2 the dynasty of Man and the Isles from its second founder Godfrey (or Godred) Crovan (*Goðrøð; Gofraid*) until the end of its rule in 1265.[1] The personal names shown are nearly all male as information on female names is limited. With the exceptions of *Paul* and *Magnus*, the male names in both dynasties are entirely Scandinavian until the appearance of *David, John* and *Henry* in the Orkney line at the beginning of the 13th century. However, although both dynasties favoured Scandinavian names, it is at once evident that they drew their names from different lexicons. Allowing for occasional exceptions, such as *Rognvald/Ragnall* and *Harald*, there is little overlap in nomenclature, although the name *Somerled* (*Sumarliði; Somairle*) appears once and early in the Orkney line, while the imported and sanctified name *Magnus* appears once and late in the Manx dynasty. Elsewhere I have characterised the names favoured by the Manx dynasty as 'conspicuously royal Norwegian names' (Sellar 2000a: 190). In fact, they are almost exclusively so, the exception being the personal name

199

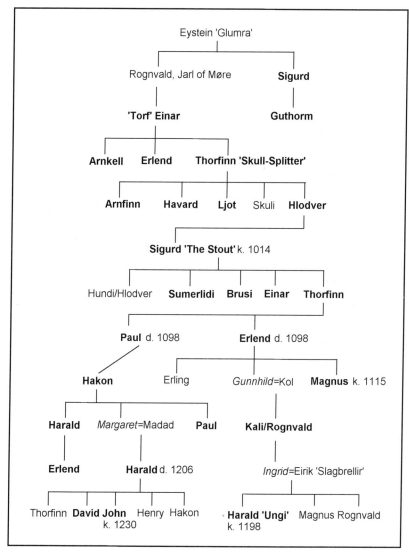

Figure 1. Jarls of Orkney.[2]

Lagman(n), also Scandinavian, which comes from the office of lawman, and gives rise to the Scottish surnames Lamont and McClymont. The names used by the Orkney Jarls do not have this same general character

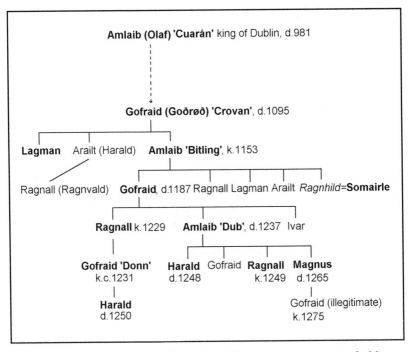

Figure 2. Kings of Man and the Isles (Kings' names appear in bold).

A second point to note is the determined use of Scandinavian names in the dynasty of Man and the Isles, to the exclusion of Gaelic. This may not seem remarkable, but there are a number of reasons why it calls for comment. The first is that it is not uncommon to find a mixture of Scandinavian and Gaelic names in Ireland from the late 10th century onwards, as Ó Cuív has demonstrated (Ó Cuív 1988). In Scotland, just such a mixture of Gaelic and Scandinavian names is to be found in the other branch of the dynasty of the Isles, the *Clann Somairle*, as discussed below. In the Isle of Man itself, one of the features of the runic inscriptions carved on the magnificent 10th and 11th century crosses is the mixture of Gaelic and Scandinavian names: 'The inscriptions on the crosses show that Vikings might give their sons Gaelic names, while men with Gaelic names chose Scandinavian names for their children' (Fellows Jensen 1978: 315; and see Page 1983). The fact that Gaelic personal names are not used by the Manx dynasty is the more remarkable given the frequency of Gaelic by-names (Megaw 1976: 16-18; Sellar 2000a: 191).

A further pointer to the gaelicised nature of Manx society is the Manx kings' patronage of Gaelic praise poetry, including what 'may be the earliest extant praise-poem in classical Early Modern Irish', a poem in praise of Ragnall, king of Man, d.1229 (Ó Cuív 1957). Elaborate praise poems of this kind, like Scaldic verse, were written for an educated audience, and point to a gaelicised court (see Megaw 1976). The poem *An Address to Aonghus of Islay*, composed c. 1250 for Angus MacDonald of Islay of the rival dynasty of the Isles, provides another early example of this type of verse, and also of a mixture of names: one stanza begins, 'Around thee are *Thorkel*, *Ivar* and *Olaf* ... heroes of Dublin of bright hazels' (Bergin 1970: 169-174). Yet the Manx dynasty used exclusively Scandinavian male names. The conclusion must be that the Manx kings attached particular significance to the Scandinavian names in question. Godfrey Crovan, himself king of Dublin as well as king of Man and the Isles, probably descended from the Uí Imhair kings of Dublin and York. The names favoured by the Manx kings were not only royal, but also carried, I would suggest, a message of royal descent, stretching back through the Uí Imhair kings to early Scandinavian royalty.

The names of Somerled's descendants – (Figure 3) the *Clann Somairle* – show a very different profile from those of the Manx dynasty, and contain a mixture of Scandinavian and Gaelic names. The Scandinavian names *Ragnall*, *Gofraid* and *Olaf* (*Amlaíb*) proudly proclaim the descent of the *Clann Somairle* from the dynasty of Godfrey Crovan, while the name of the founder Somerled (*Somairle*) also continued in regular use (for this name, see Pálsson, 1981, and Fellows-Jensen 1995: 398-400). A grandson

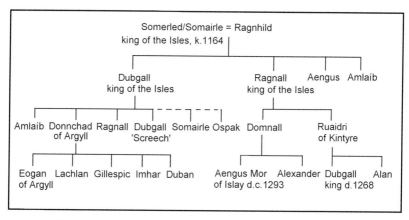

Figure 3. The Clan Somairle – the first three generations.[3]

of Somerled named *Ospak* (or *Uspak*) is also on record. It has been suggested that *Ospak* stands for the Gaelic *Gillespic*, but this remains uncertain (Duncan 1975: 547; Barrow 1981: 110). Two other popular names among the *Clann Somairle*, *Dubgall* and *Lachlan*, although Gaelic in form, appear to have Scandinavian affinities. Ó Cuív comments on *Dubgall* that, 'Although not a linguistic borrowing from Scandinavia it clearly has associations with the Vikings' (Ó Cuív 1988: 83); while Ó Corraín and Maguire note that *Dubgall* means 'dark stranger', and is 'one of the Irish names for the Vikings' (1990: Dubgall). The personal name *Lochlainn* or *Lachlan* is believed to relate to the land of *Lochlann* from which the Vikings came. Ó Corraín and Maguire gloss the name as meaning 'Viking' (1990 Lochlainn; and see Ó Cuív 1988: 83). However, reflecting Somerled's own hybrid ancestry – for he was the son of *Gilla-Brigte* and grandson of *Gill-Adomnain* – his descendants, unlike the kings of Man and the Isles, also used Gaelic names from the beginning: *Angus* in the first generation; *Duncan* (*Donnchad*), *Donald* (*Domnall*) and *Ruaidri* in the second; *Ewen* (*Eogan*), *Gillespic* and *Angus* again in the third.[4] In the third generation the foreign name *Alexander*, favoured by the kings of Scots, and soon to be gaelicised as *Alasdair*, also appears, as does *Alan*.

Given that few Scandinavian personal names, with the exception of *Magnus*, appear to have remained in regular use in Orkney down to modern times or, indeed, in the Isle of Man, the continuing popularity, in their Gaelic guise, of several of the Scandinavian names favoured by *Clann Somairle* is quite striking.[5] *Ragnall* in particular (*Raonuil*, *Ranald*) remains perennially popular. The name of Somerled's wife *Ragnhild*, the daughter of Olaf of Man, is also still popular in the Hebrides in its Gaelic form *Raonaid*, although this is often masked in English by the use of the false equivalent form *Rachel*. *Gofraid* too (or *Goraidh*) was in common use until recently, and survives still in English as *Godfrey* in MacDonald and MacAllister families. *Somerled* itself has never fallen quite out of use, whether as *Somerled* or *Somhairle* (anglicised *Sorley* or *Samuel*), and has become familiar again as the name of the Gaelic poet Sorley Maclean (*Somhairle MacGilleoin*).

The only other Hebridean kindred for which it is possible to construct even a skeleton pedigree as far back as the 13th century is that of the MacLeods. Figure 4 shows the main lines of Harris and Lewis down from the eponymous *Leod* (*Ljót*), who must have flourished towards the end of the 13th century (here following Matheson 1981, as amended by Sellar 2000b). Leod's traditional ancestry is taken back to his great grandfather *Olvir* (a name later confused with *Olaf*) '*Snoice*'. This Table resembles that of the

Clann Somairle in showing a mixture of both Gaelic and Scandinavian names. The onomastic profile, however, is different from both the *Clann Somairle* (Table 3) and the kings of Man and the Isles (Table 2). The key names *Ragnall*, *Gofraid* and *Amlaíb* (*Olaf*) do not appear; a reason for scepticism about the MacLeod claim to descend in the direct male line from the last kings of Man (Sellar 2000b: 243). The Scandinavian names most favoured by the MacLeods are *Thormod* and *Thorkell*. Indeed, the MacLeods of Harris and Dunvegan (now MacLeod of MacLeod) are known in Gaelic as the *Siol Thormoid* (the seed or family of Tormod), and those of Lewis as the *Siol Thorcuil*. As *Tormod* and *Torcuil* (anglicised *Torquil*) these names are still in use today, notably among MacLeods, although *Tormod* usually appears in English under the false equivalent form of *Norman*.

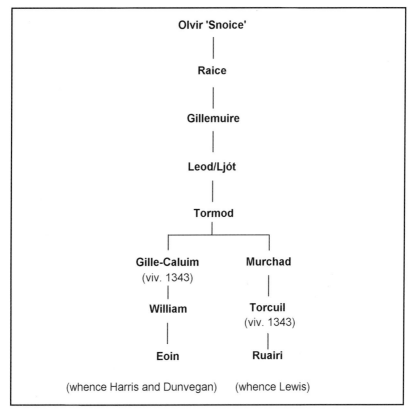

Figure 4. Early MacLeods.

The MacLeods of Lewis, who functioned in effect as a separate clan, are thought to have owed their rise, their lands and their status to marriage in the 14th century with an heiress of the family of *MacNeacail* or MacNicol (Sellar 1999). A branch of the original *MacNeacail* family remained in Skye, associated with the lands of Scorrybreac, by Portree. These Nicolsons – to use the form of surname which the chief adopted in the 17th century – used two quite distinctive forenames for many centuries, one of them Gaelic and the other Scandinavian. The Gaelic forename appears in a number of forms, some of them corrupt, such as *Malcomuill, Mulconeill, Malaneill* and *Mulcoill*. This almost certainly represents the rare name *Mael-Conghail* 'servant of Saint Congal'. The other name peculiar to the Nicolsons appears in modern Gaelic as *Armchuil*, and in the older written record under the guise of *Armiger*. The name is believed to have fallen out of use recently, although it still occurs in oral pedigrees. It emigrated to Prince Edward Island in Canada in the 19th century, where it became first *Armichael*, and then simply *Michael* (Sellar 1999: 13-14). The name appears to be the Scandinavian *Arnkell* or *Arnketil*, used, for example, by an early Jarl of Orkney. The similar name *Askell/ Asketil* gives the surname *MacAskill* in Skye, and the curious back formation *Taskill*, found once or twice as a forename; while *Torkell/ Torketil* gives MacCorquodale, a family long settled in Argyll.

The study of personal names helps to illuminate the nature of cultural contacts in the North Atlantic in the Viking Age and beyond. Ó Cuív was surely right to suggest that after the initial shock of Scandinavian invasion and settlement, contacts between Gael and foreigners 'were fairly common and often far from hostile' (Ó Cuív 1988: 85). This paper has looked at the use and adoption of Scandinavian names in a Gaelic context. The corresponding use and adoption of Gaelic names, such as *Niall, Muirceartach* (whence *Kjartan*) and Cormac in the Scandinavian context of Iceland has not been touched on, but points to the same conclusion.

Appendix: From Scandinavian through Gaelic to English

Most of the names discussed in the paper are listed below, together with a note of biblical or classical names used as equivalent forms in the Hebrides [E]. The list is conceived as a ready guide, and is not intended to be either definitive or exhaustive. It does not include Manx surnames, several of which derive from Scandinavian eponyms, as already noted. Scandinavian names appear in bold, and Gaelic names in italic.

Arnkell, Arnketil – *Armchuil* (obsolescent) – [E] Armiger – Armcholla – Armichael (Prince Edward Island). Name found among Nicolsons of Scorrybreac in Skye.

Askell, Asketil. Rare as a forename, but gives the surname MacAskill (whence the rare back-formation *Taskill*).

Dubgall – *Dugald* – *Dougall* (MacDougall).

Goðrøð – *Gofraid/Gofraidh* – *Goraidh* – Guthred – Godfrey – Godred (Isle of Man – mainly literary?) – Gorrie.

Hakon. Kenneth Nicholls suggests to me (personal communication) that this name may have given rise to [E] *Eachann/Eachunn*, whence in turn [E] Hector (see also Ó Corrain and Maguire 1990). Rendered as Hercules in Shetland.

Harald – *Arailt* – Harald. Gives the surname MacCrailt.

Ívar – *Ímar* – *Imhar* – *Iomhar* – [E] Edward (used 14th-20th century); also [E] Evander. Gives the surname MacIver.

Lagmann – *Lagman* – Laumon, whence the surnames Lamont and McClymont.

Ljót – Leod – [E] Claudius (literary; extremely rare).

Lochlainn – *Lachlan* – Lachlan – [E] Roland (12th-15th century). Gives the surname MacLachlan in Scotland.

Magnus. A name rarely used in the Hebrides, in contrast to the Northern Isles and Ireland. Gives the surnames MacManus, MacVinish.

Olaf – *Anlaf* – *Amlaíb* – *Amhlaidh* – Aulay, whence MacAulay. (*Amlaíb* was early confused with *Amalgaid*; and *Olvir* with *Olaf*.)

Ospak (**Uspak**) Gives the surnames MacUsbaig, MacCuspic.

Ragnhild – *Raonaid* – [E] Rachel/Rachael.

Ragnvald, Rognvald – *Ragnall* – *Raonail/Raonuil* – Ranald – Ronald – Randal – [E] Reginald, Reynold.

Sumarliði – *Somairlid* – *Somairle/Somhairle* – Sorley – [E] Samuel, Sam. Also [E] Socrates (rare). Gives the surname MacSorley.

Sveinn Rare as a forename, but gives *MacSuain* (MacSwan). Sometimes confused with the Gaelic forename *Suibhne*, whence the surname MacSween/MacSweeney.

Thorkell, Thorketil – *Torcail, Torcuil* – Torquil – [E] Tarquinius (literary; extremely rare). Particularly associated with the MacLeods of Lewis. Gives MacCorquodale.

Thormod – *Tormod* – [E] Norman. A favourite MacLeod name.

Literature

Bergin, O., 1970: *Irish Bardic Poetry*, D. Greene & F. Kelly (eds). Dublin.

Barrow, G.W.S., 1981: *Kingship and Unity: Scotland 1000-1306*. London.

Duncan, A.A.M., 1975: *Scotland: The Making of the Kingdom*. Edinburgh.

Fellows Jensen, G., 1978: 'The Manx Place-Name Debate: A View from Copenhagen'. In: P. Davey (ed.), *Man and Environment in the Isle of Man*. British Archaeological Reports British Series 54ii, 315-318.

Fellows-Jensen, G., 1995: 'Some Orkney Personal Names'. In: C.E. Batey, J. Jesch & C.D. Morris (eds), *The Viking Age in Caithness, Orkney and the North Atlantic*. Edinburgh, 397-407.

Matheson, W., 1981: 'The Ancestry of the MacLeods', and 'The MacLeods of Lewis', *Transactions of the Gaelic Society of Inverness* 51 for 1978-80, 68-80 and 320-337.

Megaw, B.R.S., 1976: 'Norseman and Native in the Kingdom of the Isles', *Scottish Studies* 20, 1-44. (A revised version of this paper appears in: P. Davey (ed.), *Man and Environment in the Isle of Man*. British Archaeological Reports British Series 54ii, 265-314.)

Ó Corraín, D. & Maguire, M., 1990: *Irish Names*. Dublin.

Ó Cuív, B., 1957: 'A Poem in Praise of Raghnall, King of Man', *Éigse* 8, 283-301.

Ó Cuív, B., 1988: 'Personal Names as an Indicator of Relations between Native Irish and Settlers in the Viking Period'. In: J. Bradley (ed.), *Settlement and Society in Medieval Ireland: Studies Presented to Francis Xavier Martin*. Kilkenny, 79-88.

Page, R.I., 1983: 'The Manx Rune-Stones'. In: C. Fell *et al.* (eds), *The Viking Age in the Isle of Man*. London, 133-146.

Pálsson, H., 1981: 'The Name Somhairle and its clan'. In: M. Benskin & M.L. Samuels (eds), *So Meny People Longages and Tonges: Philological Essays in*

Scots and Mediaeval English Presented to Angus McIntosh. Edinburgh, 167-172.

Sellar, W.D.H. & Maclean, A., 1999: *The Highland Clan MacNeacail (MacNicol): A History of the Nicolsons of Scorrybreac*, C.B.H. Nicholson (ed.). Waternish, Skye.

Sellar, W.D.H., 2000a: 'Hebridean Sea-Kings: the Successors of Somerled, 1164-1316'. In: E.J. Cowan & R.A. McDonald (eds), *Alba: Celtic Scotland in the Medieval Era*. East Linton, 187-218.

Sellar, W.D.H., 2000b: 'The Ancestry of the MacLeods Reconsidered', *Transactions of the Gaelic Society of Inverness* 60 for 1997-1998, 233-258.

Notes

[1] I have used the style 'King of Man and the Isles' for the original dynasty which ruled over the entire kingdom of the Isles from the Calf of Man north to the Butt of Lewis until partition in the mid-12th century, and ruled thereafter in Man and the Northern Hebrides. Both this dynasty and the Clann Somairle, who descended from it in the female line, used the style Righ Innsegall in Gaelic and Rex Insularum in Latin. It should be noted that some of the earlier names in the Orkney dynasty are on the sole authority of Orkneyinga Saga.

[2] Names are rendered here as in William Thomson's New History of Orkney. The names of Jarls appear in bold; and female names, where noticed, in italics.

[3] Gaelic forms of names have generally been preferred. The names of the brothers of Eogan of Argyll rest on later pedigree evidence.

[4] The name of Ewen son of Duncan appears in a bewildering variety of guises, including Eugenius de Argadia, Johannes Dugaldi and Jon Duncansson (see Sellar 2000a: 203).

[5] It is worth noting in passing, however, that several Manx surnames derive from Scandinavian forenames: thus Olaf (Amlaíb), Ragnall, Torkell and Tormod give Cowley, Crennell, Corkill and Cormode respectively.

Place-Names in Iceland and Shetland.
A Comparison

Svavar Sigmundsson

The place-names in Shetland and Iceland are in many cases similar, as more or less the same words, of Norse origin, have been the basis for the name-giving in both countries. John Stewart wrote in his book on the place-names of Shetland: 'In names Shetland is, in fact, a province of Norway' (1987: 36) and the same can be said about Iceland too. It has been maintained (Melchers 1994: 336) that more than 90% of the place-names in Shetland and the Orkneys are of Scandinavian origin. The similarity between the two countries can be illustrated by giving examples of parallel names in both areas (all examples of place-names in Shetland in this article are taken from Stewart 1987).

-dalur	(Deepdale Shetl. – Djúpidalur Icel.),
-fell	(Midfield Shetl. – Miðfell Icel.)
-fjörður	(Burrafirth Shetl. – Borgarfjörður Icel.)
-gil	(Swartigal Shetl. – Svartagil (Icel.)
-gjá	(Ramnageo Shetl. – Hrafnagjá Icel.)
-nes	(Stromness Shetl. – Straumnes Icel.)
-vík	(Breawick Shetl. – Breiðavík Icel.).

Figure 1. Examples of generics denoting topographical features.

The same can be said about the habitative generics like *-bólstaður* (Brebister Shetl. – Breiðabólstaður Icel.), *-bær* (Kirkaboe, Kirkaby Shetl. – Kirkjubær Icel.), *-staðir* (Tresta Shetl. – Tréstaðir or Þrasa-staðir Icel.).

In a paper I gave in Aberdeen in 1996 I discussed some Icelandic and Scottish place-names and gave some parallels of farm names in both areas, Iceland and the Scandinavian part of Scotland. At that time I did not have access to Stewart's book from 1987. I have now been able to go through it and compare it with the place-name material in Iceland. In spite of many parallels in generics between the two countries, the following ones, known in Shetland, do not exist in Icelandic place-names as a simplex or a generic.

Many of these generics or names are rare in Shetland, as the figures indicate: *bjálki* 'a beam' (1), *eyrir* 'ounce of silver'(1), *hlaðberg* 'a natural pier' (1), *hrunki* 'a big person' (1), *hytta* 'a hut' (4), *kamar* 'a privy' (2), *keyta* 'a mire' (1), *klodi* 'a lumpy hill, land with boulders' (8), *klubb* 'a lumpy hill', *klubba* 'a club' (3), *krá, kró* 'a nook, corner'(5), *kytja* 'a cottage, hut' (6), *pund* 'enclosure' (88), *skjá* 'a louver or skin frame to close a window; a window; a hut for drying fish and meat' (6), *stilli* 'an enclosure' (3), *vist* 'lodgings, an abode, provisions' (3).

As can be seen, of these *pund* is the most common as place-name or place-name element in Shetland. The word *kytja* is related to *kot*, which was very common in Iceland. Instead of *pund* and *stilli*, 'enclosure' in Shetland, Icelandic had the word *kví* or *rétt*. The Old Norse word *skjá* was not used in place-names whereas *hjallur* was used of 'a hut for drying fish'. *Krá* is nowadays only used in the sense of 'a pub' and *klodi* (as in Clothie) is unknown in Iceland.

Some comments can be made on Stewart's book from an Icelandic point of view. The place-names Sloag (Foula), Slaggan [slagin] (Aithsting) and Slukka (Bressay) are according to Stewart a parallel to e.g. Norwegian *slage* 'hollow in ground' (250). He does not mention the Icelandic word *slakki* 'hollow in ground', e.g. Skálavíkurslakki in Reykjarfjörður in Ísafjarðarsýsla. *Hérað* (Herra) is not 'a meeting place of a ting' in Iceland (130), but can among other things mean a 'ting district' (Vídalín 1846: 240).

Stewart has in most cases in his book mentioned parallels between place-names in the Nordic area which are also true about Icelandic place-names, especially farm names. He was unable to compare Shetland place-names with other place-names in Iceland, which is understandable given that they have not been published systematically, and are not all shown on maps.

I will here deal with some of the generics in Shetland place-names, according to Stewart, which he does not mention as Icelandic place-name generics or place-names or else directly states that they do not exist in Iceland. Here I will only take up Icelandic farm names which Stewart does not mention in his book (My main source is the place-name database in Örnefnastofnun Íslands.):

- *breiðr* adj., 'broad', e.g.: Brae in Breckin (Yell) : Breið in Skagafjörður.

- *burst* f.., *bust* f. 'roof-ridge', e.g.: Busts (Aithsting) : Bustarfell in Vopnafjörður.

- *gróf* f., 'a pit', e.g.: Gru (Fetlar) : Efri- and Syðri-Gróf in Árnessýsla.

– *hlaðhamar* 'a rock where boats are loaded, a natural pier', e.g.: Lahamar (Unst) : Hlaðhamar in Hrútafjörður.

– *höfuð* n., 'head', e.g.: Hellinahivda (Yell) : Strandarhöfuð in Rangárvallasýsla.

– *klúka* f., 'a little heap', e.g.: Clugan (Unst) : Klúka. Six farms in Iceland bear this name.

– *kuml* n., 'a burial mound', e.g.: Cumlins (Northmaven) : *Kuml* does not seem to appear as the final part of a farm-name in Iceland as Stewart correctly states (187), but it does occur as a name of a deserted farm in Árnessýsla.

– *merki* n., 'a boundary mark', e.g.: March [de mertsh] (Lunnasting) : Merki. Three farms in Iceland have this name.

– *skerpa* f., 'sharp, hard, dry ground', e.g.: Scarpo [skjerpa] (Unst) : Kúskerpi. Two farms have this name in Iceland, one in Húnavatnssýsla, the other one in Skagafjörður.

– *stífla* f ., 'a dam', e.g.: Stivler (Yell) : Stífla in Rangárvallasýsla.

– *svalar* f.pl., 'a balcony, walled passage round a house', e.g.: Swail [swel] (Unst). Stewart says that there are no records of this name in Iceland (264) : Umsvalir is a farm in Húnavatnssýsla.

– *sviðningur* m., 'burnt woodland (in Shetland heather)', e.g.: in Sweenie [swini] (Northmaven) : Sviðningur. Two farms bear this name, one in Húnavatnssýsla, the other one in Skagafjörður.

– *velta* f., 'cultivated (turned over) land', only in Heogravilta (Fetlar) : Flagvelta in Rangárvallasýsla.

These examples show that there are more parallels in farm names between these areas than we have been aware of.

The most common generics in compound farm names in Iceland are the topographical elements: *-nes*, *-dalr*, *-fell*/*-fjall*, *-fjörðr*, and *-vík*. Farm names with *-nes* in Iceland and Shetland are taken as examples here:

Blakknes	–	Blacksness (Scalloway)
Borgarnes	–	Burganes, Burranness (Delting, Yell, Whiteness, Cunningsburgh)
Grjótnes	–	Grutness (Dunrossness)

Haganes	–	Hoganess (Sandsting)
Hauganes	–	Heoganess (Yell)
Hvítanes	–	Whiteness
Krossnes	–	Crussaness (Yell)
Langanes	–	Langness (Aithsting)
Litlanes	–	Littleness (Whalsay, Sandsting)
Mjóanes	–	Mioness (Fetlar)
Sauðanes	–	Sodasness (Yell)
Straumnes	–	Stromness (Delting)
Svínanes	–	Swinaness (Unst)
Tjaldanes	–	Chalderness (Tingwall)
Torfnes	–	Turness (Northmaven)
Vallanes	–	Valliersness (Northmaven)
Vatnsnes	–	Watsness (Walls)

Figure 2. Examples of place-name parallels in -nes between Iceland and Shetland.

It is clear from the Icelandic farm names, that the Scandinavian generics -*vin*, -*ruð* and -*þveit* were not productive as place-name elements at the time of the settlement of Iceland soon after the year 870. On the other hand, the -*staðir* element became by far the most common habitation generic in Iceland. The *staðir*-farms were not amongst the biggest farms and seldom became church farms. The first settlement farms were normally named after topographical features. The -*staðir* farms have more or less the same distribution all over the country. They have many parallels in both countries.

Of the 33 -*staðir*-names Stewart has found in Shetland, at least the following 20 are also found in Iceland: Bardister (Barðastaðir), Basta (Bassastaðir), Baliasta (Bollastaðir), Brindister (Brandsstaðir), Busta (Býjarstaðir), Ancesti (Eysteinsstaðir), Haggersta (Hallgeirsstaðir), Hoversta (Hafrsstaðir, Hávarðarstaðir), Ringasta (Hringsstaðir), Calsta (Kalastaðir), Clousta (Klaufastaðir), Lumbister (Lambastaðir), Oddsta (Oddsstaðir), Scatsta (Skatastaðir), Skellister (Skjaldarstaðir), Ulsta (Úlfsstaðir), Vollister (Válastaðir), Wethersta (Viðar(s)staðir), Tresta (Tréstaðir, Þrasastaðir), Elvister (Ölvisstaðir) (see map in Waugh 1988: 70).

These -*staðir*-names could almost all be interpreted as having personal names as a specific, even if some of them could have another origin, e.g. Lambastaðir, from *lamb* and not *Lambi*.

Ten Shetland -*staðir*-names which are not represented in Iceland are the following: Asta (*Ásustaðir*), Bailister (*Ballastaðir*), Benston (*Beinastaðir*), Flamister (**Flámastaðir?*), Girlsta (*Geir-hildarstaðir*), Grista (*Griðstaðir*), Gunnista (*Gunnhildarstaðir*), Quendista (*Kvarndalsstaðir*), Ungirsta (*Unustaðir*), Oxensta (*Öxnastaðir*).

Stewart maintains that Flamister has as qualifier the word *flá* f 'a level part on a hillside', but in my opinion it is more likely to be ON *flámi* m (Shetl. *flomi*) 'a big area' (Icel. *flæmi*). Quendista is likely to be from *Kvíindisstaðir (*Cwindistay* 1506).

Of similar age as the -*staðir* farms in Iceland are farm names with -*bær* but they are far fewer. The *Landnámabók* refers to nine farm names in -*bær*. In sources from the Middle Ages reference is made to six farms with the simplex name *Bær*. Later on -*bær* became a common generic, independent of the Scandinavian influence. Oskar Bandle gave the explanation that this type of farm name had been dropped in preference for names in -*staðir* (Bandle 1977: 62). The use of personal names as a specific in names with -*bær* is uncommon in Iceland. In Shetland *býr*, *bær* occurs more than 30 times, and eight of them are simplexes. The compounds are not the same as in Iceland, only Icelandic Kirkjubær has its counterparts in Kirkaby, Kirkaboe in Shetland.

Younger types of farm names in Iceland are the names with *kot*. They are first mentioned in the fourteenth century but they later became very popular as croft names. Only five *kot*-names are registered in Shetland, and only one of them, Steenikots (Delting), has its parallel in Iceland in Steinskot.

In Iceland both -*gerði*, and -*hús* are amongst the most frequent farm names in later times although -*gerði* is already known in the settlement period. As is well known, farm names with -*garðr*, -*gerði* and -*hús* are common in Shetland.

In Icelandic the word *sel* was used for 'a shieling', a word known in North-Western Norway. The farm names in -*sel* are nearly 200 in Iceland, most common in the North Eastern part. The word, *setur* n., never appears in Icelandic farm names but it occurs in place-names, also the form *sætur* in North West Iceland. As known -*setur*/-*sætur* is very frequent in Shetland farm names. Here there is a clear difference between these two countries.

Some -*bólstaðir*-names are found in Iceland. I have earlier pointed out that the Breiðabólstaðir farms are nearly all found in South and West Iceland where the influence from the Western Isles has been said to be the most apparent, in place-names, personal names and in folklore. The Breiðabólstaðir-farms were bigger than the average -*staðir* farms and some of them had churches (Sigmundsson 1998: 331).

Various other compound place-names are found in both countries, e.g.:

Hurðarbak	–	Hurdiback (Papa Stour)
Kaldbakur	–	Caldback (Unst), and Calback (Delting)
Skjaldbreiður	–	Skelberry (Northmaven, Lunnasting and Dunrossness)
Vindás	–	Windhouse (Yell, Northmaven, Tingwall and Dunrossness).

Figure 3. Examples of common compound place-names.

When we take a closer look at in what parts of Shetland we find compound place-names which have parallels in Iceland, it seems as if most of them are in Unst, or 22 names, then in Yell, 16 names, and thereafter Northmaven with 12 place-names. Delting and Aithsting have nine, Sandsting eight, Walls seven and Fetlar six.

This comparison could perhaps indicate that the settlers, on their way to Iceland, sojourned in the Northern Isles, or at least had some sort of contact with people there. Only one settler in Iceland is said to have come from Shetland, according to *Landnámabók*, Þórir snepill Ketilsson, who settled in Kaldakinn and Hnjóskadalur in Suður-Þingeyjarsýsla (Benediktsson 1968: 271).

Most of the parallels mentioned here could be names coined independently in both countries on the basis of the common Norse word stock, though perhaps with one exception, namely Breiðabólstaður. The existence of so many of them in Iceland must be due to the Brebister names in Shetland and Orkney (cf. Gammeltoft 2001: 250).

Some of the existing farm name generics in Shetland have a slightly different meaning in Iceland. Hraun in Öxnadalur in Iceland and Roonan in Unst both have the word *hraun* 'rocky hill ground'; but in Iceland it means 'lava-covered ground' in the volcanic area.

Burrafirth in Shetland and Borgarfjörður in Iceland do not have the element *borg* in the same sense; it signifies a 'rocky hill' in Iceland, but a 'broch' in Shetland.

Farm names with *-dalur* in Iceland will always be found in a real valley, and is not a farm name element without the connotation 'valley', as occurs in Shetland.

The Shetland place-names are awaiting further investigation of what is Norse and what is Scottish. It might be rhetorical to say that more research is needed, but I would nonetheless like to conclude by saying that Icelandic and Shetland name studies could benefit enormously from a more thorough comparison of their place-names.

Literature

Bandle, O., 1977: 'Die Ortsnamen der Landnámabók'. In: *Sjötíu ritgerðir helgaðar Jakobi Benediktssyni 20. júlí 1977*. Reykjavík, 47-68.

Benediktsson, J. (ed.), 1968. *Íslendingabók. Landnámabók*. Íslenzk fornrit I. Reykjavík.

Gammeltoft, P., 2001: *The Place-Name Element bólstaðr in the North Atlantic Area*. Navnestudier 38. Copenhagen.

Jakobsen, J., [1936] 1993: *The Place-Names of Shetland*. Kirkwall.

Jónsson, F., 1907-1915: 'Bæjanöfn á Íslandi'. In: *Safn til sögu Íslands og íslenzkra bókmenta að fornu og nýju*. IV, 412-584. Skrá um fyrri liði í samsettum íslenzkum bæjanöfnum. Kaupmannahöfn/Reykjavík, 917-937.

Melchers, G., 1994: 'Shetland, Orkney och Caithness – tre skandinaviska utposter'. In: L-E. Edlund (ed.), *Kulturgränser – myt eller verklighet?*, DIABAS 4, 329-343.

Nicolaisen, W.F.H., 1976: *Scottish Place-Names: Their Study and Significance*. London.

Sigmundsson, S., 1998: 'Icelandic and Scottish Place-Names'. In: W.F.H. Nicolaisen (ed.), *Proceedings of the XIXth International Congress of Onomastic Sciences Aberdeen, August 4-11, 1996*, vol. 2. Aberdeen, 330-337.

Stewart, J., 1987: *Shetland Place-Names*. Lerwick.

Vídalín, P., 1846: *Skýríngar Páls lögmanns Jónssonar Vídalíns á fornyrðum íslenzkrar lögbókar er Jónsbók nefnist*. Reykjavík.

Waugh, D., 1988: 'The Scandinavian Element *Staðir* in Caithness, Orkney and Shetland', *Nomina* 11, 61-74.

Waugh, D., 1991: 'Shetland Place-Names', *Nomina* 13, 61-72.

Norse Settlement Names in *-land* in Shetland and Orkney

Inge Særheim

1. Introduction

The farm names with *land* n. as the main element form an important class of Scandinavian settlement names. In my thesis *Namn og gard. Studium av busetnadsnamn på -land* (Særheim 2001) I present a review of the settlement names of this class, i.e. of the distribution of the names and the way of naming. I have examined more thoroughly the names ending in *-land* from an area in southwestern Norway, concerning the interpretation of the names, the semantic meaning of the name element *land* and the dating of the names.

There are quite a few names of this type in Iceland, Shetland and Orkney. In this paper I will discuss *land*-names from Shetland and Orkney to see if these names may throw light on the two mentioned questions: the semantics of the name element *land* and the dating of the settlement names of this class.

2. Scandinavian place names ending in *-land*

The name element *land* is used in different ways in Scandinavian place names, according to the various semantics of the appellative *land* n. The meaning 'area, district' is found in ancient district names, like the Norwegian: Hålogaland, Hordaland and Rogaland, the Swedish: Värmland and Ångermanland, and the Danish: Jylland.

This word is also the final element in some ancient names of islands, like Gotland, Lolland and Åland. In younger names of islands and of sea-, lake- and riversides, like Hareidlandet and Eidelandet, the word is used in the meaning 'land as opposed to sea; river-, lake- or seaside'.

The name element *-land(et)* is also found in field names, in old and young names, meaning 'field; cultivated field', like Harpelandet (the growing of flax) and Hampelandet (the growing of hemp). Some of the field names ending in *-land* are old settlement names, originating from deserted farms.

Most settlement names with *land* n. as the main element are found in Norway, approximately 2,000 names, where the key area is the southwestern part of the country, i.e. Agder, Rogaland and Hordaland. More than 900 settlement names in *-land* are found in Vest-Agder and Rogaland.

Sweden has more than 300 *land-* and *landa*-names. Most of the Swedish *landa*-names – reflecting the genitive plural – are found in the southwestern part of the country: Bohuslän, Västergötland, Dalsland and Värmland. The ending *-land* is most common in Västernorrland, the key area in northern Sweden.

3. Norse settlement names in *-land* in Shetland and Orkney

According to Marwick (1952: 231) at least 35 of the 54 farm names in Orkney ending in *-land* are of Norse origin. In Shetland there are approximately 76 names of this type, according to Stewart (1987: 192).

A number of *land*-names in Shetland and Orkney are identical with names of this type in Norway. ON *Há(va)land, with the adjective ON hár/hór 'high' as the first element, describing the situation of the farms, appears in 12 Holland-names in Orkney (two of them are probably young), and 18 Houlland in Shetland (two are young), cf. also Holland in Caithness. The similar Norwegian Håland/Holand is found 67 places, 24 of them in Rogaland. Other names with parallels in Norway are:

- Bigland (Ork.) vs. Byggland (Norw.); ON *bygg* n., 'barley'.
- Hamarsland (She.) vs. Hamarsland (Norw.); ON *hamarr* m., 'rock'.
- Heyland (Ork.) vs. Høyland (Norw.); ON *hey* n., 'hay'.
- Leyland (Ork., cf. Litherland, Lancashire) vs. Liland (Norw.); ON *(h)líð* f., 'slope'.
- Litlaland (She.) vs. Litlaland (Norw.); ON *lítill* adj., 'small'.
- Mai(l)land (She.) vs. Meland and Mæland (Norw.); ON *meðal* adv., 'middle'.
- Russland (Ork.) vs. Rossaland (Norw.); ON *hross* n., 'horse'.
- Stanesland (She.) vs. Steinsland (Norw.); ON *steinn* m., 'rock'.
- Stockaland (Isle of Man) vs. Stokkaland (Norw.); ON *stokkr* m., 'log, trunk'.
- Vatsland (She.) vs. Vatland (Norw.); ON *vatn* n., 'water, lake'.

More examples could have been mentioned.

Marwick underlines that the final ending *-land* in some names might reflect Scots *land*, with similar semantics. Also the first element appears to be Scots in some names, e.g. Butterland (Birsay, Ork.; *Buttirland* 1595), containing Scots *butter*.

In some of the names it is more difficult to decide whether the first element is of Norse or Scots origin:

- Heyland (Sandwick, Ork.; *Heyland* 1739); either ON *hey* n., or Scot. *hey/hay* 'hay'.
- Twartland (Bressay, She.); probably Scot. *twart* 'across' (or ON *þverr* 'across').

Orklandquoy (Paplay, Ork.; *Orklandquy* 1492, *Orklandisquoy* 1500) probably contains a pre-Norse element, cf. *Ork* from Shapansay.

Quite often an adjective or an adverb appears as the first element in *land*-names from Shetland and Orkney. There are 20 examples in Shetland (i.e. 26 % of the *land*-names, including four with an adverb), In Orkney there are 13 examples (30 % of the names, two names with an adverb):

- Everland (Fetlar, She.; *Overland* 1628-); ON **Øfra-* 'upper land, i.e. farthest inland' (Stewart op. cit. 194).
- Greenland (Walls, She.; *Gronyland, Grunoland* 1507); ON *grœnn* adj., 'green'.
- Holland (Ork., 12 ex.: North Ronaldsay, Stronsay, Papa Westray, Eday, Faray, Shapansay, Deerness, St. Andrews parish, St. Ola, Firth, South Ronaldsay; *Holland* 1492); ON *hár* adj., 'high' (maybe ON *haugr* m., 'hill, mound' in a few instances).
- Houland (She., 18 ex.: Unst, Yell 2 ex., Northmaven 4 ex., Nesting, Walls, Sandsting 4 ex., Aithsting, Tingwall, Sandwick?; *Holand* 1507); ON *hár* adj., 'high'.
- Mailand (Unst, She.; *Metheland* 1524), Mailland (Whiteness, She.; *Mailand* 1507-); ON *meðal* adv., 'middle'.
- Midland (Ork., 2 ex.: Orphir; *Midland, Mydland* 1492; Rendall; *Mydland* 1492, 1500); ON *miðr* adj. (or *meðal* adv.), 'middle'.
- Litlaland (Fetlar, She.; *Litlaland* 1628); ON *lítill* adj., 'small'.
- Sulland (Westray, Ork.; *Suyirland* 1492, *Sutherland* 1500); ON *suðr* adv., 'south'.
- Swartland (Ork., 2 ex.: Sandwick, Graemsay); ON *svartr* adj., 'black' (the soil).

The most common type of appellatives used as the first element in this area is words for topographical features, which are found in 21 names in Shetland (i.e. 30 % of the names), and nine names in Orkney (21 %):

– Backaland (Eday, Ork.; *Backaland* 1733); ON *bakki* m., 'hill, slope'.

– Graveland (She., 2 ex.: Northmaven, Yell; *Gravaland* 1602-); ON **Grafa-*, *gröf* f., 'a hollow' (Stewart op. cit. 193).

– Hamarsland (She., 3 ex.: Whiteness, Tingwall 2 ex.; *Hamirisland* 1507); ON *hamarr* m., 'rock'.

– Heogland (Unst, She.; *Hugaland* 1523-, *Howgaland* 1627); ON *haugr* m., 'hill, mound' ('a cairn', Stewart op. cit. 193).

– Hogaland (She., 5 ex.: Northmaven, Whiteness, Trondra, Burra (2); *Howgaland* 1580); ON *haugr* m., 'hill, mound' ('cairn', Stewart loc. cit.).

– Hugoland (Northmaven, She.; *Hugoland* 1577-); ON *haugr* m., 'hill, mound' ('cairn', Stewart loc. cit.).

– Howland (Sanday, Ork.); ON *haugr* m., 'hill'.

– Holland (Sanday, Ork.; *Holland* 1500); ON *hóll* m., 'hillock', cf. the toponym *Hool*.

– Ireland (Stenness, Ork.; *Areland* 1492, *Airland*, *Irland* 1500; Sandwick, She.; *Yirland* 1507); ON *eyrr* f., 'delta, sandbank' ('a sandy or pebbly shore', Stewart op. cit. 200).

– Leyland (Sanday, Ork.; *Lyrland*, *Leyland* 1500); ON *(h)líð* f., 'slope'.

– Nifland (Dunrossness, She.; *Neffiland* 1741); cf. the toponym *Niv* < ON *nef* n., 'nose'.

– Stanesland (Walls, She.; *Stannisland* 1577); ON *steinn* m., '(standing) stone'.

– Vatsland (Tingwall, She.; *Weisland* 1570-79, *Vatsland* 1782-); ON *vatn* n., 'water, lake' (on a peninsula).

Also first elements describing the vegetation, the hay-lands and the keeping of livestock are common in the names of this class in Shetland and Orkney:

– Barkland (Fair Isle); Scot. *bark* 'tormentil', less probable ON *börkr* m. According to Stewart (op. cit. 200) 'Bark in Shetl. Dialect is tormentil (Potentilla erecta), whose root was used in tanning'.

- Bigland (Rousay, Ork.); probably ON *bygg* n., 'barley'.

- Bruntland (She., 2 ex.: Walls, Bressay); probably composed of Scot. *brunt* 'burned', cf. *bruntland* (*burnt-land*) 'rough, mossy ground, formerly burnt over periodically' (*SND* 1941: 293). Stewart (op. cit. 197) suggests ON **Brennu-*.

- Fethaland (Northmaven, She.; *Phedeland* 1530-, *Fethaland*   1748-), Fedelands (Scatness, Dunrossness, She.); ON *fit* f., 'meadow'.

- Findlins (Northmaven, She.; *Findeland* 1577-); ON *finna* f., 'wire grass'.

- Heyland (Sandwick, Ork.; *Heyland* 1739); ON *hey* n., 'hay' or Scottish *hey/hay*.

- Noltland (Ork., 4 ex.: Sanday; *Noltland* 1500; Westray; *Noltland* 1500; Westray; *Nouteland* 1492; Deerness; *Noutland* 1492); ON *naut* n., 'cattle'.

- Redland (Ork., 2 ex.: Evie; *Roithland*, *Rothland* 1492; Stromness, *Raland* 1492, 1500); ON *rjóðr* n., 'clearing' (later misinterpreted as ON *rauðr* adj., 'red').

- Rusland (Westray, Ork.); ON *hross* n., 'horse'.

- Swinland (Sandness, She.; *Sweenaland* 1860); ON *svín* n., 'pig'.

- Tarland (South Ronaldsay, Ork.; *Tarland* 1492); probably ON *tari* m., 'sea tangle'.

Other types of first elements:

- Broland (Rousay, Ork.; *Brewland* 1562, *Browland* 1595); according to Marwick (op. cit. 61f.) maybe ON *brún* f., 'brow, hill-slope'; another possibility is ON *brú* f., 'bridge'.

- Browland (Sandsting, She.; *Broland* 1507); probably ON *brú* f., 'bridge'.

- Burland (She., 2 ex.: Trondra, Gulberwick; *Burraland* 1567-); ON *borg* f., 'fort'.

- Burraland (She., 3 ex.: Northmaven, Walls, Sandwick; *Burroland* 1507); ON *borg* f., 'fort'.

- Burrowland (at present: *Braeland*; South Ronaldsay, Ork.; *Burrowland* 1492, *Brunaland* 1595); ON *borg* f., 'fort'.

- Mailand (Unst, She.; *Magneland* 1577); ON *Magni* (male name, < *Magnús*).

- Roveland (Westray, Ork.; *Roveland* 1740); according to Marwick (op. cit. 42) ON *rófa* f., 'tail'.

- Skolland (Dunrossness, She.; *Scholland* 1507-); ON *skáli* m., 'hall' or *skál* f., 'bowl'.

- Twattland (Birsay, Ork.; *Twaitland* 1595); contains the toponym *Twatt* (*Tuait* 1564).

Some names ending in *-land* seem to contain a compound appellative:

- Foreland (Fetlar, She.; *Forland* 1628; St. Ola, Ork.; *Forland* 1492); ON *forland* n., 'a flat piece of land under a hill'.

- Scattlands (Yell, She.; *Scatlandishouss* 1577); ON *skattland*, cf. *skattr* m., 'tax', i.e. 'land-tax'.

- Uresland (She., 3 ex.: Fetlar 2 ex., Tingwall; *Urisland* 1507-); ON *øyrisland* n., 'land which paid one eyrir in rent'.

In several of the names the origin of the first element is uncertain:

- Clouk(land) (Stromness, Ork.; *Cloukland* 1492, *Cluck* 1739).

- Hackland (Rendall, Ork.; *Halkland* 1500, *Haukland* 1664), Halkland (Sandwick, Ork.; *Halkland* 1581); probably ON *haukr* m., 'hawk', as suggested by Sandnes (2003: 199f.), less probable is Marwick's suggestion (op. cit. 120): ON **Akslar-* 'shoulder'.

- Howbustirland (Stromness, Ork.; *Howbustirland* 1492); contains maybe a *bólstaðr*-name, compounded of ON *haugr* m., 'hill'.

- Hundland (Birsay, Ork.; *Houndland* 1595, *Hundland* 1727); maybe a personal name ON *Hundi*, or a topographical name ON **Hunda* f., or **Hundi* m.

- Mousland (Ork., 2 ex.: Westray; *Mobisland* 1492, 1500, *Mousland* 1595; Stromness; *Mousland* 1492, 1500). Mobisland (= *Mobisyord*, Sanday, Ork.; *Mobisland* 1492, 1595). According to Marwick (op. cit. 33f.) maybe a personal name, cf. *Mavius (Magnus?) Maibsoun* 1492.

- Redland (Firth, Ork.; maybe *Renaland* 1425, *Raynland* 1500); Marwick (op. cit. 116) mentions a possible river name ON **Renna* (cf. *renna* vb. 'flow, run').

- Sotland (Paplay, Ork.; *Sotland* 1492); Marwick (op. cit. 91) suggests a personal name ON *Sóti* m.

- Tratland (Rousay, Ork.); Marwick (op. cit. 70) suggests ON *þræta* f., 'quarrel'.

- Trebland (Westray, Ork.; *Trebland* 1740); Marwick (op. cit. 43) suggests Celtic *treb* 'old dykes'; another interpretation is Scot. *threap* 'quarrel'.
- Trumland (Ork., 2 ex.: Westray; *Trumland* 1664; Rousay; *Trymland* 1500); according to Marwick (op. cit. 44, 65) the last mentioned might contain ON *þrömr* m., 'edge, brim, verge'.
- Weland (Ork., 2 ex.: Shapansay; *Weland* 1492, *Weyland* 1595; Egilsay). Weyland (St. Ola, Ork.; *Weiland* 1536). Marwick suggests ON *víðir* m. 'a kind of willow', or *vé* n. 'a holy place, site of pagan worship'.

4. The semantics of the name element -*land*

The first elements of the *land*-names from Shetland and Orkney – as well as the situation of the farms – indicate that the last element -*land* has had a semantic connection with the agricultural use of the land, as hayland, cornfield or pasture, corresponding to the semantics of the Scandinavian names.

For the original semantics of -*land* in ancient settlement names, some onomasts (cf. Lindroth 1946: 25, Lundahl 1972: 22) have suggested 'river- or lakeside', describing a field by a river or a lake. They emphasize that this semantics suit the situation of many *land*- and *landa*-farms, and that many names have a name of a river or lake as the first element.

Other Swedish onomasts (cf. Sahlgren 1942: 3f., Ståhl 1970: 81f., Karlsson 1968: 24) have suggested a denotation connected with farming, like 'piece of land, land as property', or the more specialized 'cultivated field'. The agrarian semantics have been preferred by Norwegian onomasts (cf. Olsen 1928: 143ff., Stemshaug 1985: 64, *NSL*: 280).

By studying the farms with a name ending in -*land* in Southwest-Norway one gets the impression that these are often secondary farms, in a peripheral situation, as seen from a mother-farm. Some *land*-names contain the name of an older neighbouring farm as the first element, like Valland (ON *Vallarland*) by Voll, and Skrettingland by Skretting, which indicates that the farm land earlier belonged to the older farm.

Deserted farms with names ending in -*land* give the same impression. These farms are often situated between older and more central farms, often on the outskirts of the parishes, lying on less fertile ground. It was not without reason that the settlement on these farms was abandoned during a period of crises and changes, in some districts as early as 550 A.D.

It is a common view among onomasts that many settlement names in -*land* are original field names, in other words names used of the fields – meadows, pastures etc. – of an older farm. Some of these field names in -*land* have later become settlement names, as the result of the clearing of farms and thus establishing permanent habitation in these places. An original denotation 'fields that are suitable for farming' – i.e. 'hay-fields, meadows, cultivated fields', and possibly 'pastures' – therefore seems to suit well, while the content 'fields by a river, a lake or the sea' is less probable.

By studying the first elements of Nordic settlement names in *-land*, one also gets the impression that the original semantics of *land* is closely connected with the function of the places. Words for different species of plants and trees are very common and account for about 20 % of the Norwegian and Swedish names, cf. Eikeland (ON *eiki* n., 'oak trees', 63 ex.), Birkeland (ON *birki* n., 'birch trees', 46 ex.).

A number of first elements are words for meadows, hay-lands and the storing of hay, cf. Høyland (ON *hey* n., 'hay', 31 ex.), Fidjeland (ON *fit* f., 'meadow', 3 ex.), Engeland (cf. ON *engi* n., 'meadow', 7 ex.), Tjelmeland (ON *hjalmr* m., 'haystack (-helmet)', 14 ex.) and Løland (ON *hlaða* f., 'barn', 13 ex.).

Other names relate to the growing of crops, like Byg(g)land (ON *bygg* n., 'barley', 3 ex.), Rugland (ON *rugr* m., 'rye', 7 ex.), Haveland (ON *hafri* m., 'oats', 3 ex.), Linland (ON *lín* n., 'flax', 8 ex.), Akland (ON *akr* m., 'cornfield', 2 ex.). Some names contain words for different traditions in older agriculture, like Kvern(a)land (ON *kvern* f., 'cornmill', 3 ex.).

Quite a few first elements describe pastures and the keeping of livestock: Nautland (ON *naut* n., 'cattle'), Kalvaland and Kåveland (ON *kalfr* m., 'calf', 9 ex.), Rossaland and Rosseland (ON *hross* n., 'horse', 15 ex.), Svinland (ON *svín* n., 'pig', 8 ex.).

First elements of the agrarian type are mainly found in the southern part of Norway. Appellatives describing the topography are more common in the northern part of the country, including Trøndelag.

In Swedish place-names, too, first elements containing words for trees, plants and farming are typical for the southern part of the country, while topographical appellatives dominate in the material from northern Sweden.

Some of the Norwegian names in *-land* seem to consist of a compound appellative. ON *Aukland* (19 ex.) and *Ruðland* (3 ex.) probably originate from the cultivation of the land, with the semantics 'additional land' and 'cleared land', while ON **Øyrisland* (2 ex.) describes the value of the land.

Some common settlement names with the first element *Land-* are also likely to have had appellatival character, e.g. ON *Landsefni* 'fit for land (field)' (e.g. *Landsem*) and **Landroð* 'cleared land, cultivated land' (e.g. Landro, Landrø, Landråk).

In this context it is interesting to notice that Gelling in ancient settlement names ending in *-land* in England has suggested an original denotation 'new arable area' (1984: 245f.). These names reflect 'new settlements of the Anglo-Saxon period in areas colonized or reclaimed in response to an increasing need for arable'. Many names of this type are found in northern England, where the Scandinavian settlement and influence was strong. In some cases it is difficult to decide whether the name is of English or Scandinavian origin, and Gelling concludes (op. cit. 245): 'It is reasonable to regard the ON word *land* as subsumed in the use of the OE term'.

The appellative *land* appears in all Germanic languages, with fairly similar semantics. There are closely related words in other North-European languages, i.e. in Celtic, Baltic and Slavic. The Swedish *linda* f., 'fallow land' is an ablaut form of *land*, as is probably the common Nordic *lund* m., 'grove'.

A study of the use of the appellative *land* in Germanic languages and of closely related words, gives evidence of an original semantic content 'open terrain, open field, uncultivated land, heath'. In Old Germanic a meaning in connection with the agricultural use of the land has possibly been developed, i.e. 'land that can be used as a hay field (meadow), cultivated field', possibly 'pasture'. In this period there have probably been coined field and settlement names ending in *-land* with this denotation. Younger names may have been coined with later developed denotations, like 'soil'.

5. The historical background of the *land*-names in Shetland and Orkney

Stewart (op. cit. 192f.) writes that the many *Houlland*-names in Shetland 'can hardly represent anything but a late settlement from a specific part of Norway'. He mentions several identical *land*-names in Norway and Shetland and adds: 'The style of naming is, as in Norway, from situation, nature of land, or surroundings'. He underlines that the 76 *land*-names in Shetland 'although early, are not on harbours or among the best land, which would have been taken first'. The *land*-farms are situated inland, 'off the beaten track, often on elevated ground'. The names represent 'the land-takings of latecomers'. He takes the view that the names 'indicate settlement from south-west Norway', and that they represent 'an influx at the time of the Icelandic settlement, when much of the readily available farmland had been taken up'.

Waugh (1991: 19f.) suggests that the *land*-names in the south and west mainland reflect 'block portioning out of land with arable potential to incomers at a slightly later date, when prospective settlers were arriving from Scandinavia in larger numbers and were requiring land for immediate use'.

Marwick (1952: 231f.) points out that a number of the *land*-names in Orkney are tunship names, and continues: 'in general, they are substantial fertile farms (or tunships) lying in the body of the parish, so to speak. They are without any doubt very early and venerable settlements. And yet – not I think the earliest!'.

Several archaeologists and historians have studied Norse settlement and settlement names in the northern isles. Brøgger (1928: 42f.) mentions the distribution of the *land*-names in Southwest-Norway and the northern isles, and he concludes that a substantial number of the settlers in Shetland and Orkney came from Agder, Rogaland and Sunnhordland.

Brøgger also mentions the deserted farms with *land*-names in Rogaland and Agder, which were deserted before the Viking Age. He thinks that they give an archaeological proof that a number of the settlers in Shetland and Orkney came from Agder and Rogaland. The emigrants left the peripheral *land*-farms to start a new life on these islands where the conditions were more favourable.

A problem with this reasoning is the fact that the deserted farms in South-Rogaland were left approx. 550 AD. The Norse settlement in Shetland and Orkney is believed to be much later.

Sveaas Andersen (1971 [1995: 16f.]) regards the earliest waves of Viking emigration as 'an overpopulation phenomenon in the *-land* and *-setr* regions'. The settlement in Shetland and Orkney and later Iceland must be regarded as 'a settlement movement which had begun inside Norway in the Merovingian period'. He writes that the *land*-farms in Southwest-Norway represent:

> a settlement extension farther into the hinterland and also towards the outer coastal area. These farms, mostly on marginal land and much exposed to crop failure, would soon be deserted when better opportunities became available. The propitious time came in the ninth century.

6. The dating of the Scandinavian *land*-names. Some linguistic and historical criteria

The various types of first elements have sometimes been used as a base of dating the different classes of settlement names. The fact that the Scandinavian *land*-names do not contain first elements that reflect Christian culture, is regarded as evidence that these names have, as a rule, been coined prior to (900-) 1000 A.D.

It has been reckoned that there are more words for pagan cult in the *land*-names than in the *heim-*, *vin-* and *staðir*-names, in the total number of names as well as per cent, cf. Frøyland (ON *Freyja*, 14 ex.), Frøytland (ON *Freyr*, 6 ex.), Nærland (ON *Njörðr*, 4 ex.), Totland (*af Þorslande* about 1175, ON *Þórr*, 10 ex), Osland (*a Odenslande* 1322, ON *Óðinn*, twice), Hovland (ON *hof* n., 40 ex.), Helgaland (ON *heilagr* adj., 40 ex.).

However, it is not obvious that the reason for this is a difference in age between the types of names. Maybe this is due to the different types of farms, to the use of the names and the function of the places. The fact that some interpretations of the first element as a word for pagan cult are controversial, is an important reason not to base the dating on this criterion.

Most *land*-names seem to contain linguistic elements that are known in the Scandinavian languages, and many names of this group are fairly easy to interpret. This fact could possibly lead to the conclusion that these names are relatively young. It is not obvious, however, that names like Håland and Høyland, which from a linguistic point of view could very well be made in the Mediaeval period, and which are identical with names in the areas of Norse settlement, are in fact young compositions simply because they are linguistically transparent. From a linguistic point of view, these names might have been coined in the early Iron Age. In some districts farms with these two names are central habitations with a long continuous settlement.

A few *land*-names probably contain personal names that have come from German in historical times, e.g. Hindersland (ON *Heinrekr*), Hobbåsland and Håbbesland (ON *Hagbarðr*). However, these examples are few and the whole group of names cannot be dated on this basis. Still, this signifies that *land*-names have been coined in historical times.

Some of the appellatives used as the first element probably reflect historical events that can be regarded as more recent phenomena, not older than the Viking age, e.g. *kvern* f. (Kvernaland), 'water mill', a tradition which was probably introduced by Christian monks.

Even though the dating of settlement names by using historical criteria is methodically very complicated, this type of criteria is useful as a supplement to the linguistic base. It is, however, very important to be aware of what the different criteria actually say something about, and avoid circular conclusions (cf. Sandnes 1967, 1973).

The land rent valuation of the farms in Mediaeval times gives information about the size – and probably the age – of the farms with the various names, and of the relationship between the types of settlement names. Farms with *land*-names from southern Rogaland that appear in the cadastres, have on average had a lower land rent valuation in Mediaeval times than farms with names ending in *-vin, -heim* and *-staðir*. There are, however, great variations within the *land*-group. Many farms are small and registered with low tax figures, while some big and central farms have high figures.

During the agricultural crisis that followed the Black Death, more farms with *land*-names in the examined area – in total number as well as per cent – were deserted than farms with *heim-, vin-* and *staðir*-names. In southern Rogaland 57 % of the *land*-farms were deserted, 45 % of the *vin*-farms, 36 % of the *staðir*-farms and 33 % of the *heim*-farms.

The fact that the desertion of the farms in times of crisis has been more typical for *land*-farms than for *heim-, vin-* and *staðir*-farms, seems to be due to the more peripheral situation of the *land*-farms, and the poor soil. A study of the situation of the farms with *land*-names registered in the cadastres, gives the same impression.

The collection of other names ending in *-land* in the examined area has revealed quite a few defunct settlement names of this type. In several cases the names are connected with farms that were deserted around 550 A.D. These names are in general regarded by archaeologists and historians as the original settlement names. Some of them are found as the first element in another place name, like **Eigeland* in Eigelandsskogan (Birkeland in Sokndal) and **Berkland* in Berklandshagane and Berklandskleiva (Njå in Time).

In Jæren there are archaeological finds from the Bronze Age and the earliest Iron Age (1500 B.C. to 300 A.D.) on 19 of the *land*-farms, i.e. on 22 % of the material. An archaeological find does not, of course, date the farm name. On the other hand there seems to be a certain correlation between the finds and the type of farm name represented (cf. Myhre 1984). In comparison there are finds from this period on 4 of the *vin*-farms (33 %), on 11 of the *staðir*-farms (31 %) and on 3 of the *heim*-farms (17 %).

The archaeological material on historic farms with *land*-names and on deserted farms with names of this type in the examined area, seems to indicate that many *land*-farms were cleared in the important expansion period within agriculture which is dated around 200-550 A.D. In the same period farms with names ending in *-heim, -vin* and *-staðir* were cleared. The names of these farms were probably also coined in this period, passed on in the oral tradition up to present time (and in literature the last 500-800 years). A few *land*-names are probably older than 200 A.D. There are archaeological finds from earlier periods, e.g. from the Bronze Age, that signify continuous agriculture on several places where a *land*-name is used today. This early dating is likely for some of the uncompounded ON *Landir*-names.

However, many settlement names ending in -*land* must be younger. A large group of them was probably coined in the expansion period that began in the last part of the 7th century. Settlement names in -*land* made after 1000 A.D. are the exception.

The fact that there are many *land*-names in the areas of Norse settlement, especially in Shetland and Orkney, that are identical with Norwegian settlement names of this type, clearly signifies that this class of names was productive when people from Norway settled on these islands, i.e. in the Viking Age. Recent research indicates that the contact with the northern islands – and probably the Norse settlement there – is older than earlier believed. There have been connections, at least, in the 8th century, maybe as early as in the 7th century (cf. Lillehammer 1994: 223f.).

Inge Særheim

Literature

Andersen, P.S., [1971] 1995: 'The Norwegian Background'. In: B. E. Crawford (ed.), *Scandinavian Settlement in Northern Britain*. London/New York, 16-25.

Brøgger, A., 1928: *Gamle emigranter. Nordmennenes bosetning på norskehavskysten*. Oslo.

Christensen, V. & Sørensen, J.K., 1972: *Stednavneforskning* 1. *Afgrænsning. Terminologi. Metode. Datering*. København.

Gelling, M., 1984: *Place-Names in the Landscape*. London.

Karlsson, H., 1968: *Bebyggelsehistoriska problem kring land(a)-namnen*. Uppsats för Seminariet i historia vid Göteborgs universitet den 9 december 1968. Göteborg.

Lillehammer, A., 1994: 'Fra jeger til bonde – inntil 800 e.Kr'. In: K. Helle (ed.), *Norges Historie* 1. Oslo.

Lindroth, H., 1946: 'Bohuslänska ortnamn och bohuslänsk bebyggelsehistoria', *Göteborgs och Bohusläns Fornminnesförenings Tidskrift* 1945, 1-116.

Lundahl, I., 1972: *Ortnamnen i Skaraborgs län* 1. *Inledning*. Ortnamnsarkivet i Uppsala. Lund.

Marwick, H., 1952: *Orkney Farm-Names*. Kirkwall.

Myhre, B., 1984: 'Bosetning og gårdsnavn på Jæren'. In: V. Dalberg *et al*. (eds): *Bebyggelsers og bebyggelsesnavnes alder*. *NORNA-rapporter* 26. Uppsala, 169-198.

NSL = *Norsk stadnamnleksikon*. J. Sandnes & O. Stemshaug (eds). 4. utg. Oslo. 1997.

Olsen, M., 1928: *Farms and Fanes of Ancient Norway. The Place-Names of a Country Discussed in their Bearings on Social and Religious History*. Instituttet for Sammenlignende Kulturforskning. Serie A: Forelesninger 9. Oslo.

Sahlgren, J., 1942: 'Svenska ortnamn och svensk bebyggelsehistoria'. *Ortnamnssällskapets i Uppsala Årsskrift* 1941. 3-7.

Sandnes, B., 2003: *Fra Starafjall til Starling Hill. Dannelse og utvikling av norrøne stedsnavn på Orknøyene*. Dr.art.-avhandling, Norges teknisk-naturvitenskapelige universitet. Trondheim.

Sandnes, J., 1967: 'Kilder til busetningshistorien i eldste tida', *Heimen* 14, 3-20.

Sandnes, J., 1973: 'Datering av navneklasser ved landskyld-metoden', *Maal og Minne*, 12-28.

SND = *The Scottish National Dictionary*. 2. 1941. Edinburgh.

Steinnes, E., 1951: 'Alvheim', *Historisk Tidsskrift* 35, 353-404.

Stemshaug, O., 1985: *Namn i Noreg. Ei innføringsbok i norsk stadnamngranskning*. 3. utg. Oslo.

Stewart, J., 1987: *Shetland Place-Names*. Lerwick.

Ståhl, H., 1970: *Ortnamn och ortnamnsforskning*. 1. utg. Stockholm.

Særheim, I., 2001: *Namn og gard. Studium av busetnadsnamn på -land*. Tidvise Skrifter 38. Stavanger.

Waugh, D., 1991: 'Place Name Evidence for Scandinavian Settlement in Shetland', *Review of Scottish Culture* 7, 15-25.

Some Place-Names from Twatt
– on Da Wastside

Doreen Waugh

1. Introduction

The Westside, or 'Da Wastside' as it appears in the written vernacular and as I shall refer to it in this paper for the most part, is a generic term for a wide area of land in the middle-west of mainland Shetland. It roughly equates with the land which juts out like a clenched fist to the west of an imaginary line running from Aith to Bixter on the modern map, with a degree of elasticity in the line to permit the inclusion of Tresta and Tumblin on the Bixter side and, most would argue, East Burrafirth on the Aith side. The borders of Da Wastside, in other words, are not absolutely fixed but there is a considerable degree of current local agreement about its perceived geographical extent. In addition, if locals are asked where, in Shetland, they live, a common answer is 'Da Wastside' rather than the specific place where the person has his or her home in that part of Shetland. I suspect that this is because Da Wastside is more than a geographical concept; it also encompasses dialectal and cultural features which mark people as coming from that area, just as other Shetlanders are marked as coming from Da Ness (Dunrossness) or Northmavine (to the north of Mavis Grind) and so on. The islands of Shetland, of course, can have their own cultural and dialectal markers due to isolation but islands such as Vementry, Papa Stour and Vaila are, in my opinion, culturally and geographically part of Da Wastside.

What I hope to do in this short paper is to start building up a toponymic picture of Twatt (Figure 2), a typical Shetland crofting township which owes some of its place-names to the Norn language and some of them to the Shetland dialect. The latter is essentially a dialect of Scots or Scottish English, the language which finally superseded Norn in the 18th century or possibly earlier. I shall consider etymology in some instances but, as is the case in many other parts of Shetland, early forms of Twatt place-names are not always easy to find and some of the comments here rely on local knowledge and lore about the origins of names.

Figure 1. The Westside or 'Da Wastside' of Shetland.

My chief informant has been Jim Johnston, who is now Headmaster of Farr High School in the north of mainland Scotland but who was born and brought up in Twatt. His family lived at Upper Langaskule – a name which will be discussed later – and he recorded a great deal of local information for me. I have also received some information from a current Twatt resident, Herbert Nicolson, formerly of Lower Langaskule, and from Andy and Betty Abernethy, residents of the neighbouring village of Clousta. In addition, my grandparents were Taits who lived at Northhouse in Twatt and I have some personal knowledge of many of the locations and their names.

2. The Place-Names of Twatt

I shall begin with the name Twatt itself which appears regularly in documents from the 16th century at least. J. Jakobsen derives Twatt from:

> ON þveit, f., a parcel of land, etc. (which) occurs in the form *twatt* in a few Shetl. farm-names, all in "Westside". *Twatt* (Aithsting). *Brunatwatt* [*"bruna-þveit", where "bruni" must refer to the burning of the soil], *Foratwatt, Germatwatt* [*Geirmundar-þveit ...], *Stennestwatt* [*steinhús-þveit? ...] – all in Walls (Jakobsen 1936: 110-111).

It has been suggested, by Jakobsen, that 'Thveitathing' seems to denote the 'Westside':

> A couple of old (now obs.) thing-names are found in some of the ancient charters concerning Shetland: 1) "Thveitathing", in two Latin charters of 1 September 1321 and 6 April 1322 (Nidaros), and 2) "Raudarthing", in a Latin charter of 1 Sept. 1321 (Nidaros). "Thveitathing" [*Þveita-þing] seems to denote the "Westside" (M.), comprising Walls and Aithsting, where all the farms named *Twatt* [*þveit] are to be found; see "þveit" (Jakobsen 1936: 126).

I have an open mind on the suggestion that 'Thveitathing' and the 'Westside' were one and the same but I am inclined towards it, and the medieval historian, Ronald Cant, whose knowledge of Shetland church organisation was immense, indicated that he was equally willing to consider the idea, and to take it a little further with the suggestion that Twatt itself might conceivably have been the centre of the parish of 'Thweitathing':

> Eastwards of Walls and Sandness are the parishes of Sandsting and Aithsting, associated since the Reformation and possibly before. ... The principal church of Aithsting seems to have been much where it still is at Twatt and this might conceivably have been the centre of the parish of 'Thweitathing' mentioned in 1321. Chapels have been suggested at Uyeasound [now Vementry, according to Stewart 1987: 263], Biggings (Aith) and Tumblin' (Cant 1975: 18).

Some further references to Twatt are underlined below and references to the other place-names which are to be discussed later are also underlined:

February 1543-44: 'Aytht in parish of Twayt' (Ballantyne & Smith 1999: 49).

August 1561: 'all and sundry my 12 marks land of Unyafirth, 2 marks land of Twat in Langskoill [Langskaill], 2 marks land of Samlasetter, with their pertinents, lying in the parish of Sandsting in Eisting' (Ballantyne & Smith 1999: 95).

May 1610: 'and in the parishes of Aithsting, Sandsting ... 19? marks land, 9 pennies the mark, in Twot, 1? marks land, 8 pennies the mark, in Kirkhous, 3 marks land, 8 pennies the mark, in Langascoill, 2? marks land, 9 pennies the mark, in Breck ...' (Ballantyne & Smith 1994: 247).

2.1 Langaskule, Breck and Gairden

Langaskule – to use the form of the name recorded on the 1882 6" OS map – is mentioned above in the context of the name Twatt as *Langskoill* and *Langascoill* (1561 and 1610) and it appears in further early documents as follows:

August 1582: 'Edsting parish ... Languaskaaill, 2 marks land, 8 pennies the mark: 16 marks butter, 6 ells wattmell' (Ballantyne & Smith 1994: 21).

October 1589: '4½ marks land in Tumbling in Twat' ... '4? marks land in Langasole' (ibid: 67).

December 1602: '1½ marks land, 8 pennies the mark, in Langaskoill in Tuait, in the parish of Aithsting' (ibid: 156).

October 1605: '2 marks land of Twait in Langoskaill, 2 marks land of Samlesetter, in the parish of Sandsting and Esting' (ibid: 187).

July, 1609: '3 marks land, 6 pennies the mark, of Langaskaill, 2 marks land, 8 pennies the mark of Brek' (ibid: 240).

Before discussing Langaskule, I shall note that the other place-name mentioned along with *Langaskaill* in the 1609 and 1610 documents is *Brek* or *Breck*, which is still extant as a place-name in Twatt, now commonly spelt Breck. It refers to a house located on the slopes of the hill near Langaskule and is a commonly recurring name in Shetland for a house in such a situation, derived from ON *brekka* 'a slope'. The word is recorded by Jakobsen in his *Etymological Dictionary of the Shetland Norn* (Jakobsen 1936: 72) where he suggests that in some areas it was used as a common noun but, for the most part, it seems to have been used only in place-names. Stewart gives several early forms, as follows: *Y westhri brecko* 1516; *Brek* 1576-1636; *Breck* 1603-1951; *Breck of Twat* 1645-1853; *Break* 1784; *Brake* 1954 (Stewart 1987: 62). A place-name which could be contemporary with Brek is Gairden, although, as yet, I have no incontestable proof of that. It is adjacent to Breck, further down the slope, and it is also a very common place-name in Shetland, derived from ON *garðr* 'an enclosure'.

According to Jim Johnston (aged 50-55) who lived in Upper Langaskule, his mother (Christina Margaret Abernethy, known as 'Kirsty', who was born in Bonhouse, Clousta) said that Lower Longaskule was the original kernel of Twatt and there was 'a biggins' there from which most of the existing houses of Twatt (but not Kirkhouse) were 'set oot' at some earlier time; probably early 19th century, although this date has proved difficult to confirm exactly. Early travellers who wrote accounts of the Shetland Islands were irritatingly coy about Twatt. For example, Samuel Hibbert's account of life in the islands, published in 1822, says: 'From Bigsetter Voe I again crossed the hills, and arrived at Aithsvoe' (Hibbert 1822: 238). Twatt, of course, lies between Bixter and Aith and Hibbert chose to pass it by without even a glancing comment about its dwellings. George Low, writing his account in 1774, is even less communicative: 'Scarce touched Aithsting Parish, as but a small point of it lies this way' (Low 1774: 80).

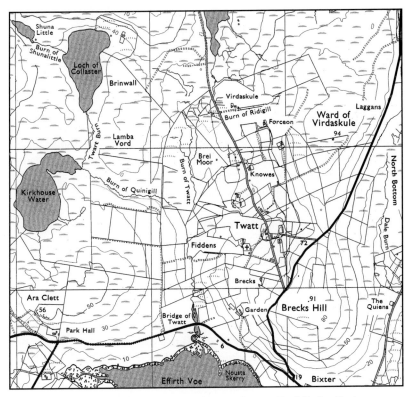

*Figure 2. Twatt, as on the Ordnance Survey Pathfinder Series
(Sheet HU 15/25).*

The stones from the original houses of Twatt were, according to Kirsty
Johnston, carried out from Lower Langaskule by the occupants and new,
separate houses were built in their current locations.

'A biggins' is the Scots collective noun 'biggings' for a
collection or cluster of houses 19th-early 20th century [chiefly
nME big(ge) etc; ON byggja inhabit, dwell in; build] (*Concise
Scots* 1985: 41).

The dictionary record of this collective noun suggests that early 19th century
is likely to be correct.

Langaskule itself was obviously in existence from the 16th century at
least and possibly earlier and is identified by Jakobsen as *langi skáli*, with

the definition of 'long shed, hut' (Jakobsen 1936: 96). When the same name occurs in a farming context in Orkney, however, it is associated by Hugh Marwick in his magisterial study of Orkney farm names with 'good, old fertile land' and a more substantial farm than the description 'shed or hut' would imply. Marwick points out that 'the term Skaill seems never to have been applied as a tunship name. In point of fact, however, many or perhaps most of the skaills represented the chief farms in their several tunships ...' (Marwick 1952: 238-239) and it seems reasonable to suggest that the same applies to the Twatt example of the name. Its very longevity as a place-name suggests importance and its present situation is certainly on good, meadow land. As can be seen from the above examples, Langaskule often appeared in the same context as Twatt itself in early documents.

2.2 Kirkhouse, Pinch, Twatt Kirkyard

Lower Langaskule is adjacent to Kirkhouse and to the present church which, as we have seen, Cant thought stands on the site of the medieval church. The modern church is now falling into disrepair, having been closed within living memory, presumably after 1975 when Cant was writing. I can remember attending harvest thanksgiving in the church as a child in the 1950s.

Jim Johnston has a splendid story that an officer of the press gang is buried under the Twatt church doorstep so that everyone would step on him as they went in and out of the church. According to local folklore, he fell to his death in Da Loch o Setter or Kirkcaldy's Loch because the local hero of the tale, being familiar with the loch, ran across stepping stones through the water and Kirkcaldy (the press gang officer) being a stranger to the area fell in and drowned. Jim's grand-uncle, John Robert Nicolson, told Jim that he found the bones when he put in a step for a new porch in the 1920s.

There are several examples of the name Kirkhouse in Shetland, always referring to property near churches or belonging to the church. The 1610 reference to *Kirkhous* above is the earliest certain mention of the Twatt instance of Kirkhouse which I have found thus far. The situation is confused by the fact that there is also a *Kirkhous* in neighbouring Aith and it is sometimes difficult to distinguish between the two. There is also an Upper Kirkhouse in Twatt, still known locally as Pinch. John Stewart records it as *Pund of Northhouse* in 1789 but I am doubtful that Pund – which is a common term in the Shetland vocabulary for a pound for animals, often also used as a place-name – would have mutated towards Pinch. The former house at Pinch was absolutely tiny. Could the name have been a humorous description of the building?

The churchyard adjacent to Kirkhouse – Twatt Kirkyard – was very typical of rural churchyards throughout Scotland in that there were stepping stones in the high wall to the west of the yard so that people could scramble in over the wall from that direction. It was, in fact, frequently the case that churchyards were totally enclosed, with the aim of protecting the dead bodies from whatever marauding animals might be tempted to attack the graves. On mainland Scotland the animals were wolves but that would not have been the case in Shetland. The kirkstile was often the place where biers were received into the churchyard for burial. One 1617 reference to 'the kirkyard of Twat' does not reflect well on a particularly riotous visitor from Nounsbrough in neighbouring Clousta:

> William Sinclair of Rawick cautioner that Nicoll Manssone in Nusbruch would satisfy the sheriff depute for a riot committed by him in the kirkyard of Twat on 'Sonday was twentie dayis' and would compeer before 'the ministrie' and underlie their punishment on the first Thursday of August next, on pain of £40 (Donaldson 1991: 48).

2.3. Da Daals, Da Lewis Knowe

The flat ground, south of the meadow, between Lower Langaskule and Kirkhouse is known as Da Daals (Shetland dialect 'daal' from ON *dalr* 'a valley'); the use of the Shetland dialect form of the English definite article in this name confirms that it, and other names which are similarly combined with 'da', is either a comparatively recent coinage or, while it may have been coined by a Norn-speaker, it continued in use when the language spoken was no longer Norn but Scots. Jim Johnston mentions an interesting feature to the north of Da Daals, which should be recorded although it has now vanished from the landscape. Jim knows the name of the feature as Da Lewis Knowe and he describes it as 'a kidney-shaped grassy mound with a small tank-like declivity to the north of Da Daals'. He describes it as having been 'right on the *banks*' (i.e. the edges) of the small un-named burn that comes down there and eventually flows into the meadow. It was removed in the course of agricultural work about ten years ago and apparently consisted entirely of angular fragments of burnt stone; i.e. like others in neighbouring Clousta, it was a burnt mound and would probably have been of archaeological interest. I have no theories about the name – Da Lewis Knowe – and would welcome any further comments, particularly from local readers.

2.4. Northhouse, Da Meadow

Northhouse is one of the houses in the new biggings mentioned by Kirsty Johnston. It lies to the north of the church and to the north of Lower Langaskule, and adjacent to Da Meadow. Ironically, Northhouse is difficult to pin down, not because it is etymologically opaque but because it is a common and utterly transparent name, meaning 'north house' and, being common, it is difficult to identify an individual example in early documents, if the name existed prior to the creation of the biggings, which I believe it did. The Twatt example of Northhouse is not recorded in any of the documents which feature in Ballantyne & Smith, but John Stewart lists it in *Shetland Place-Names* (Stewart 1987: 153). His earliest reference is from 1577-1603, when the form is *Northous*. It is probably named from its location in relation to the church and the likelihood is that the name was also in existence when Twatt and Langaskule were being recorded in 16th century documentary sources, but I cannot prove that conclusively. The presently ruinous croft house at *Northous*, in which my mother spent her childhood, almost certainly dates from the time of the establishment of the 19th century biggings and probably replaces whatever earlier building stood on the site.

Adjacent to Northhouse is the Northhouse Meadow which was divided between Kirkhouse and North and South Northhouse. There was also a Breck Meadow nearer the sea at Bixter or Effirth Voe. The diphthongal pronunciation of the English word Meadow ['møidu] is one of the dialectal markers of a Wastside origin but spelling of the local pronunciation is challenging and I have opted for Standard English 'meadow' in the following discussion. Jim Johnston remembers 'Da Meadow' as a 'haavers meadow' in which several crofts had shares or divisions but, interestingly, his Meadow was different from Da Northhouse Meadow or Da Breck Meadow. I have this information from Herbert Nicolson who still lives in Twatt and who was able to give some more local details. Apparently, in the early 20th century at least, there were three shareholders in each section of Da Meadow, each with his own sign of ownership of the stacks, or 'cols' (ON *kollr* 'top, summit') of hay. In Da Meadow, as remembered by Jim Johnston and Herbert Nicolson, the Johnstons from Upper Langaskule had a docken (dockleaf) to mark their cols of hay; the Nicolsons from Lower Langaskule had a 'widdie' twig ('widdie' meaning wooden); the family from the Gilbraes had a gowan (ox-eye daisy). This tripartite division makes me think again of the discussion of run-rig agriculture by W.P.L. Thomson in which he states the following, which is very apt for the Twatt meadow situation and use:

Run-rig agriculture in Shetland involved three levels of organisation, the township, the 'house' and the tenant-holding. A township can be envisaged as a confederation of 'houses', bound together by an encircling hill-dyke and united by shared interests in unevenly distributed resources such as arable land, grass and meadow hay. These constituent 'houses', sometimes known as 'farms' might each be occupied by a single tenant, but they were often divided into two, three or more quite distinct tenant holdings (Thomson 1998: 107).

2.5. Stackwall Park, Da Trottems

The meadow was an important part of any Shetland crofting community. It provided lush summer grass and hay for winter fodder. The Twatt Meadow was very wet and could be flooded in winter. The area was, once again, divided in the 1960s with each croft getting a park and, in turn, giving these newly acquired parks an identifying name. The Johnstons called theirs the Stackwall Park, from an earlier name, Stackwall, which was applied to a patch of raised ground on the interface between Da Daals and Da Meadow. I find this fascinating because Jim Johnston actually commented that he thought this name unjustified because Stackwall, the geological feature, did not fall within the new park and yet the name was borrowed into the new context. One wonders how often this happened and how many place-names have moved around the countryside in this way, and how often researchers are duped into thinking that they have remained in one place. Incidentally, Stackwall is a name which occurs more than once in rural Shetland as a description of an area of raised ground with rocks sticking out of it.

Jim Johnston remembered a further previously unrecorded place-name from the Twatt Meadow. It is the very puzzling name Da Trottems, which was the western part of the meadow, going towards the Burn o Twatt. I could make an informed guess at the etymology of Stackwall but, without early references, I have no idea what the origin of Da Trottems might be. The 1" map records another name for the same area. It is Fiddens (from ON *fitjar* 'meadowland'), which occurs more than once in Shetland.

2.6. Da Knowes, Da Brei Moor, Virdaskule

Next, at the side of the road going towards Clousta from Northouse, there is Da Knowes. According to the 1st edition 6" map, the area of land between Northouse and Da Knowes is called Da Brei Moor but the name is no longer

239

used, as far as I have been able to ascertain. Knowes is a Scots word meaning 'hillocks', which fits well with the creation of the houses in the biggings in the late 18th/early 19th century. Stewart lists it in a number of places in Shetland, often as an alternative to an existing name, but there is no alternative name for Da Knowes in Twatt. The initial [k] was always pronounced, although it has, for the most part, vanished from the dialect, except in humorous presentation of a past age in Shetland dialect plays. The spelling of 'Brei' in Da Brei Moor suggests that it might have had the meaning 'broad' from ON *breiðr* rather than 'on the slope' from Scots *brae*. Certainly, the location is fairly flat and, nowadays, it is not moorland but it may well have been in the past before land improvement. Speculation leads nowhere without earlier spellings of the name.

Beyond Da Knowes, and delimiting the northernmost edge of Twatt and of the biggings described by Kirsty Johnston, there lies the now deserted house at Virdaskule. *Virda-* is not an uncommon specific in Shetland place-names as is pointed out by Jakob Jakobsen who proposes derivation of *Virda-* from ON *varða* 'a beacon or cairn'. Jakobsen does not list Virdaskule and neither does it appear in the two sets of early documents by Ballantyne & Smith but, once again, Stewart has an unattributed early form, *Virdascoll* 1580 (Stewart 1987: 324).

The 1882 6" OS map records that the hill above Virdaskule is known as the apparently tautologous *Ward of Virdaskule* and it is certainly true that a beacon or cairn would be more readily associated with a hilltop than with the flat ground where Virdaskule is situated. It would also explain why an apparently modern house with no evidence of any earlier buildings round about has a Norn name, borrowed from the hill behind it. Stewart suggests ON *skáli* for the generic which is a possibility, particularly in a place which already has the place-name Langaskaill as proof that the element *skáli* was in use, although it rather contradicts my earlier argument about the relative importance of *skáli* names. In other words, when a name was required for the boundary croft at Virdaskule in the 19th century, the name of a small dwelling on the slopes of the neighbouring beacon hill was commandeered, but with no remaining understanding of the component parts of the name. We have already seen that names are moved around the landscape of Twatt as required by new name-givers. In his discussion of the name, Stewart records it as *Virdascoll* 1580, becoming *Virdascule* by 1888, and he further notes *Virdshill* 1951 and *Verdshill* 1954. There is clearly considerable uncertainty about the generic in the name.

2.7. Force, Forceon, Da Gilbraes

On the side of the Ward of Virdaskule there is a place called Force. The name is an old one and probably describes the waterfall (ON *fors*) in the Ridigill Burn. Jim Johnston describes this as a burn with little gorges and plunge pools joining the Twatt Burn at Virdaskule, and I was reminded that there is an Achrìdigill in Sutherland. This place-name is mentioned by William J. Watson in an article entitled 'Some Sutherland Names of Places' (Watson 1906: 71), in which he suggests derivation of Rìdigill from ON *rjóta-gil* 'roaring gully' with reference to the rushing of the water, which certainly fits the Ridigill Burn in Twatt with its waterfalls and plunge pools. Force is recorded on the 1882 map as *Forceon* which may possibly preserve the Norn definite article **fors-inn*. At the time of reading this paper to the conference, I had thought Forceon had vanished as a place-name but since then I have had information from Betty Abernethy of Clousta, whose family owned Virdaskule, that Forceon is certainly still known and used, pronounced with the stress on the second syllable, which does not serve to reinforce my definite article theory but the current pronunciation could be map-derived. Stewart records an early form *Fuirso* 1604 (Stewart 1987: 91). Unfortunately, the conclusion has to be that this is yet another name with a puzzling origin.

As we continue mentally walking the bounds of Twatt, the next name we come to is Da Gilbraes on the slopes or 'braes' beside the Burn of Ridigill. This is really a Scots name, although *gil* 'a gully or ravine' is originally Norn. I think the Scots form *brae* 'a slope' must be the generic in this name, which suggests that it was created some time in the last two or three centuries. As already noted elsewhere, the use of the Shetland dialect form of the English definite article also supports relatively recent creation of the place-name.

2.8. Lochs and burns

Da Wastside has numerous lochs and burns or small streams and Twatt has its fair share. Da Northouse Loch, or Da Loch o Northouse (used interchangeably), lies up the hill from Da Gilbraes and, although at a considerable distance from Northouse, it is likely that the link between the loch and the house is to be logically explained because the loch supplied the water for the mill which was located in the Twatt Burn on Da Brei Moor to the north of Northouse. A small burn called Sturaleog, which cuts deeply into the peat of the hill, flows into Da Northouse Loch. Jakobsen mentions the name and derives it from ON *lækr* 'a brook' (**stóri lækr*), which becomes *ljog* in Shetland and is used frequently as a common noun in the sense of 'a small brook running quietly in a deep channel' (Jakobsen 1936: 80). On the opposite side of the valley, there is a deserted house and croft next to Da Collaster Loch and, joined to Da Collaster Loch by Da Burn o Shunlittle, there is a loch called Shun Little, probably from ON *tjörn* 'a small lake' (now more commonly a pond, pool or swamp). Da Collaster Loch is, in turn, joined to Da Kirkhouse Loch by Da Twart Burn – the same word as 'athwart' (ON *þvert*). Coming full circle we find Da Twart Burn joining Da Quinnigill Burn just as it leaves Da Kirkhouse Loch and Da Quinnigill Burn joins Da Burn o Twatt. I am not sure about the derivation of the specific in Quinnigill (ON *kvern* 'a mill' has been suggested by Stewart) but I wonder if it could be ON *hvann*, the word for angelica, a plant which is native to Shetland and is notably common, particularly on Da Wastside, with Sandsound and Bardister in Waas being singled out as places where the plant grows (Scott & Palmer 1987: 214).

3. Conclusion

There is much more to Twatt place-names than I can do justice to in this short paper. I could talk about paths such as Skurdigaet (path through the notch or defile – ON *skarð*) and Slidderygaet (slippery path), or about Da Wirlie (an opening in the base of a fence through which a burn runs) (Jakobsen 1932: 1066) where there was a source of fireclay, but I think I shall end with Geurwal, the name of a trowie hill (hill inhabited by trolls) on the road between Twatt and Clousta, which leads towards another of the places in my research project to write about the village names of Da Wastside. Jakobsen lists it in his dictionary as *de Gørhul* 'a hill inhabited by trolls' (ON *gýgr* (gen. *gýgjar*) 'a giantess or witch') (Jakobsen 1932: 281-282). It fits well with the trowie places mentioned elsewhere in this volume, about which I enjoyed hearing at the conference. Local folk certainly have plenty of stories of the supernatural in one form or another, but it is for their knowledge of the real world round about them in Twatt that I would pay tribute to them and thank them all for their help in preparing this paper.

Literature

Ballantyne, J.H. & Smith, B., (eds), 1994: *Shetland Documents 1580-1611*. Lerwick.

Ballantyne, J.H. & Smith, B., (eds), 1999: *Shetland Documents 1195-1579*. Lerwick.

Cant, R., 1975: *The Medieval Churches and Chapels of Shetland*. Shetland Archaeological and Historical Society. Lerwick.

Concise Scots = Robinson, M. (ed.), 1985: *The Concise Scots Dictionary*. Aberdeen.

Donaldson, G. (ed.), 1991: *Court Book of Shetland 1615-1629*. Lerwick.

Hibbert, S., [1822] 1931: *A Description of the Shetland Islands*. Lerwick.

Jakobsen, J., [1928-1932] 1985: *An Etymological Dictionary of the Norn Language in Shetland*, 1-2. Lerwick.

Jakobsen, J., [1936] 1993: *The Place-Names of Shetland*. Kirkwall.

Low, G., 1879: *A Tour through the Islands of Orkney and Schetland, Containing Hints Relative to their Ancient, Modern and Natural History – Collected in 1774 by George Low*. Kirkwall.

Marwick, H., 1952: *Orkney Farm-Names*. Kirkwall.

Scott, W. & Palmer, R., 1987: *The Flowering Plants and Ferns of the Shetland Islands*. Lerwick.

Stewart, J., 1987: *Shetland Place-Names*. Lerwick.

Thomson, W.P.L., 1998: 'Township, "House" and Tenant-Holding; the Structure of Run-rig Agriculture in Shetland'. In: V. Turner (ed.), *The Shaping of Shetland*. Lerwick, 107-127.

Watson, W.J., [1906] 2002: 'Some Sutherland Names of Places'. In: *Scottish Place-Name Papers*. London, 56-75.

The Semantics of *Stöng/Stang*

Diana Whaley

1. Introduction

Readers of Icelandic sagas or voyagers on the internet may have encountered situations where one person or group ridicules and curses another by raising an actual or virtual *níðstöng* 'scorn-pole' against them. Egill Skallagrímsson, poet, rune-master, warrior and farmer, provided the most famous example, raising a pole topped by a horse's head and turning it in the direction of his deadly enemy King Eiríkr blóðøx (Blood-axe) of Norway and his queen Gunnhildr (*Egils saga* ch. 57; typing 'nidstang' or 'nidstong' into a search engine produces interesting modern applications). In early modern England, 'riding the stang' was also a form of public humiliation, this time inflicted on miscreants by carrying them, or effigies of them, astride a pole around the village or town. Somewhat more benignly, the reflex of *stöng* enters into the English dialect compound *gammerstang*, 'a tall, awkward person, usually a woman' (*OED*, first citation 1570), or 'a rude, wanton girl' (1788).

These are among the more picturesque uses of ON *stöng* and its derivatives, and they remind us of the versatility of the word and the objects it denotes. As a place-name element, *stöng* is found throughout the Scandinavian-speaking world, where it has puzzled and intrigued successive scholars.[1] The object of this paper is therefore to investigate the toponymic usage of *stöng* throughout the North-Atlantic region, with the emphasis on the range of possibilities. Meanwhile, since the problem of this element came to my attention through work on the place-names of the English Lake District, my subsidiary aim is to suggest interpretations of the Lakeland names in *stang*. The rich material from other geographical areas will be represented, but it is beyond the scope of the present study to draw systematic conclusions about the range of usage or the meaning of individual *stöng* names in those areas.

2. *Stöng* as lexical word

Stöng is a feminine noun of the strong 'u-stem' type, with variant plural forms of the 'i-stem' type; hence genitive singular *stangar*, dative singular *stöng(u)*, nominative plural *stangir/stengr*, genitive plural *stanga* and dative plural *stöngum*.[2] The reflexes may reflect the *a* or *ö* vowel, and both Stang- and Stong- names occur in the British Isles. *Stöng* is related to the verb *stinga* 'stab, pierce' (see de Vries 1977, s.v.). Before proceeding to the usage in place-names, let us examine the semantic range of the ON lexical word, following Fritzner's *Ordbog*, s.v. *stöng*.

● Pole, staff. Applications include poles on which nets are hung to dry; staves to beat people with (cf. the nickname of Þorsteinn stangarhögg 'Staff-bash', hero of a short tale), or poles over which performing dogs jump to amuse the fine folk. Thus the basic sense is a long, straight, slender pole, presumably of wood, which can be erected vertically, wielded at an angle, or held horizontally.

● The simplex *stöng* can have the same specific meanings as *stöng* compounds, including:
= *merkisstöng* '(shaft of) a standard', on which the *merki* 'banner, emblem' hangs;
= *fjallstöng* 'fell-pole', a walking pole or stick;
= *mælistöng* 'measuring rod', of 5-8 Norwegian *alen*, or approx. 3-5 metres.

● Compounds, in addition to those mentioned, include: *fiskistöng* 'fishing rod', *krosstöng* 'cross-shaft', and *stýris(s)töng* 'rudder-post' (Fritzner IV, s.v. *stöng*). Various special idioms using *stöng* are not relevant here.

3. Select corpus of *stöng* names

ON *stöng* spread, and was deployed in place-names, wherever there were significant numbers of Scandinavian speakers.[3] I will be referring to these as '*stöng* names', shorthand for 'place-names probably or possibly containing ON *stöng* or its reflex in the appropriate local form'. The principal reflexes of ON *stöng* are: Icel. *stöng*, Faer. *stong*, Nwg. *stang*, *stong*, Swed. *stång*, Dan. *stang*, Shetl. *steng*, *stong*, Hebrid. *staing*, Scots *stang*, *staing*, N. Eng. dial. *stang* (after de Vries 1977, s.v.). Although there are West Germanic cognates, its distribution in the British Isles seems to point to Scandinavian origins.

The Appendix contains a selection of over 280 *stöng* names arranged mainly by (modern) country, and references to the Appendix will henceforth use the letters D (Denmark), E (England excluding Lake District), ELD (English Lake District), F (Faeroes), I (Iceland), N (Norway), SC (Scotland & the Isles), and SW (Sweden).[4] Only for a minority are pre-1550 spellings available, though many of the names may be substantially older than their first record, such as *Stangana* (Moss), recorded in 1837 but possibly an inversion compound from the period of Scandinavian-Gaelic contact (*PNWestm* 1, 51). A large proportion of the names refer to topographical features, often minor ones, but topographical habitative and habitative names also abound.

Morphologically, *stöng* occurs frequently both as a simplex, singular or plural, and as the specific (first or qualifying element) or the generic (second or basic element) of compounds. Some of the *stöng* specifics are themselves compounds, e.g. Fågelstång (SW). It should be noted that not all dithematic names containing *stöng* were created as compound formations, for some may be secondary derivatives of a simplex, such as Stang Gill, from (The) Stang (E). Other dithematic names derive from compounds, with ellipsis of the original generic, e.g. Stangebro, Stangemark and other Bornholm names derived from Stangegaard (D). Meanwhile in Lerstang, Jonstang and Gjestang (N), appellatives or personal names have apparently been added as distinguishing prefixes to existing *Stang(ir)* names (*NG* 2: 212, 6: 95, 140).

In the absence, so often, of early spellings, there is a possibility that some apparent *stöng* names are of different origin, though the problem is more restricted than with many other toponymic elements. Among the examples are Stanghill (*Stayngill* 1471, *PNWRY* 6: 96), clearly from ON *steinn* 'stone, rock' and ON *gil* 'ravine with stream', and Stanger, Birsay, Orkney (*Nether, Over Stansgar* 1595, Marwick 1952: 138), which is again from *stei(n)n*, plus ON *garðr* 'enclosure, farm'. The standing stone NW of the farm, and the pronunciation, rhyming approximately with *stranger*, emphasise the true origin here. Again, two place-names in Jarlsberg & Larvik are named Jonstang (N), but the early forms show that only the Ramnes example is definitely a *stöng* name, while the Vaale one could be from ON *tunga* 'tongue (of land)', *tangi* 'pointed end, spit of land' or *stöng*. Similarly in Denmark some apparent *stöng* names may originate in *tang, stage* or *stafn* (e.g. *DS* 3: 6, 59, *DS* 20: 160, 168), while in Gaelic-speaking areas there is scope for confusion between *staing* from *stöng* and the Gaelic *staing* 'ditch', as, presumably, in the Strathclyde Staing Mhor (Grid Reference NM8108) and Staing Tealan (NN 0425), names of straight watercourses.

Conversely, although most *stöng* names are readily detectable from their modern forms, some may appear in disguise, e.g. Stank Top, a 1000-ft/300m. height in Lancashire (E), where *stang* appears to have been influenced by *stank* 'pond' (OFr *estanc*).

It should be emphasised that while the corpus in the Appendix below is a useful tool for investigating the range of possible toponymic applications of *stöng*, the disparate coverage of different countries inhibits direct comparisons, and the corpus is far from complete. The Swedish material, for instance, could be supplemented significantly from the online Ortnamnsregistret, currently in progress.

4. The meaning of *stöng* in place-names

While the sense 'pole' or similar accords with most occurrences of the lexical word *stöng*, its derived compounds and modern reflexes, the *stöng* place-names are a good deal less straightforward. Hugh Marwick, considering Stangasetter, Orkney, commented that '*stang-* is ... common in Norse place-names but its exact significance is quite uncertain ... O.N. *stöng* ... meant a pole, but one cannot be sure that it had any such meaning in place-names' (1952: 14); and entries for individual *stöng* names in place-name surveys repeatedly note with a shrug that the etymon is *stöng/stang*, but in an unknown sense. An attempt to fathom the meaning of *stöng* as a toponymic element will involve considering whether poles might be referred to, and if so, what sort; and whether there are applications that go beyond the basic sense of 'pole'.

4.1. Pole, post, rod

The simplest hypothesis is that *stöng* has the literal meaning 'pole, post' in place-names, and this might find support in the incidence of plural forms of the word. Lakeland examples (Appendix ELD) include Stanger (NY1327), a hamlet in Embleton, (The) Stangs, a tract of fellside at Dove Crag, Patterdale, and Big and Little Stanger Gill. The early Norwegian material (N) also contains several simplex names in the dative plural, normalised *á/í Stöngum*, though in some instances these are pairs of places called Stöng.

What material feature could *stöng*, taken literally, designate? Hallberg lists some of the possibilities for the numerous Swedish *stång* names as: 'vägbommar, rågångsmärken, gärdsgårdar, mätstänger, fångstfällor' (waymarks, boundary markers, enclosures, measuring poles, (bird-) catching poles, 1990: 51). Clearly a major difficulty is that these would normally have been wooden, hence biodegradable, making it impossible in most cases to verify specific hypotheses (as pointed out by Olsson, 1984: 51). Nevertheless, there is definite evidence for some specific uses of *stangir*, and we begin with sea-marks or waymarks.

A number of coastal *stöng* names seem to refer to sea-marks, the clearest examples being from Sweden. At Stångskären off Arkö, 16 posts 40 feet high formed a beacon with a container on top in the 18th century (Franzén 1982: 90), while at Stångudden, Värmland, *stänger* were used as sea-marks before the lighthouse was erected (Rosell 1984: 123); there are several more probable examples from the Stockholm archipelago (Appendix SW). At Stangenes in Norway, Stangen is seemingly the name of a beacon standing on a distinct headland and marking a harbour much frequented in the Middle Ages (*NG* 9: 25).

The use of *stöng* to refer to landmarks or waymarks is not, to my knowledge, directly attested in England, but there is Swedish evidence, as when Hellquist noted references in early Swedish laws to *stänger* (including *vaþstang* '?ford-post') in support of his suggestion that *stång* in Stångby, like the first elements of Råby, Rörby, Skälby, and Stafby should probably be interpreted as boundary markers or landmarks (1918: 27). The N. English Stangerthwaite (Appendix E), standing at a crossing of the R. Lune, is similarly likely to be 'the ford marked by a post'. As well as marking individual points, posts erected singly or in a row could have helped travellers to negotiate the peat bog at Stang Moss, for instance, or the precipitous ravines at Big and Little Stanger Gill (both ELD). This notion is encouraged by the names of two famous Lakeland passes, Sticks Pass and Stake Pass, both potentially treacherous in mist or snow, and the collocation elsewhere of *stöng* with generics referring to wet, marshy terrain, such as *kær* or *mose* (D) or *myr* (Ortnamnsregistret, Uppsala and Kopparbergs län) could suggest waymarks. Collocation with hill terms (e.g. *howe* from ON *haugr* 'hill, mound' in N. England) is still more frequent, and these are likely sites for landmarks or beacons. Stangrah (ELD) is a possible example, which like Stangergill (Caithness), and Stangobreck (Orkney) stands on a slope under a mile from the coast and could therefore have been the site of a sea- or landmark. Stångberget (SW), meanwhile, is a known beacon site (Hellberg 1985: 126).

Some *stöng* names refer to boundary markers. Among the likely examples is Fourstangs in Yorkshire, seemingly '"four poles" ... used to mark a boundary or the like' (*PNWRY* 2: 3) – compare Fourstones (Fourstanes 1307) on the border with Lancashire (*PNWRY* 6: 239). Similarly, the specific of Stångeseter, Västergötland, probably refers to boundary marker(s) (Linde 1982: 64), as does the Sydslesvig name of Stangsbjerg, which stands at the meeting of three parishes (*SSS* 7: 138, cf. Stangled, Stangroj, Appendix D).

The marking of assembly sites is another strong possibility. The likely equivalence of the parish-name Garstang in Lancashire to the wapentake-

Diana Whaley

names Gartree in Leicestershire and Lincolnshire and to the Swedish names Gertre, Gärtre and Hjärterum (*i gertrem* 1377) has been noted, and their significance in relation to assemblies or boundaries discussed, especially by Franzén (1967) and Arngart (1978, 1979), though they differ over the identity of the specific. Franzén suggested ON *geiri* 'gore, triangle (of land)', perhaps referring to a distinctive marking on a post, while Arngart favoured ON *geirr* / OE *gār* 'spear', referring to a symbolic spear-structure. Girsten(wood) (SC) looks like another instance of the same name as Garstang, and one wonders whether the Yorkshire Gearstones (E) might be another. Other significant places marked by poles may be indicated by *stöng* names, though the significance now eludes us. Kettlestang was glossed as 'Ketill's pole' by Smith, who added, 'the site of a cross is noted on the top of the hill' (*PNWRY* 5: 203); the enigmatic Mallerstang could be a similar case (both Appendix E).

The surmise that some *stöng* names may refer to posts forming an enclosure is *a priori* attractive given the ubiquity of place-names referring to enclosures, and it may be encouraged by its collocation with *gård* (ON *garðr* 'enclosure') in Gårdstånga, a name particularly exciting because it appears, in dative plural *karþ:stąkum*, normalised *Garðstöngum*, in an early 11th-century runic inscription on the Forsheden stone, Småland (Pamp 1983: 94-95, following Jansson). Pamp suggests a *stång* used to close an opening in a fence, and similar explanations have been given, e.g., for three instances of Stanggab (the fourth, in Højrup, being on a boundary; D). Stanger in Embleton, mentioned above, may allude to a fence, since the gentle terrain makes waymarks unlikely (unless indicating the nearby saline springs), and since the R. Cocker forms a boundary, making markers superfluous (Stangerhill, NY2038, is also near a boundary stream).

We might well expect the application of *stöng* 'pole' to exploitation of woodland, in the same way as, OE *stocc* and *stæf* in the Lakeland names Stockley and Staveley (see Whaley, forthcoming), and Stangarholt (I) has been proposed as an instance (see below, p. 283). In general, however, the typical situations of *stöng* names do not favour this, and *stöng* only exceptionally co-occurs with generics referring to woodland or woodland clearance.

As well as commemorating poles or stakes driven into the ground for various purposes, *stöng* may denote slighter, more portable poles or rods with special functions. The sense 'fishing-rod' or 'fish-trap' has been proposed for *stöng* in some Danish lake- and river-names, including six examples of Stangebæk and two of Stangesø; however, where a medial -*e*- seems organic, the verb *stange*, used of spiking eels or fish, has been favoured (*DSÅ* 6: 311,

249

8: 375). Stanghelle, Norway may refer to a cave for storing fishing rods, though there is also a topographical solution (*NG* 11: 317).

Meanwhile, in the Stockholm archipelago and elsewhere around the Swedish coast, we find names containing *stång*, *fågelstång/flöjstång* and *bak(slag)stång* (SW), all apparently related to fowling with nets, as practised well into the 19th century. In seven places such names are complemented by oral traditions of bird-catching recorded in the 1930s, and Stahre prints a fascinating map of 1713 showing a 'Fogelstång' at two points, one on the islet Stångskiären. A contemporary note to the map explains that nets were slung across the channel between islets during the spring migrations (1986: 188). The Faeroese practice of fowling by climbing bird-cliffs is also commemorated onomastically, and Matras glosses *stong* as 'stang, spec. Fuglestang' (1933: 272).

4.2. Topographical uses

There can be no doubt that *stöng* and its reflexes denote landscape features of various sorts in place-names. It is compounded with *nes* 'headland' in most of the Nordic countries, e.g. at Stångenäs, Bohuslän, where Wadström notes that the point of the long, rocky headland was known as Stangen in 1594 (1983: 27). He also notes that there is no evidence for sea-marks so early as the period when the name must have arisen, hence back-formation is unlikely, at least here. In Norway Stang(e)nes is a frequently occurring compound (*NG* Indledning: 80), and the specific may often refer to a narrow, straight promontory, hence 'headland with a sharp point / at Stang / called Stang'. Where a medial vowel points to **Stangarnes* rather than **Stangnes*, the last option, an *ex nomine* construction, is less likely (Olsen, discussing Stangnes, Hedmark (*NG* 3: 222, 9: 25)). The topography is not necessarily decisive in interpreting such names, since a long, prominent headland or *stöng* is a very likely place for a sea-mark or *stöng*. The Shetland Stonganes is one such case, where the headland, of peat on boulder clay, is eroding and was probably more *stöng*-like in the past, but where a post also stands, doubtless successor to earlier ones, warning of rocks in the approach to the harbour. [5]

As well as referring to promontories, Stang(en) occurs as an island name or skerry name (e.g. *NG* Indledning: 80, 9: 25), and at least some instances are '*stöng*-shaped island' or 'island called Stang', just as the long, narrow inlets or channels in the Norwegian Stangervaag and Stangringen seem to have been visualised as *stangir* (*NG* 11: 131, 15: 362). *Stöng* also appears in river-names, by far the grandest being the Swedish Stångån in

Östergötland which divides Västanstång from Östanstång and is bridged at Stångebro, though the meaning is uncertain, and it is unclear whether the river gave its name to the royal manor of Stång or vice versa (Franzén 1982: 10-11, 103, Hallberg 1983: 115). But there is also an Icelandic Stangará, a Norwegian Stangeraa in Klingen and some Stangviks, including one in Romsdal, which may refer to straight rivers – compare ON *stafr* 'stave, shaft' and *spjót* 'spear' in river-names (*NG* 13: 400).

Stöng also denotes mountains in Norway and Iceland, just as simplex words meaning 'pole' or similar form the Norwegian mountain-names Staven, Stauren and Sneisa, or as *áss* 'beam, ridge', pl. *ásar*, enters into Norwegian and Icelandic topographical names. Where the heights in question are high and steep, *stöng* might indicate, albeit exaggeratedly, a natural, vertical 'pole', as in the Alpine *aiguilles* 'needles'. However, the 'pole' may alternatively be horizontal. A Lakeland example is Stang in Patterdale (NY3517), which is far from Alpine in scale, but is a long, prominent ridge terminating at Stang End in a steep drop to the valley below; Stang End, Durham is a similar landform. The Icelandic farm of Stöng in Árnessýsla, famous because preserved for centuries under lava from Hekla, excavated and reconstructed down the valley, stood underneath the elongated height of Stangarfjall, and one might conjecture that the name refers to that.

Finally in this section, *stang* was used in Middle and Early Modern English as a measure or unit of land equivalent to a rood or, in Wales, an acre. This sense is attested in place-names, in fact it is the only usage other than 'pole' recognised in Smith's *English Place-Name Elements*, who illustrates it with the ME field-names *le Stongs*, *Scortstonges*, *Twelfstong* (1956, 2: 157).

4.3. Bridge

Alongside the basic sense 'pole', *stang* in Cumbrian dialect takes on the specialised sense of an important item made of wooden poles or planks: a footbridge. A will of 1582 from Hawkshead parish, for instance, provides for the maintenance of 'the Stang or bridge at Esk waterfoote' (= foot of Esthwaite Water; *CW* 1904: 148). *Stang* also appears as the generic of bridge names. Still in Hawkshead, the drowning of Edward Satterthwaite of Colthouse beneath Pool Stang is recorded in 1632 (PR, p. 178), and a gibbet near *the Pooll-stang* is mentioned in 1672 (p. 298). Similarly, *Mansergh stang* is recorded in a list of Westmorland bridges of 1656 (BL MsAdd 37,721 23/13v), and where *stang* collocates with *bridge* it may again mean 'bridge', e.g. Stang Bridge (SD2490) and two cases of Stangs Bridge (E, SC; the plural perhaps referring to the individual poles or planks comprising the bridge).

Several *stang* names are associated with streams, among them Stang Dub (NY2515), a deep pool in the upper Derwent close to what is now a single-arched stone bridge, and Stang Hill (SD4285), where a rudimentary bridge known, at least until recent times, as 'the stang', crosses the R. Winster. Further, three places named Stangend(s) are situated near crossings of the Irt (NY1103), Brathay (NY3202), and Leven (SD3484), and the sense 'bridge' for *stöng* again seems very likely, though as the first two are also below blunt headlands, a topographical reference is not impossible.

We can safely assert that, although not all individual instances can be proved, *stang* is definitely used to mean 'bridge' in some Lakeland place-names alongside other dialect terms for minor, plank bridges: *clapper* in Clappersgate (*PNWestm* 1, 209) and *hebble* in Hebblethwaite (*PNWYorks* 6, 264). This usage is seemingly only demonstrable in post-medieval examples, which prompts the question whether it is a late post-colonial development, peculiar to N.W. England, or whether it could be more widespread. *Stång* collocates with *bro* 'bridge' in a handful of Danish and Swedish place-names, and the possibility that it means 'bridge' in some Danish place-names was raised by Nordén (1928-1929) but dismissed by Eile (1930-1931; cf. *DSÅ* 6: 311). *Spång* 'bridge' is among the possible meanings entertained for the specific of Stångby, Skåne, by Pamp (1983: 50) and for the river-name Stångan by Hallberg (1983: 115). However, other and perhaps preferable explanations are usually to hand.

4.4. Personal names

No investigation of a toponymic element would be complete without reference to the possibility that some of its claimed instances are personal names. Unsurprisingly, *stöng* appears as a nickname, for instance of Þorbjörg (or Þordís) stöng, sister (or daughter) of Þórir Þurs ('giant') in *Landnámabók* ch. 111 and *Egils saga* ch. 28. She was presumably tall and slim – of the enviable build that English speakers describe as a beanpole (see Lind 1921, *bolstöng, stöng*, for male Norwegian bearers of this nickname in the 10th to 16th centuries). Þorbjörg stöng settled *í Stangarholti*, Mýrasýsla, and the clear implication is that the place was named from her. However, scepticism about the apparent eponyms which abound in early Icelandic sources has been encouraged, above all by Þórhallur Vilmundarson (e.g. 1986), and we might wonder whether the specific of Stangarholt, and of nearby Stangarvatn and Stangarhylur, might instead refer to the small, narrow knoll on which Stangarholt stands (cf. the above discussion of Stöng), or, as Þórhallur suggests, to exploitation of woodland, as probably at other -*holt* sites such as Stafholt and Skíðsholt (1983: 97).

Elsewhere, the presence of a personal name is also possible but difficult to prove. It is tentatively suggested as the specific of Stangeby, Jarlsberg & Larvik, though without reasons being adduced (*NG* 6: 245). More certain is that *Stange* becomes a surname (perhaps via the nickname), present, e.g., in several instances of Stangegaard, Bornholm (two of them inhabited in 1625 by Hans Stange and Rasmus Stange, *DS* 10: 317), as well as in Stangerup, Falster. Stanger also appears in England as an occupational term and as a surname of uncertain origin (Reaney 1976: 331, Hanks & Hodges 1988: 508), so that a place-name containing 'Stanger' as first element and lacking medieval spellings might well derive from the surname.

5. Conclusion

Stöng is a prolific element which spread throughout the Scandinavian(-influenced) lands, occurring in several hundred names and giving rise to regional clusters of stereotyped formations, e.g. numerous instances of Stangeland in Stavanger and Søndre Bergenhus (N), of Stanggab and Stangebæk in S. Jutland (D), of Stångskär in the Stockholm archipelago (SW), and repeated collocation with *howe* (ON *haugr* 'hill, mound') and with *end* in N. England (E, ELD).

Shetland is typical of the islands and coastal regions of the North Atlantic in using *stöng* mainly in names of coastal features, and the evidence of the generic elements to which *stöng* is joined in the corpus of names below suggests an association especially with relatively remote, infertile spots. It co-occurs particularly frequently with terms for 'hill/slope', 'islet/skerry', 'headland', and 'stream'; almost never with terms for valleys, woodland or (except in Denmark) fields, and only rarely with habitative generics, although a large number of names are topographical habitative. It is also noticeable that when *stöng* acts as a generic, it is rarely qualified by a personal name.

The possible toponymic applications of *stöng* include literal reference to poles – fixed or portable, and for multifarious purposes – and figurative reference to landscape features. Both seem to be widely attested throughout the North-Atlantic area, and in names of pre-modern origin, allowing us to surmise that both usages are pan-Scandinavian. Exactly which of the potential literal and figurative meanings are realised in particular areas remains a fertile subject for study, but clearly depends on local geography, culture and toponymic fashion. From meaning a measuring pole, *stöng* comes to denote a measurement or unit of land (the examples known to me are

English). It also gives rise to personal names that enter into place-names. That *stang* can refer to a bridge both within and outside place-names is certain in Northern England – a usage not, to my knowledge, registered in the onomastic literature to date and possibly a local, 'post-colonial' development.

Given the rich array of interpretative possibilities, many individual *stöng* names will always remain elusive. Nevertheless, with evidence from morphology, collocations, topography and local usage, many individual names can be explained with a fair degree of probability, and the solutions tentatively proposed for the small set of Lake District examples are summarised in Appendix ELD. The semantics of *stöng* would certainly repay further investigation on a regional basis, and it is hoped that the present survey of the range of potential meanings throughout the North-Atlantic area will provide a useful contribution to such studies.

Appendix: Select corpus of probable or possible *stöng* names in alphabetical order of country

D: Denmark

Note: The former *amter* in which places are located can be traced through the volume numbers of *DS*: 1: Samsø, 2: Frederiksborg, 3-7: Sønderjylland, 8: Vejle, 9: Viborg, 10: Bornholm, 11: Maribo, 12: Århus & Skanderborg, 13: Svendborg, 14: Odense, 15: Svendborg (Naturnavne), 16: Præstø, 17: Ringkøbing, 18: Rander, 19-22: København, 23-24: Vestsjælland. Parishes or districts (*herreder*) are also specified since multiple occurrences of names are frequent.

Pre-1550
Specific

Stangebro Musse Herred *Stongebro* 1475/1552 (*DS* 11: 166)

Stangerup Maglebrænde *Stangæthorp* 13th cent. (*DS* 11: 169)

Stanghede Dollerup *stange hee* 1525 (*DS* 9: 133)

Stangsig Bølling Herred *Stongsigh* 1484 (*DS* 17: 549)

Post-1550
Simplex singular

Stang Jørl – meadow *sein Stang*, *Stang* 1806 (*SSS* 4: 404)
Specific

Stangager Karlum *Der stangh acker* 1694 (*SSS* 4: 130)

Stangager Kværn *Stang-Acker* 1762 (*SSS* 7: 300)

Stangager Medelby (*SSS* 4: 173)

Stangager Vonsild *Stacker-*, *Lang Stengagger*, *Stangagger Ende* 1716-18
  (*DS* 3: 82)

Stangborg Frørup 1716-18 (*DS* 4: 320)

Stangborg Ødis – wood & meadow *Stangborrig* 1789 (*DS* 3: 103)

Stangdam *Stavendam* 1744, *Stongdamm* 1758 (*DSÅ* 6: 309-10)

Stangebæk Glemminge *Stångabäckskrokarne* 1843 (*DSÅ* 6: 310)

Stangebæk Købelev *Stange Bechs Eng* 1682 (*DSÅ* 6: 310)

Stangebæk Østofte *Stange Becks Wenge* 1682 (*DSÅ* 6: 310)

Stangebæk Povlsker *Stange-bekken* 1746-50 (*DS* 10: 459, *DSÅ* 6: 310)

Stangebæk Såby *Stangebeck* 1682 (*DSÅ* 6: 310)

Stangebæk Vallensved *Stange Becks Agere* 1682 (*DSÅ* 6: 310)

Stangebakker Øster-Larsker (*DS* 10: 317)

Stangebro Klemensker *Stangebroe* c. 1779 (*DS* 10: 226)

Stangeenge Klemensker (*DS* 10: 226)

Stangegaard Aaker *Stangegd* 1746-50 (*DS* 10: 496)

Stangegaard Klemensker *Stangegd* 1634 (*DS* 10: 208)

Stangegaard Øster-Larsker *Stanggegd* 1661 (*DS* 10: 317)

Stangegaard Øster-Larsker *Stanggegd* 1661-62 (*DS* 10: 317)

Stangegaard Rø (*DS* 10: 290)

Stangegade Øster-Larsker – part of Stangemark (*DS* 10: 331)

Stangehus Øster-Marie (*DS* 10: 358)

Stangekær Smørum *Stangekiers Aas* 1682 (*DS* 20: 84)

Stangekrogsbakke Øster-Larsker *Stangekrogs Bakken* 1813 (*DS* 10: 331)

Stangeland Taps 1790 (*DS* 3: 124)

Stangemark Klemensker 1715-21 (*DS* 10: 226)

Stangemark Øster-Larsker/Øster-Marie *Stange Marken* 1801 (= habitation), *Stange Marck* 1727 (topographical feature) (*DS* 10: 317, 331-332)

Stangemølle Allinge Kobstad – skerry 1923 (*DS* 10: 54)

Stangeng Brede 1704 (*DS* 5: 428)

Stangeng Hostrup *Stangwisch* 1717 (*DS* 5: 538)

Stangeng Taps *Stang Eng* 1716-18 (*DS* 3: 122)

Stangenge Bylderup (*DS* 5: 607)

Stangerende Aaker *Stangerenden* 1795 (*DS* 10: 511, *DSÅ* 6: 311-312)

Stangerum (*DSÅ* 6: 311)

Stangerup Engestofte *Stangerop* 1682 (*DS* 11: 132)

Stangesø Hvalsø *Stange Søe*, *Stonge Søe* 1792 (*DSÅ* 6: 312)

Stangesø N. Mellby *Stångsjö* 1842 (*DSÅ* 6: 312)

Stangestykke Hasle Købstad *Stange Styket* 1760 (*DS* 10: 38)

Stangetsagre Sengeløse *Stangets Agerne* 1682 (*DS* 19: 258)

Stanggab Agerskov 1785-88 (*DS* 4: 717)

Stanggab Branderup *Stang-Gabet* 1771-77 (*DS* 4: 748)

Stanggab Stepping (Anderup) *Stang Gaff* 1716-18 (*DS* 4: 329)

Stanggab Stepping (Højrup) *Stanggaff* 1716-18 (*DS* 4: 334)

Stangholm Siversted – meadow 1787 (*SSS* 4: 333)

Stanghøj Øster-Larsker Probably 20th cent. (*DS* 10: 319)

Stanghøj Sengeløse 1898 (*DS* 19: 258)

Stanghøjsagre Glostrup *Stanghøys agre* 1682 (*DS* 19: 71)

Stanghøjsagre Ledøje (*DS* 20: 50):

> Brydernes St. *Brydernis stanghøis agre* 1682
>
> Krogede St. *Kraaged [S]tanghøis Agre* 1682
>
> Nørre St. *Norre Stanghøis Agere* 1682
>
> Søndre St. *Søndre Stanghøis agre* 1682

Stanghøjsvang Ledøje *Stanghøffs Vang* 1635 (*DS* 20: 50)

Stangkær Aller *Stangkehr* etc. 1715 (*DS* 4: 264)

Stangled Sterup *Stangeleier-Lücker* 1777 (*SSS* 7: 348)

Stangled Esgrus *bi dem Stangeheck* 1607, *Stangled* 1858 (*SSS* 7: 382)

Stangled Øster-Løgum *Stanglei* 1704 (*DS* 6: 119)

Stangled Varnæs 1857-58 (*DS* 6: 456)

Stanglyk Esgrus (*SSS* 7: 419)

Stangløkke Varnæs *Stanglük* undated (*DS* 6: 478)

Stangmade Ullerup (Blans) (*DS* 7: 68)

Stangmade Ullerup (Ullerup) *Stangmay* 1783 (*DS* 7: 74)

Stangmoseled Vejstrup *Stagemoos Ley*, *Stangmosled* 1775 (*DS* 3: 48, 8: 161)

Stangmoseled Vonsild (*DS* 3: 75); cf. Stangmoseled Have *Stangmosled have* 1788 (*DS* 3: 82)

Stangroj Sterup *Stangrad* 1776 (*SSS* 7: 354)

Stangsagre Galten *StungsAgre* 1683 (*DS* 18.1: 86)

Stangsbjerg Grumtoft *Stangs-Berg* 1787 (*SSS* 7: 138)

Stangstykker Hammelev 1922 (*DS* 4: 420)

Stangvraa Bov *Stang Vraa* 1802 (*DS* 6: 591)

Generic

Bustangeren Pedersker *Bustångarijn* 1906/23 (*DS* 10: 470)

Eekstang Gelting *Eeckstang* 1791 (*SSS* 7: 424)

Egstang Gelting *Eckstam* 1583, *Eckstang* 1790 (*SSS* 7: 440)

Flagstangen Allinge-Sandvig *Flagstangsbakken* 1867 (*DS* 10: 68)

Flagstangen Vrads Herred 1872-74 (*DS* 12: 173)

Halverstang Joldelund *(der) Hal(l)werstang* 1805 (*SSS* 4: 430)

Kiæbstangs Toft 1800 (*DSÅ* 4: 253)

Røstang Esgrus *Rostang* 1723 (*SSS* 7: 398)

Signalstang Sønder-Stenderup – hillside (*DS* 3: 14)

Skalmstang Ikast *Schalm stangs Agre* 1683 (*DS* 17: 308)

Tappestang Toftlund *Tapstang Enge* 1777-78 (*DS* 4: 663)

E: England (excluding Lake District)
Note: Places can be located through the source volumes or through grid references; counties are post-1974 in *OSG*, pre-1974 in other sources.

Pre-1550
Specific

Stangdail 1339 (*PNERY* 83)

Stangerbarrow 1278 (spelling not specified, *VCHLancs* 8: 142 and n. 29)

Stangerhau 14th cent. (*PNLancs* 250)

Stangerthwaite SD6289 *Stangerwath* 1279 (p), *Stangrewath* 1340 (*PNWestm* 1, 40)

Stanghow *Stanehou* 1273, *Stanghou(e)* 1280 to 1575 (*PNNRY* 146)

Stank Top *Stanghend* 1524, *Stang Toppe* 1546 (*PNLancs* 68)
Generic

Fourstangs *Fourestangeg* [sic] 13th cent., *Fourestanges* 1349, *Lefour Stanges* 1380 (*PNWRY* 2: 3)

Garstang *Cherestanc* 1086, *Gairstang* 1195 (*DEPN*, cf. *PNLancs* 163, Lindkvist 1912: 47-48)

Kettlestang *Ketelsang* [sic] 1379 (p), *Ketellstang Head* (collem montis) 1481 (*PNWRY* 5: 203)

Mallerstang *Malrestang* 1223, 1284, 1312, 1322, *Malvestang* 1228,
   Marlestang 1268, *Mallerstang*(e) 1272 to present (*PNWestm* 2: 11)

Wrangstang 1352 (*PNWRY* 7: 252, Elements list only)

Post-1550
Simplex singular/plural

Stang NZ0107 NYorks (*OSG*)

Stangs (field-name) 17th cent. (spelling not specified, *VCHLancs* 8: 243).

Stangs (*PNWRY* 7: 252, Elements list only)

Stang, The NZ0208 Durham (*OSG*)
Specific

Stang Brae 1840 (*PNWRY* 5: 213)

Stang Gill NZ0208 Durham (*OSG*); cf. The Stang above

Stang Hill (*PNERY* 83; near *Stangdail* above)

Stang Hill SD4283 Cumbria (*OSG*)

Stang Holme (*PNWRY* 7: 252, Elements list only)

Stang Howe NZ7613 NYorks (*OSG*)

Stang Ings (*PNWRY* 7: 252, Elements list only)

Stang Lane (*PNWRY* 5: 91, listed only)

Stang Side NZ0105 NYorks (*OSG*)

Stang End, Stangend Currick, Stangend Rigg NY8443 Durham (OS 1:
   25,000)

Stanggill (Fell) *Stranggill* [sic] 1577, *Stang-gill* 1663 (*PNWRY* 6: 141)

Stanghow (Moor) NZ6514 Cleveland (*OSG*)

Stangs Bridge Cf. *Ulton stanges* 1578 (*PNCumb* 307)

Stangs Laithe (*PNWRY* 6: 80, listed only)
Generic

Birkstang (*PNWestm* 2: 290, Elements list only)

Gearstones *Gearston* 1621, *Gearstange* 1631 (*PNWRY* 6: 243)

Mansergh stang 1656 (in list of bridges, BL Ms Add37721 23/13v)

Peestang (*PNWestm* 2: 290, Elements list only)

Stang, Stang Green Westmorland 1851 (Census)

Stangana (*Moss*) 1837 (*PNWestm* 1: 51)

ELD: English Lake District
With *suggestions* as to most likely reference of *stöng*

Pre-1550
Simplex plural

Stanger NY1327 *Strangre* 1298, 1332 (p), *Stanger* 1322 to 1777 (*PNCumb* 384) = stakes, enclosure

Specific

Stangrah SD1185 *Stangerhovet* 1180-1210 (*PNCumb* xxv, 449) = landmark

Post-1550
Simplex singular/plural

Stang NY3517 *Stang* 1859 (OS) = long ridge

Stanger Newlands Valley, late 18th cent. (Thomas Kitchin map) = waymarks

Stangs / The Stangs NY3811 = waymarks

Specific

Stang Bridge SD2490 *Stang Bridge* 1851 (OS) = footbridge

Stang End NY3202 *Stange End* 1663-64 (*CW* 20,1920: 178) = footbridge (or ridge)

Stang End SD3484 *Stang End* 1851 (OS) = footbridge (or ridge)

Stang End Broughton-in-Furness 1547 (spelling not specified, *CW* 57, 1958: 58)

Stangends Lorton 1651 (*CW* 14, 1897: 201)

Stangends NY1103 *Stangendes* 1563 (*PNCumb* 404) = footbridge (or ridge)

Stanger Gill, Big NY2613, **Stanger Gill, Little** NY2612 = waymarks

Stanger How NY1427; cf. Stanger above = (hill at) Stanger

Stangerhill NY2038 *Stanger Hill* 1851 (Census) = surname

Stang Dub NY2515 (OS 1:25,000) = footbridge

Stang Hill SD4285 (OS 1:25,000) = footbridge

Stang How NY2113 (OS 1:25,000) = landmark

Stang Moss SD3090 (OS 1:25,000) = waymark

Diana Whaley

Generic

Lammer Stangs Hawkshead 1851 (OS)

poole stong 1631/2, *the Pooll=stang* 1672 (Hawkshead PR) = footbridge

F: Faeroes

Source: Matras 1933: 272; no early spellings

Simplex singular/plural

(Sandurin) á Stongum Myrkjanoyri

Stangir / Norðr á Stongum / á Stongunum Klakksvík

Stongin Nólsoy

(Úti) á Stongum Miðvágur

Specific

Stanga(r)klettur Hvannasund

Stanga(r)nes Tórshavn

Generic

Mirkjanastong Klakksvík

Vaags-Stong Klakksvík

I: Iceland

Principal source: database of Örnefnastofnun Íslands; places are located by sýsla (s.)

Pre-1550

Stangarholt Mýras. (*Grímnir* 2, 1983: 97)

Post-1550

Simplex singular

Stöng Árness. – deserted farm

Stöng Austur-Barðastrandars. – long, narrow sea-stack

Stöng Dalas. – islet

Stöng Múlahreppur, Austur-Barðastrandars. – islet

Stöng Norður-Þingeyrars. – long lava spit (Stangaroddi at point; Stangarboðar nearby)

Stöng Reykhólahreppur, Austur-Barðastrandars. – islet

Stöng Snæfellsness. – rock stack

Stöng Suður-Þingeyrars. – farm

Stöng Vestmannaeyjar – high peak on Heimaey (Þorkell Jóhannesson 1938: 76)

Specific

Stangá Dalas.

Stangará Árness.

Stangarbás Vík í Mýrdal

Stangarbásar Vestmannaeyjar (Þorkell Jóhannesson 1938: 74, near *Stöng*)

Stangarhaus Vestmannaeyjar (Þorkell Jóhannesson 1938: 74, near *Stöng*)

Stangarhlaup Vestur-Skaftafells. – narrows in river

Stangarhólar Árness.

Stangarhólar Austur-Skaftafells.

Stangarhólmi Dalas.

Stangarhylr Mýras. (near Stangarholt)

Stangarlækur Árness.

Stangarlækur Mýras.

Stangarsvelti Austur-Skaftafells.

Stangarvatn Mýras. (near Stangarholt)

Generic

Háastöng Snæfellsness. – sea stack

Hóleyjarstöng Mýras. – rock peak

N: Norway

Note: The former *amt(er)* in which places are located can be traced through the volume numbers of *NG* (*Norske Gaardnavne*): 1: Smaalenenes, 2: Akershus, 3: Hedemarken, 4: Kristians, 5: Buskerud, 6: Jarlsberg og Larvik, 7: Bratsberg, 8: Agdenes, 9: Lister og Mandal, 10: Stavanger, 11: Søndre Bergenhus, 12: Nordre Bergenhus, 13: Romsdal, 14: Søndre Trondhjem, 15: Nordre Trondhjem, 16: Nordland, 17: Tromsø.

Pre-1550

Simplex singular / plural

Stang *Stong* c. 1400 (*NG* 1: 291)

Stang *i Stongum* c. 1400, *Stong* 1520 (*NG* 2: 212)

Stang, Store & Lille *Stangh, Stongh* c. 1400 (*NG* 6: 224)

Stange *a Stöngum* (*Hákonar saga Hákonarsonar* ch. 126), *a Staungum* 1334 (*NG* 3: 158)

Stange *i Staungum i Skarde* c. 1400 (*NG* 4: 56)

Stange *a Stongom, i Stanghom* c. 1400 (*NG* 6: 139)

Stange *Stange* 1520-70 (*NG* 10: 407)

Stange, Nordre *a Stangom* 1384 (*NG* 6: 269)

Stanger *á Staungum* (*Magnúss saga Erlingssonar* ch. 25), *Stanger* (*Fagrskinna* ch. 105), *á Stöngum* (*Sturlunga saga* II, 361), *Stanger* 1578 (*NG* 1: 368)

Stanger *i Stongum* c. 1400 (*NG* 2: 409)

Stanger, Vestre & Østre *i / a Stongom* c. 1400 (*NG* 2: 310)

Specific

Stangeby *i Stangaby* c. 1400 (*NG* 6: 245)

Stangeland Austevold *Stangeland* 1520-70 (*NG* 11: 249)

Stangeland Fjelberg *Stangaland* 1341 (*NG* 11: 93)

Stangeland Høiland *Stangaland* 1484 (*NG* 10: 175)

Stangeland Klep *Stangeland* 1520-70 (*NG* 10: 126)

Stangeland Kopervik *Stangeland* 1520-70 (*NG* 10: 392)

Stangeland, Vestre & Østre Haaland *a Stangalande* c. 1270 (*NG* 10: 126)

Stangenes, Søndre & Nordre *Stangha nes* c. 1350, *Stangarnese* c. 1370 (*NG* 17: 20)

Stangerholt *af Stangarholte* c. 1430 (*NG* 15: 155)

Stangnes *Stanganæs* c. 1400 (*NG* 3: 222; cf. 9: 25)

Stangvik Nordmøre *Stangarvík* 'middelalderske Form' (*NG* 15: 375)

Stangvik, Indre med Finviken *Stagwighen (!)* 1520-70, *Stanguig* 1559 (*NG* 13: 400)

<u>Generic</u>
Gjestang *Gestongh* c. 1400, *Gestangh* 1520 (*NG* 2: 212)
Jonstang Ramnes *i Jonstongom* 1378, *Joenstang* 1593 (*NG* 6: 140)
Lerstang *i Lœirstangum, i Lœirstanghom* c. 1400, *Lerstanng* 1574-77 (*NG* 6: 140)
Morstang *i Notstongom* (!) c. 1400, *Morstangh* 1604 (*NG* 1: 131)
Rokstang *Røgstoe* 1520-70 *Rockstang* 1559 (*NG* 13: 366)

Post-1550
<u>Simplex singular/plural</u>
Stange *Stonghe* 1566 (*NG* 3: 90)
Stong – mountain (*NG* 10: 126)
<u>Specific</u>
Stangefjeldet (*NG* 11: 317)
Stangenes *Stangenes* 1610 (*NG* 13: 253)
Stangenes *Stanngenes* 1601 (*NG* 9: 25)
Stangervaag *Stangwog* 1668 (*NG* 11: 131)
Stangfjeldet (*NG* 17: 68)
Stanghelle *Stanndhelle* 1610, *Stanghelle* 1620 (*NG* 11: 317)
Stangringen *Stanngerengh* 1590 (*NG* 15: 362)
Stangvik *Stangwiig* 1669 (*NG* 15: 375)
Stångmóbakken – local name for Elvegaarden (*NG* 16: 287)
<u>Generic</u>
Jonstang Vaale *Jonßthunngi* 1574-77, *Joenstang* 1593 (*NG* 6: 95)

SC: Scotland & the Isles
<u>Scottish mainland</u>
Girstenwood Dumfries *Gairstang* 1305 (Lindkvist 1912: 48, n.1)
Stangergill, Stangergill Burn ND1967 Caithness (OS 1:25,000)
Stangs Bridge NY2452 Dumfries
<u>Western Isles</u>
Stan(n)graidh NB4122 Lewis (*OSG*)
Stangram NF7775 N. Uist (*OSG*)

Orkney

Stangasetter HY6744 Sanday *Stangasetter* 1500, 1595 (Marwick 1952: 14)

Stanger Head HY5142 Westray (*OSG*)

Stanger Head ND 3792 Flotta (OS 1:25,000)

Stangobreck HY4702 Mainland (OS 1:25,000)

Shetland

Haa of Stong and **Stonga Banks** HU2985 Mainland (*OSG*)

Stonga Ness, Stonganes HP5402 = de Ness o'Cullivoe, Yell (Jakobsen 1936: 105)

Stongerholm Mainland (Jakobsen 1936: 104-105)

Stongir Holm HU5994 Fetlar (*OSG*)

SW: Sweden
Note: The *län* to which names belong can be traced through the volumes cited: see Literature.

Pre-1550
Simplex plural

Stånga *Stangum* 14th cent. (Olsson 1984: 51)
Specific

Stångberga *Stangaberghom* 1384 (Calissendorff 1986: 126)

Stångenäs (härad) *j Stanganesi* 1338 (Wadström 1983: 27)

Stångsmåla *Stangsmala* 1337 (Hallberg 1990: 50)
Generic

Gårdstånga *karþ:stąkum* Forsheden stone, early 11th cent. (Pamp 1983: 94-95)

Hanskastang Västergötland *Hanzkastang* 1356 (*NG* 16: 270)

Post-1550
Simplex singular

Stång – royal estate (Franzén 1982: 10-11, Hallberg 1983: 115, *DSÅ* 5: 73)

Stången – beacon (Hallberg 1990: 124)
Specific

Själstångsvitje 1936, *Skäl Stång Viken* 1786, *Skäl stångsviken* 1800 (Stahre 1986: 202)

Skräddarstängslan – field (Stahre 1986: 215)

Stångberget (Hellberg 1985: 126)

Stångby (Pamp 1983: 50; *DS* 13: 113)

Stånge huvud cf. Stångenäset (Wadström 1983: 103)

Stångeholme sund cf. *Stangesund* 1589 (Wadström 1983: 27)

Stångesäter (Linde 1982: 64)

Stångrör (Hellberg 1985: 128)

Stångskär (Hallberg 1990: 137)

Stångskärsflöt (Hallberg 1990: 131)

Stängslan – field (Stahre 1986: 210)

Stångån – river > **Västanstång**, **Östanstång**; also **Stångebro** (Franzén 1982: 10-11, 77, 103)

The following probably refer to sea-marks and are from Stahre 1986: 187, unless otherwise specified

Stangnöudd *Stångnäsudd* end 17th-early 19th cent.

Stångehall (Hallberg 1990: 78)

Stångkobben *Stankobben* 1703

Stångören 1691

Stångskär 1690s

Stångskären (Franzén 1982: 90)

Stångskaten *Skatan* 1691

Stångudden

Stångudden (Rosell 1984: 123)

The following certainly or probably refer to posts for fowling nets, and are from Stahre 1986: 185-189 unless otherwise specified:

Backstanskobben *Bakstangskubben, Baakstångskubben, BakStadz K:* 17th-18th cent.

Bakstangskär 1691

Flogstångsudden 1773

Flygstångsudden 1776, probably = Flögstångsudden

Flögstångsvassen

Flöjstångsudden = Fågeludden Möjasidan

Flöjstångsudden Möja

Fågelstångsholmen

Fågelstångsholmen (Stahre 1986: 109)

Fågelstångsudden

Fällstångskobben

Stången

Stångklabben (Franzén 1982: 90)

Stångkobbarna

Stångkobben

Stångskär

Stångskär (Franzén 1982: 90)

Stångskär *Stor Stangskär* 1630-40

Stångsundet

Stångsundet *Stång-Sund* 1691

Stångudden

Literature

Arngart, O., 1978: 'Three English Hundred Names', *Namn och Bygd* 66, 13-17.

Arngart, O., 1979: 'Gertre, Gartree, Garstang', *Sydsvenska Ortnamnssällskapets Årsskrift*, 50-53.

Calissendorff, K., 1986: *Ortnamn i Uppland*. Stockholm.

Census = 'Index to Places covered in the 1851 Census', at: http://rolyg.members.beeb.net/CensusPlaces.htm (accessed December 2003).

CW = *Transactions of the Cumberland and Westmorland Antiquarian and Archaeological Society*.

DEPN = Ekwall, E., [1936] 1960: *The Concise Oxford Dictionary of English Place-Names*. Oxford.

DS = *Danmarks Stednavne*. København 1922-. [See Appendix D]

DSÅ = Sørensen, J.K., 1968-1996: *Danske sø- og ånavne* 1-8. København.

Eile, A. 1930-1931: '"Stång" i ortnamn', *Sydsvenska Ortnamnssällskapets Årsskrift*, 37-43.

EPNS = English Place-Name Society county surveys

Franzén, G., 1967: 'Svensk Gertre och engelsk Gartree', *Namn och Bygd* 55, 15-19.

Franzén, G., 1982: *Ortnamn i Östergötland*. Stockholm.

Fritzner, J., 1883-1896: *Ordbog over det gamle norske Sprog* I-III. IV, Rettelser og Tillæg, by F. Hødnebø, 1972. Kristiania, Oslo/Bergen/Tromsø.

Hallberg, G., 1983: *Ortnamn i Småland*. Stockholm.

Hallberg, G., 1985: *Ortnamn på Öland*. Stockholm.

Hallberg, G., 1990: *Ortnamn i Blekinge*. Stockholm.

Hanks, P. & Hodges, F. 1988: *A Dictionary of Surnames*. Oxford.

Hawkshead PR = Cowper, H.S. (ed.), 1897: *The Oldest Register Book of the Parish of Hawkshead*.

Hellquist, E., 1918: *De svenska ortnamnen på -by*. Göteborg.

Jakobsen, J., 1936: *The Place-Names of Shetland*. London/Copenhagen.

Jesch, J., 2001: *Ships and Men in the Late Viking Age*. Woodbridge.

Jóhannesson, ?., 1938: *Örnefni í Vestmannaeyjum*. Reykjavík.

Lind, E.H., 1921: *Norsk-isländska personbinamn från medeltiden*. Uppsala.

Linde, G., 1982: *Ortnamn i Västergötland*. 2. utg. Stockholm.

Lindkvist, H., 1912: *Middle-English Place-Names of Scandinavian Origin*. Uppsala.

Lindqvist, N., 1926: *Bjärka-Säby Ortnamn*. Stockholm.

Marwick, H., 1952: *Orkney Farm-Names*. Kirkwall.

Matras, C., 1933: *Stednavne paa de færøske norðuroyar*. Kjøbenhavn.

NG = *Norske Gaardnavne* 1-19. Kristiania/Oslo, 1897-1936 [See Appendix N].

Nordén, A., 1928-1929: '"Stång" som bronamn', *Sydsvenska Ortnamnssällskapets Årsskrift*, 35-44.

OED = Simpson, J.A. & Weiner, E.S.C., (eds), *The Oxford English Dictionary*. 2nd edition. 1989. Oxford.

Olsson, I., 1984: *Ortnamn på Gotland*. Stockholm.

OSG = *Ordnance Survey Gazetteer of Great Britain*. 2nd edition. 1989.

OS = Ordnance Survey maps [six inch to mile unless otherwise specified]
Ortnamnsregistret vid SOFI, Språk- och folkminnesinstitutet, Uppsala, at:
http://www.sofi.se/SOFIU/topo1951/_cdweb/ (accessed December 2003).

Pamp, B., 1983: *Ortnamn i Skåne*. Stockholm.

PNCumb = Armstrong, A.M., *et al.*, 1950-1952: *The Place-Names of Cumberland*, 1-3. EPNS 20-22. Cambridge.

PNERY = Smith, A.H., 1937: *The Place-Names of the East Riding of Yorkshire*. EPNS 14. Cambridge.

PNLancs = Ekwall, E., 1922: *The Place-Names of Lancashire*. Manchester.

PNNRY = Smith, A.H., 1928: *The Place-Names of the North Riding of Yorkshire*. EPNS 5. Cambridge.

PNWestm = Smith, A.H., 1967: *The Place-Names of Westmorland*, 1-2. EPNS 42-43. Cambridge.

PNWRY = Smith, A.H., 1961-1963: *The Place-Names of the West Riding of Yorkshire*, 1-8. EPNS 30-37. Cambridge.

Reaney, P.H., 1976: *A Dictionary of British Surnames*. 2nd edition, by R.M. Wilson. London.

Rosell, E., 1984: *Ortnamn i Värmland*. Stockholm.

Smith, A.H., 1956: *English Place-Name Elements*, 1-2. EPNS 25-26. Cambridge.

SSS = *Sydslesvigs stednavne* Inledning, 1-7. København, 1979-1993.

Stahre, N.-G., 1952: *Stångskäret, Kåksna och Kummelberget : studier över ortnamn från Stockholms skärgård*. [Lidingö].

Stahre, N.-G., 1986: *Ortnamn i Stockholms skärgård*. Stockholm.

Ståhl, H., 1985: *Ortnamn i Västmanland*. Stockholm.

VCHLancs = Farrer, W. & Brownbill, J., (eds), 1914: *The Victoria County History of the Counties of England. A History of Lancashire*, vol. 8. London.

Vilmundarsson, Þ., 1983: 'Safn til íslenzkrar örnefnabókar 2', *Grímnir* 2, 51-144.

Vilmundarsson, Þ., 1986: 'Um persónunöfn í íslenzkum örnefnum', *NORNA-Rapporter* 33, 67-79.

Vries, J. de, 1977: *Altnordisches Etymologisches Wörterbuch*. 2nd edition. Leiden.

Wadström, R., 1983: *Ortnamn i Bohuslä*n. Stockholm.

Whaley, D., forthcoming 2005: *A Dictionary of Lake District Place-Names*. Nottingham.

Notes

[1] Among the more extended discussions are those by Rygh (NG Indledning: 80), Kjær (NG 9: 25), Lindqvist (1926: 318-328), Matras (1933: 272). Stahre (1952: 172), and Sørensen (DSÅ 6: 310-311, summarising Lindqvist and Stahre).

[2] Normalised Old Icelandic spellings are used as the 'default' form throughout this paper, except that for technical reasons it has been necessary to substitute ö (o umlaut) for hooked o (o ogonek) in stöng.

[3] Stöng was also adopted into Gaelic; into Lappish, Finnish and Estonian (de Vries, s. v.); and into Russian by 1096 (Jesch 2001: 253, citing Svane).

[4] I am greatly indebted to Peder Gammeltoft for performing a search of the index of Danish place-names at the Afdeling for Navneforskning, Copenhagen, to Svavar Sigmundsson for performing similar wizardry at Örnefnastofnun Íslands, Reykjavík, and to Doreen Waugh for guidance on Scottish examples. I would also like to thank Peder Gammeltoft and Paul Cullen for providing me with photocopies of sources not available to me. Thanks are also due to the British Academy for a small research grant, and to the Arts and Humanities Research Board (now Council) for funding a period of research leave, both of which grants have greatly assisted my work on Lake District place-names.

[5] I am grateful to Mr D.R.A. Rushton of Stonganes for this information.